AFFECTIONATE
COUSINS

T. Sturge Moore and Marie Appia

AFFECTIONATE
COUSINS

T. Sturge Moore and Marie Appia

SYLVIA LEGGE

Oxford   New York   Toronto   Melbourne

OXFORD UNIVERSITY PRESS

1980

Oxford University Press, Walton Street, Oxford OX2 6DP

OXFORD LONDON GLASGOW
NEW YORK TORONTO MELBOURNE WELLINGTON
KUALA LUMPUR SINGAPORE JAKARTA HONG KONG TOKYO
DELHI BOMBAY CALCUTTA MADRAS KARACHI
NAIROBI DAR ES SALAAM CAPE TOWN

British Library Cataloguing in Publication Data

Legge, Sylvia
   Affectionate cousins.
   1. Moore, T Sturge – Relationship with women
   – Marie Moore
   2. Moore, Marie   3. Authors, English –
   20th century – Relationship with women
   I. Title
   821'.8   PR6025.0582/   79–41265

   ISBN 0–19–211761–0

Printed in Great Britain by
Fakenham Press Limited, Fakenham, Norfolk

To the Memory of
Christopher Connlagh Legge

Preface

IT has been my good fortune to have known the Sturge Moores for as long as I can remember, for my parents were their near neighbours in Hampstead during the First World War. When I was about five years old Mrs. Sturge Moore tried to teach me to knit squares in garter stitch to be made up into blankets for refugees, gaily reassuring me that they would still be useful as dishcloths if they failed to end up as squares. Later, when the Sturge Moore parents and my own had moved to Steep in Hampshire so that their children could attend Bedales School, Mr. Sturge Moore, the poet, emerged more clearly, and opened unfamiliar paths for the eye and imagination to follow. For a twelve-year-old child, knowing nothing of the Noh plays of Japan, it was an awe-inspiring experience to take part in his verse-drama, *Medea*, summoned by the masked Curtain Bearer to help unfold his symbolic curtain

> From off an acre of the Arcadian field,
> Till what occurred three thousand years ago
> Be watched again to-night by these choice friends.

Later still, back in Hampstead, I sometimes shared the hilarious family meal-times at 40 Well Walk before the Friday evening poetry readings, conducted in a more solemn atmosphere.

An outcome of this happily continuing association was that some years ago Dan and Riette Sturge Moore asked me if I would look through their father's papers, placed after their mother's death in the University of London Library, with the object of assessing their potential as material for a biography or an edition of letters. What emerged inescapably for me from the perusal of the contents of these seventy-two boxes was the family story told here, beginning with an unorthodox marriage between cousins in the 1830s and ending two generations later with a marriage between cousins who had surmounted more complex obstacles. I am therefore doubly grateful to the son and daughter of the second pair of cousins for the constant encouragement and indulgence they have shown me in the writing of a book that is not the scholarly biography of Thomas Sturge Moore and critical assessment of his work that should be written.

Other members of the family have also helped me greatly. The late Mrs. Dorothy Moore was generous in lending letters and sharing recollections, Mr. Edmund Williams-Ashman produced the Sturge legal documents, Mme Beatrice Appia-Blacher, besides providing a crucial series of letters, gave me the benefit of her scholarly historical perspective, Professor Henry Appia, also a mine of information, kindly read the typescript, and the portraits of Henry and Lydia Sturge are from an Appia collection. Descendants of men and women appearing in the book have given me valuable information: I have to thank Mrs. James Wilson for the letter to her mother, Gwendoline Bishop, Mr. Julian Trevelyan for the photograph of his father, Professor David Pye for the photograph of his aunt Sybil and permission to print her letters, Senator Michael and Miss Anne Yeats for permission to print their father's letter, and Laurence Binyon's three daughters, Mrs. Nicolete Gray for access to letters and permission to print, Mrs. Margaret Higgens for the photograph of the William Strang etching, and both her and Miss Helen Binyon for drawing my attention to published material previously unknown to me.

Fellow researchers into the same period have provided details on various subjects: Mr. Victor Cassidy on Wyndham Lewis, Mr. Paul Delaney on Charles Ricketts, M. Henri Locard on Michael Field, Professor Ronald Schuchard on the Literary Theatre movement, Professor Smallbridge on R. C. Trevelyan, and Colonel Francis on the sources of the Sturge fortune. And here I must also record my gratitude to my generous friend Mrs. Marcella Carver, whose scholarly mind and feeling for language has supported me throughout the composition of the book.

To the staff of the University of London Library I have been deeply indebted over a protracted period, particularly to Miss Joan Gibbs for her kindly and efficient response to my erratic demands, and to Miss Mary Grant, whose interest and practical help has gone far beyond her professional duties. I am also beholden to the following libraries, institutions, and organizations: the Library of the Religious Society of Friends (and the Clerks of several Meetings), the British Library, the Bodleian Library, the Denver Public Library, Colorado, the Fitzwilliam Museum, the Hastings Public Museum, the Church Missionary Society, and Dulwich College, and I am pleased to acknowledge the Master and Fellows of Trinity College, Cambridge, for permission to quote the passage from R. C. Trevelyan's 'Cambridge and Sturge Moore'.

Though presented as a story, this book is as factually accurate as I could make it, areas of conjecture or tentative deduction being, I hope, clearly indicated as such. Knowing that an appraisal of TSM's artistic and literary achievement is matter for a better qualified hand, I have refrained from personal comment on the work that appears in the course of the narrative. The translation of the Appia letters has been done by Dan Sturge Moore and that of parts of TSM's letters written in French is my own. The French place names of the period in Piedmont have been retained. Except in TSM's childhood letters, spelling has been conventionalized and punctuation and paragraphing occasionally added in the interest of clarity. Where not otherwise indicated, quotations in Chapters Two and Three are from the correspondence between the Sturge sisters, and later in the book from that between TSM and his parents.

S.M.L.

1979

Contents

Illustrations

ILLUSTRATIONS IN THE TEXT

CHAPTER ONE

❦

The Quaker Sturges

IN 1832 Lydia Sturge, the grandmother of Thomas Sturge Moore, opened a diary modelled on *The Secret Journal of a Self-Observer* by the Swiss poet and theologian Lavater. She was twenty-seven years old and living in Croydon with her widowed mother, her sister Maria, and two young nieces.

The Sturges were members of the Society of Friends. Debarred, like all Nonconformists, from entering the universities and learned professions, Quakers then engaged mainly in manufacture and trade—and few more successfully than Lydia's eldest brother Thomas. While still in his teens he had rescued his father's whale fishery from financial rocks and in due course become a prosperous spermacetti-oil merchant; later he took over from its inventor the manufacture of Portland cement, for which he found markets at home and abroad. He was tenderly devoted to his invalid sister Esther, with whom he lived at Northfleet, Gravesend, where, with a touch of un-Quakerly flamboyance, he erected a fiercesome-looking fence of crossed harpoons around his estate. Brother Samuel, on the other hand, is described as 'the most Quaker of them all'. He wore the dress of the previous century and adhered strictly to traditional forms of speech and conduct. In his grocery shop in London he sold candles manufactured by Thomas and later, no doubt, Montserrat lime juice from the plantations his cousin Joseph Sturge had bought for the freed slaves. The youngest brother, George, a partner in some of Thomas's enterprises, was also a bachelor, and perhaps expected to remain so. An accident in childhood had torn the muscles of his face, leaving him shockingly disfigured. It may have been partly this that led to his interest in all forms of provision for the sick and handicapped; he served on the committees of numerous hospitals, asylums, and homes and contributed liberally to their support. Of the fourth brother, Nathan, little is known except that as a young man he rushed imprudently into marriage with a Jeanette de St. Dalmas, who had a beautiful singing voice but was not a member of the Society of Friends. The censure incurred by this marriage was cruelly endorsed, for the young wife proved periodically so deranged as to be incapable of bringing up any of their ten children, some of whom inherited her mental instability. These children became to a large extent the responsibility of their celibate uncles and aunts. Lydia, who had herself attended one of the Quaker boarding-schools providing 'a liberal education' for boys and girls alike, took the tuition of the two nieces entrusted to her care very seriously.

Her diary was intended to be a record 'of *all* my deviations from what I know to be right'. As such it is inevitably a melancholy account of 'failures to grow in grace' over a period of seven years. 'Impatience and temper' she believed to be her besetting sins, leading her 'to speak inadvisedly' to her brothers, express disagreement with undue vehemence, and be reluctant to accept reproof. She also deplored her tendency to indulge in 'foolish talking and jesting'. But far more than by such sins of commission she was oppressed by the deadness and indifference of her soul, her lack of response to God's love, her blindness to the Inner Light. In silent Meetings, the value of which to one of her wavering faith she several times questioned, her thoughts usually wandered in selfish, worldly paths. In other Meetings she often found comfort, especially when the ministry came from Elizabeth Dudley, Elizabeth Fry, or John Barclay. If, however, she dared to hope that she had truly profited, this, she feared, was only the turning of her 'corrupt and deceiving heart' towards spiritual pride. She was trapped in a treadmill, a word she herself uses, in which all her resolutions and prayers led to no upward progress. Such an underlying sense of unworthiness was not uncommon among devout Quakers, nor did it necessarily inhibit their effectiveness in life.

Between the lines of pious introspection events and movements of Lydia's life within the concentric spheres of family and the Society can be traced. She regularly attends all Meetings—the Monthly, the Quarterly, the Yearly, the Bible, the Missionary—as well as two or three a week in Croydon. There are occasional stays with relatives in the Midlands and the West, and more frequent journeys accompanying some invalid to a seaside resort, such as Bexhill, Hastings, or Worthing, whose 'more retired pleasures' Lydia preferred to 'the gay and bustling scene of Brighton'. Sickness and death are always in the foreground. Lydia herself often suffers prostrating rheumatic pains; her mother's chronic illness has acute phases; the erratic behaviour of her two pupils causes forebodings; her eldest niece, near to Lydia in age and her dearest friend, is consumptive. Several deaths in childbirth occur among the relatives. When her three-year-old niece dies of whooping cough, Lydia finds it particularly hard to accept the formula of consolation for such 'sanctified afflictions', a phrase often heard in 1833 when many of their circle died in the cholera epidemic.

In June of that year Lydia noted a visit from 'cousin Henry', with the reflection that since he was last in Croydon 'he has become a husband, a father and a widower—how uncertain are all earthly possessions! all earthly enjoyment!' Henry Sturge, whose second wife Lydia was before long to become, belonged to the branch of the family living in the Midlands. The outstanding member of this family, and one who broadened the horizons of the entire Sturge clan, was Henry's elder brother Joseph, known as 'The Philanthropist of Birmingham'. A corn merchant by trade, unlike most good paternalistic employers of the time Joseph became deeply concerned by the permanently depressed condition of the working classes. His consequent work for adult education, his founding of the National Complete Suffrage Union, and his standing for Parliament on a mainly Chartist platform were all denounced by many 'weighty Quakers'. This did not, however, prevent his becoming one of the leading representatives of the Society in its anti-slavery campaign, and he worked with the same pertinacity for the cause of peace, lobbying ceaselessly for the principle of arbitration at home and abroad. By contrast, Henry was a relatively obscure figure. He seems to have been of a gentle, contemplative nature, not particularly suited to the kind of employment open to him. With the help of his brothers he had been launched as a carpet manufacturer in Bewdley, Worcestershire. There he met Helen Newman, the daughter of a local glover, whom he married in 1830. The young couple lived in the wooded countryside outside Bewdley, at Northwood Cottage, where Henry made a beautiful garden. A daughter was born on 9 June 1831, and a few weeks later Helen died. Henry's unmarried sisters, Lucretia and Rebecca, then came to look after his household and his baby daughter Helen, the future mother of Marie Appia.

Henry's visit to Croydon renewed a close friendship with his cousin formed in childhood and it is clear that its continuance was a comfort and support to Lydia in the sorrows and anxieties of the next three years. It was not, however, until after her mother's death in January 1837 that she felt free to consider the possibility of marriage. Two obstacles then confronted these cousins. Henry's carpet manufactory had by this time failed, and mismanagement of one's worldly affairs leading to bankruptcy could then also lead to disownment by the Society of Friends. This difficulty was apparently overcome within the family, for Henry became a corn factor, probably as agent for his brother Joseph's firm. More distressing to such a hitherto devoutly conforming couple was the objection of the Society to marriage between cousins, yet entries in Lydia's diary show that her resolution was never seriously shaken:

Two Friends visited on sixth day morning to dissuade me from the intended connexion, and threaten, or rather intimate, the certainty of disownment if it is not abandoned; I hope that I desire to act consistently with the divine will in this matter, but feel it trying to incur the censure of our Society.

There is no evidence that Lydia's immediate family exerted such pressure on her, but there was presumably much consultation between them and the Elders of the Meeting as to what countenance such a union could receive, for the date of the marriage was postponed three times.

Meanwhile the marriage settlement had been drawn up. Under its terms Lydia's 'considerable fortune' of over £7,000 was to be administered for her 'sole and separate use and benefit ... exclusively and independently of Henry Sturge ... not in any manner subject to his power control interference debts engagements or encumbrances'. The Friends were always careful to safeguard the position of married women, but here the stipulation that were he to become bankrupt Henry should be regarded 'as though dead' rings harshly. The marriage at last took place on 15 April 1838 'after the manner of Friends, though not in a Friends' Meeting House' and with only six Witnesses. Some weeks later the official notification of disownment by the Society was received; Lydia wrote in her diary, 'I feel grieved at this act of theirs, but as I cannot doubt the good providence of God conducted me to my present happy station I hope to feel satisfied and remember that true Christianity is open to all men and not confined to any sect or party'.

During the honeymoon Henry's seven-year-old daughter Helen stayed with Newman relatives in Worcester. Lydia prepared to welcome her home to 'the sweet sequestered abode' of Northwood Cottage with a shade of apprehension, 'as she has been so much indulged and made the centre of attention'. Helen's later recollections of her early childhood with her father and her two aunts were indeed of the happiest. She remembered feeding the cats, playing long hours in the garden, watching the rabbits in the neighbouring fields, making houses in the corn stooks, and climbing on farm wagons with visiting cousins. She adored her father. He spent a little time after breakfast every morning teaching her to read, sometimes took her riding in front of him on his rounds, and allowed her to pick a red flower for his buttonhole when he went to Radical meetings. She loved her aunts too, particularly Aunt Rebecca, who indulged her in most things, but checked her demonstrations of affection by crying, 'Helen dear, *don't* crumple my white collar!' In spite of difficulty in retaining her attention, Aunt Lucretia taught her to write, count, and sew. Only on Sunday mornings did time seem to drag; the sole means she could devise of passing the long silent hour in the bare Meeting House was to count the number of buttons in sight, those sober-coloured buttons which were the nearest approach to ornament on the garb of the assembled Quakers. Lydia and Henry had given much thought to their 'difficult and delicate responsibility' towards this child who had known no rival in her father's affection so they were not surprised when her first delight at having a new mother turned to jealousy, nor when she rebelled against a firmer control than she had experienced before. It was not long, however, before Lydia's patient understanding prevailed and Helen responded to her affection.

Disownment by the Society made little difference to their way of life, for they continued to attend Meetings and move in familiar circles. What disturbed Lydia more deeply at that time was the realization that she was pregnant. The experience of assisting at her sister Maria's second confinement, when an agonizingly protracted labour had resulted in a second still birth followed by fever and delirium, had given her a lasting dread of childbirth. She reproached herself for her weak and wicked attitude to what should be considered a blessing, but could not overcome her terror of the coming ordeal. When, on 19 March 1839, the dreaded confinement came, she was safely delivered of a daughter, named Henrietta. So, on her first wedding anniversary, Lydia was able to list among her blessings 'the kind, affectionate companionship of my dearest earthly friend', 'the affection of the dear little girl who was once so loth to call me Mamma', and 'the little baby I was so loth to possess, so blessed with health and sweetness of temper as to be almost too fondly loved and dangerously dear; a universal favourite indeed, and especially so of her admiring sister who does affectionately love her'. At this point Lydia closed her diary, with the reflection that even the most unworthy of believers could be richly blessed by an All-Merciful God.

Lydia could long continue to regard the affectionate relationship of the step-sisters as a blessing; the strong bond between them remained unbroken throughout their married lives in different countries, and was to lead to the childhood friendship between Thomas, the eldest son of Henrietta, and Marie, Helen's youngest daughter. But Henry was not to see his daughters grow up, for in the autumn of 1841 he contracted a fever. Hoping that a change of air might do him good, Lydia sent the two girls to their Uncle Joseph's home in Birmingham and took Henry to Northfleet. It was a very cold winter and he grew worse. He was then moved into London where Lydia's brother George could ensure that the best medical attention was always available. No treatment had any lasting effect and on 25 June 1842 Henry died.

For some months Lydia's grief overwhelmed her entirely; she wished only to be reunited with Henry by her own death. Though she was never, it seems, fully to regain the power to 'walk cheerfully over the world' as Quakers were enjoined, her piety and her affection for the two girls whom she regarded equally as her own daughters gradually moved her to resume responsibility for the burdens of life. A painful dispute had arisen over Helen, who was now again staying with her Newman relations. They argued that, as she was now an orphan and they were her next of kin, her home should in future be with them. Eleven-year-old Helen reacted to this suggestion with distress and indignation and insisted on returning at once to the only mother she had ever known. Because Henry's affairs had been neglected during his illness, Northwood Cottage had to be sold to pay his debts. Lydia, unable to decide where to settle, accepted a series of invitations from the many relatives anxious to succour her. The succession of visits during 1843–4 to homes where she had once been with Henry often served only to revive her grief. Their mother's prolonged mourning must have had a depressing effect on the two girls, most lasting perhaps on the impressionable five-year-old Henrietta. It was

7

George who eventually decided that his sister needed a complete break from all familiar, painful associations and in the summer of 1844 carried her and the children off for a holiday in Paris. And in Paris, with only one significant break, Lydia remained for the rest of her life.

What induced her to transplant herself so unconventionally is a matter for conjecture. She had probably been well grounded in French at school, for the Friends favoured modern rather than classical languages as more helpful both in spreading the gospel and in furthering trade. The small Quaker community may have persuaded her to prolong her stay. It is known that at a quite early stage someone took her to hear the great preacher Adolphe Monod. From that occasion on, she seems to have found in the more structured gospel ministry of the French Reformed Church a form of worship more satisfying to her needs, at once more rousing and less demanding than that of the Friends. Like her Quaker circle in England, the Protestants in Paris were a closely knit religious minority. She soon became acquainted with the Monods and with their friend Pasteur Meyer, to whom she entrusted the religious instruction of her daughters. The educational opportunities in the city were also a great attraction. At first Helen, so much a country child, had felt lonely and imprisoned in their gardenless apartment off the Champs-Élysées, but her life was transformed when her mother learned of the excellent lectures held at the Muséum d'Histoire Naturelle in the Jardin des Plantes. Beginning with 'The Drawing of Animals' and 'The Painting of Plants', Helen and some young English neighbours, sometimes accompanied by Lydia, attended a number of courses on natural history and the sciences, all given by distinguished professors. As this meant walking right across the city for the morning session at eight, Lydia moved to the rue Buffon, close to the Jardin des Plantes.

There was no breach with the family, for part of almost every summer was spent in England, and Lydia maintained a steady correspondence with her sister Esther. In June 1847 came a letter from Thomas telling of Maria's death from cerebral fever; knowing how profoundly Lydia would be affected by this news, he added a postscript: 'For the sake of thy children I hope and trust thou wilt look on this event with the Eye of a Christian and be able to perceive the great gain for our departed Sister. Grieve not.' The following year all the Sturges were shocked by George's marriage to Jane Sturge of Bristol, a cousin more than twenty years his junior. Both these events made Lydia's family desire the companionship of her and her daughters. By 1851 the decision to return to England was made. The furniture was brought out of store in Bewdley and installed in a cottage on Thomas's estate. Within a year, however, Henrietta, whose health had not fulfilled the promise of her babyhood, developed an intermittent fever, thought to be caused by damps arising from the Thames. Haunted by memories, Lydia fled back to Paris. As far as Henrietta's health permitted, the family resumed their old life there. A letter from George to his nieces, written just before the outbreak of the Crimean War in 1854, shows with what kindly interest the wider family links were still maintained:

Dear Helen and Dear Henrietta,

I seem unwilling to let your Aunt's letter go without a few lines to say how pleasant it is to hear of you often thro sister Esther and to express the hope that when fine summer weather comes Henrietta will feel stronger and better ... many people like some plants make no progress in the winter season. ... Does Helen attend any lectures—if so no doubt she has pleasure in relating what is interesting in them to Henrietta. I suppose that Pastor Meyer is gentle and interesting. I imagine he is like Baptist Noel whom I heard in John St, Bedford Row last autumn—is he like in any respect? ... Yesterday I had a letter dated 5 Feb 1854 from Adolphus [son of Nathan] in Cleveland, Ohio, U.S.A. He writes happily and his wife Caroline seems industrious and judicious. ... Lately we have seen a good letter from Frederick Douglass, a talented Black Man who escaped from slavery and now edits a Newspaper, addressed to H. B. Stowe asking her to pay attention to his coloured brethren by assisting them to become Mechanics

9

and thus become useful members of Society . . . which we thought very good. It seems Cousin Joseph has seen the Tsar of Russia but not altered his warlike views and it is supposed Joseph will now return home.

With very dear love to your mother, affectionately G.S.

The Emperor of Russia treated Joseph and his companions with respect and introduced the Empress to them.

Past II. Aunt Jane gone to sleep.

Lydia's health was by this time beginning to fail, so that Helen shouldered many household responsibilities. Nevertheless, she continued her studies at the Muséum d'Histoire Naturelle and at the Observatoire, winning praise for the clarity of her *résumés* and the thoughtfulness of her essays. They were now living in the rue Marché aux Patriarches, where the Chapelle Tournefort was their place of worship. Although no longer Friends, they remained faithful to the simple manner of life of the Society; their friends called the demoiselles Sturge 'les Chrysalides' because their plainness of dress made no concession to the prevailing fashion of the crinoline. This plainness of living, indeed, concealed the extent of Lydia's income, much of which was quietly used to support evangelist causes and help needy members of the Protestant community.

It was at the Annual Protestant Assembly in April 1857 that the family heard a Georges Appia speak on behalf of his people in the Vaudois Valleys of Piedmont. The fervour of this dark, intense young pastor made a deep impression on his hearers, and moved Helen to read as much about the history of the Vaudois as she could lay hands on. Shortly afterwards Georges Appia was made responsible for services in the Chapelle Tournefort. Even before Lydia approached him concerning a blind Italian she was befriending, Georges had become aware of three gravely attentive members of his congregation, a soberly dressed mother and two daughters, the elder of whom took notes during his sermons.

Georges, then thirty-two, had recently written to his mother, in whom he confided without reserve, 'Quand Dieu me fera-t-il trouver une compagne selon son cœur et le mien? Prier beaucoup à ce sujet.' After his first meeting with the Sturges he resolved to visit these ladies on every pretext that arose. Soon he was to write,

I think that Mlle Hélène is not altogether indifferent to my visits. . . . Her head has already more than one grey hair, although she is only 28. This suggests that she is no stranger to inner experience and that life will not find her entirely a novice; she has evidently received a careful upbringing. I believe she is eminently a woman of silence and duty.

When the following year Lydia fell mortally ill, Georges visited her daily. Before she died she gave a thankful blessing to his be-trothal to Helen. Georges took the service at her burial in the cemetery of Père Lachaise in November 1858. Their Uncle George then took the bereaved sisters back to England, and Georges returned to Piedmont.

❦

CHAPTER TWO

The Vaudois Appias

T HE career of the man Helen Sturge was to marry had been largely determined by a historic family allegiance of exceptional intensity. The Vaudois, known in England as Waldenses, were members of a religious sect older and more cruelly persecuted than the Quakers. The name derives from Pierre Valdo of Lyon, a half-legendary figure who in the late twelfth century inspired a primitive Christian movement that rejected the authority of the Pope and turned to the teaching of the Bible in the vernacular. Persecuted as heretics, Valdo's followers dispersed to various parts of Europe, a substantial number of them congregating in the hitherto uninhabited valleys of the Cottian Alps in Piedmont. Here, despite repeated attempts to dislodge them, these resourceful 'mountain men' lived austerely and practised their faith discreetly, while training evangelist preachers known as the 'Barbes'. Their emblem was an anvil, on which all hammerings served to forge faith. In the general movement of the Reformation they allied themselves with the Calvinist church of Geneva, but still retained their historic identity and, like all Vaudois wherever they settled, continued until recent times to use the French language. The Edict of Nantes failed to protect them; the indignation aroused in England by the Piedmont massacre of 1655 is voiced in Milton's sonnet:

> Avenge, O Lord, thy slaughter'd Saints, whose bones
>   Lie scattered on the Alpine mountains cold,
>   Ev'n them who kept thy truth so pure of old
>   When all our Fathers worship't Stocks and Stones,
> Forget not; . . .

After the repeal of the Edict, Louis XIV resolved to eradicate these obstinate heretics completely. In 1668 the Valleys were stormed and all Vaudois not killed in resisting arrest were thrown into prison, where many more died; the survivors were then deported to Switzerland. Only three years later, with support from England, the exiled Vaudois rallied to make their first attempt to return to their Valleys. A Daniel Appia, from whom Georges was directly descended, was captured in this attempt and died in prison. Because of the sympathy for the Vaudois cause in England, his son Paul was enabled to study divinity at Oxford. After being ordained in Fulham in 1706 he returned to minister to his people, by then precariously reinstated in the Valleys and with years of repression still before them. Georges's father, another Paul born in 1782, never realized his wish to work in his ancestral homeland, for the Valleys bred more pastors than they had churches. After completing his studies in Geneva he was appointed to the French Reformed Church in Hanau in Germany founded in 1792 by Huguenot refugees. In 1814 Paul Appia married Caroline Develay who came of a Swiss banking family; she was a woman of great vitality and independence of mind, of whom her youngest son was to write, 'Ma mère avait le cœur gros comme un melon, chacun pouvait y mordre.' Theirs was a home full of music and learning, which became quite a centre of intellectual life when five years later Paul was appointed to the French Reformed Church in Frankfurt.

Here, in 1827, Georges was born, the youngest of six children. While he was still at school two sisters had married pastors, a third, less predictably, a Swiss artist, and his only brother, Louis, was studying medicine at Heidelberg. Georges himself remained for sometime uncertain of his vocation. He had a huge appetite for knowledge—languages, history, science, mathematics. Whereas he played the piano and violin by way of relaxation, he sketched with a passionate enthusiasm, particularly in his last school year in Geneva, where the mountain scenery intoxicated him and his young brother-in-law Gabriel de Beaumont egged him on. His idealistic nature made him wish to be of the greatest possible service to mankind, but whether as a scholar, a pastor, or an artist was not clear to him when he was awarded a scholarship for university study in Germany.

The circumstantial letters that he wrote to his parents during two terms at Bonn, where he 'sketched all day and worked all night', and three at Halle, show the zest and rapidity with which he assimilated, and evaluated, new knowledge and experience. As a student caught up in the revolutionary ferment of 1848 he remained loyal to his social and religious upbringing. Nevertheless, he was one of the self-appointed 500-strong 'Delegation of Halle', which in March commandeered a train to Berlin, marched to the Palace, some rattling their sabres and some shouting 'Peace!', and demanded to see Kaiser Friedrich Wilhelm IV. When the little old man came out to them wearing a red cap, he was met by an embarrassed silence, which he finally broke by asking, 'Well, gentlemen, does the River Saale still flow under the bridge in Halle?'— an episode which moved Georges to tears. At the demonstrations and meetings that followed, Georges's was a lone anti-revolutionist voice, shouting, 'But the bourgeois are also the people!' and he was booed for a speech attacking radical policies. In May he joined his family who were staying with his sister Pauline and her husband Pasteur Louis Vallette in Paris, and so witnessed the bloody events of the June rising. He went through the barricades to his brother-in-law's church to find the cloisters heaped with corpses and was in the streets with his brother Louis helping to tend the wounded.

It was not, however, revolution that frustrated his now burning desire to study theology at Tübingen. Too much sketching in bright sunlight and reading by candlelight had affected his eyesight. The enforced break of six months from all study at this juncture was almost intolerable to one of his impatient, impulsive nature. During this period he taught at a college for Protestant teachers and complained bitterly to his father of the lack of mental stimulus in this milieu of 'le médiocre et très médiocre', words for which he was sharply rebuked. After his father's death the following year his mother made a home for her two sons and her unmarried daughter Louise, in Geneva, where Jacques Claparède, the husband of her daughter Marie, had his parish. Here Georges resumed his studies, now concentrating exclusively on theology and allowing himself little recreation. To spare his eyes during his final year his mother studied with him. In 1851, having passed his examinations with distinction, he began his pastoral career at the age of twenty-four as assistant to Louis Vallette in Paris.

The expectation that his intellectual and personal gifts would find their natural outlet in the vocation of his choice was not fulfilled. He had evidently pressed himself too hard, for he now fell into a deep depression. While forcing himself to perform his parochial duties, he refused to take communion because he had not truly repented of his sins. Although his brother Louis joined with the family doctor in urging a period of complete rest, and Louis Vallette, who had been in the army before he entered the church, issued orders to the same effect, Georges was compulsively driven to further self-mortification; he refused food and set himself bizarre tasks, such as hopping a certain distance down the street or learning so many pages of the Bible by heart. A diary kept by his mother records her anguish at not being able to help him as he deteriorated physically and became increasingly isolated in a black misery. The first help that came was from his brother-in-law Gabriel de Beaumont. He was a man of benignly eccentric character, a respecter of nature in all its aspects who would rather have moved his house than cut down a tree growing too close to it, a natural therapist perhaps. Somehow, in June 1852, he succeeded in taking Georges away with him on a tour of the south of France, which ended up, almost by chance, in the Vaudois Valleys of Piedmont.

This was the first time that Georges had been to the region with whose history he was so familiar and where the name of Appia made him everywhere welcome, yet his letters to his mother are flat, factual records, untouched by excitement or delight. Nevertheless, he stayed on in the home of a pastor in La Tour (now

Torre Pellice), the little capital of the Valleys, where he again gave
lessons to student teachers, this time with a pathetic humility.
According to his own account, his deliverance came through
readings from the first chapters of the Book of Isaiah at family
prayers in April. The words 'the whole head is sick and the whole
heart faint/From the sole of the foot even unto the head there is
no soundness in it' described his own condition to him and
in the asceticism he still practised he recognized a form of 'vain
sacrifice':

Then flew one of the seraphims unto me, having a live coal in his
hand . . .
And he laid it upon my mouth, and said, Lo, this hath touched thy
lips; and thine iniquity is taken away, and thy sin purged.
Also I heard the voice of the Lord, saying, Whom shall I send, and
who will go for us? Then said I, Here I am; send me.

Georges was not tempted to identify himself with the prophet, but
this passage had so powerful a relevance for him that he was able
to walk out of his darkness. In May he began preaching again, in
July he delivered his thesis on Moses at Strasbourg University, in
August he was consecrated in La Tour and for the next four and a
half years he worked for the people of the Valleys with inexhaustible energy.

Although the Vaudois had attained religious and civil freedom
after the revolution of 1848, the years of persecution had left them
physically stunted and culturally deprived. Having no parish of
his own, Georges made the peasants in the outlying farms, the
poorest and most isolated members of the community, his pastoral
concern. When in 1854 he was made Directeur of the École
Normale, he made provision for the children of these families by
introducing school meals (*soupe d'Appia*) and opening a simple
boarding-house. Education he saw as the vital factor in regenerat-
ing the former vigorous spirit of the Vaudois. The lectures he
continued to give at the college for teachers were now inspired by
this conviction; fired by his enthusiasm, his sister Louise came

from Geneva to be head of the École Supérieure for girls, also with its boarding-house. At the same time Georges preached by invitation in the Valley churches, was active and eloquent at conferences of Vaudois pastors, and made incursions into the south of France to encourage the small Vaudois settlements there in the practice of their faith. By 1857, however, his family and friends considered he was spreading his energies too widely and should now concentrate on parish work with time for meditation and study. Louis Vallette commanded him to return to Paris to fulfil his original undertaking there. Reluctantly, Georges obtained from La Tour the year's secondment to the Reformed Church in Paris that led him to the Chapelle Tournefort and so to his future wife. When after Lydia's death and Helen's return to England, he went back to the Valleys as pastor of Pignerol it was not at a moment in history conducive to quiet concentration on parochial duties.

His letters to his fiancée early in 1859, though not without tender passages, are full of the excitement of preparations for war with Austria, and hopes that it would lead to the liberation of all Italy. With his mother he made a collection of prayers and passages from the Bible under the title *Petit Compagnon du Soldat* which, printed in French and Italian, he distributed to the volunteers who were gathering to serve under Garibaldi in the brilliant campaign that was to free Lombardy. His brother Louis, now a Swiss citizen with a medical practice in Geneva, was to play a far more significant part in this conflict. Ever since his experiences in the streets of Paris in 1848, Louis had been making a careful study of methods of treating casualties on the battlefield. He now offered his services, as a civilian doctor from a neutral country, to the military authorities in Turin, and remained throughout the war, working and observing in the fighting areas and the field and base hospitals. For this humanitarian work, he was awarded, along with his better-known compatriot Henri Dunant, the Order of St. Maurice and St. Lazare by King Victor Emmanuel. Back in Geneva, Dunant consulted Louis while writing his stirring *Un Souvenir de Solferino*, with its closing plea for the establishment of permanent relief societies, sanctioned by international agreement for use in time of war. Both men were on the committee which later became the Committee of the International Red Cross. If Dunant had the vision and the crusading fire, Louis Appia understood the medical, administrative, and diplomatic requirements; for most of the rest of his life he served the Committee as medical adviser, negotiator, and watch-dog for the principles of the first Geneva Convention of 1864.

Before Louis had even arrived in Turin, however, Georges was on his way to England for his marriage. Reaching Gravesend in a 'désagréable brouillard' he penetrated the harpoon fence at Northfleet to be welcomed with open arms by the uncles and aunts and Henrietta, as well as by Helen. Uncle Thomas authoritatively satisfied his interest in the commercial traffic on the Thames and took him to see two Quaker schools, Uncle George showed him over Greenwich Hospital, while a visit to Westminster Abbey in the company of Uncle Samuel was abruptly curtailed, for, on being politely asked by the sacristan to remove his broad-brimmed beaver hat, the old man left the building, saying 'I owe no respect to bricks and mortar'. In deference to the claims of Helen's Newman relations, the marriage took place on 15 July 1859 from the home of a maternal aunt in Peckham. The next fortnight was spent in the Midlands, unhappily just after the death of Uncle Joseph, but much to the joy of the aunts Lucretia and Rebecca, and Helen was then introduced to her in-laws in Geneva. The letter announcing Georges's return to Pignerol with his bride on the evening of 14 August had meanwhile gone astray. They found the door of the house locked and nothing prepared; the next morning they rose at four to ride up to Prali in time for the annual Vaudois Festival of Reunion, at which Georges was speaking.

Helen had been fully prepared by Georges for the strenuous life in the service of God and the Vaudois into which she was thus immediately plunged. What she can hardly have foreseen was the nomadic form this life was to take as her husband responded to a succession of calls. After only eighteen months in Pignerol, where a daughter, Cécile, was born, Georges felt his duty lay in Sicily, where Protestants were still not permitted the freedom of worship that was legally theirs. Despite fierce opposition, during their eighteen months in Palermo he succeeded in founding a Reformed Church there. In Palermo a son, Henry, was born and the infant Cécile died. The next call was to Naples, where l'Église de la langue française was apparently threatened by schism on political lines. Here the family remained for three years; a second son, Louis, was born in 1863 and a third, Jean, in October 1865. Georges had by this time agreed to spend a year as Professor at the Vaudois College of Theology, which had recently been transferred to Florence. His departure was delayed by a cholera epidemic and it was not until January 1866 that the family embarked for Florence in a ship called the *Marco Polo*.

Three months later the Italo–Prussian treaty heralded another attempt to free the north-east of Italy from Austrian domination; Piedmontese volunteers were again gathering to serve under Garibaldi. Georges set about recruiting young Protestants for a small religio-medical mission of aid to the wounded under his brother's leadership. A mission so constituted was not acceptable to the authorities, so the unsponsored brigade that assembled in Milan on 20 June finally consisted only of the Appia brothers, the English-born curator of the Turin Museum, and a Neapolitan lawyer turned theological student. Wearing white arm-bands with a red cross and carrying stout sacks stuffed with medical supplies, they reached the Volunteer headquarters in Storo at the foot of the Dolomites just as Garibaldi arrived to review his troops. Louis presented a personal letter of recommendation from the president of the Red Cross Committee. Garibaldi was moved by Louis's explanation of their aims and, after cross-examining Georges as to his role as a pastor, he signed the passes without which the brigade could not have proceeded. All its members were regarded as doctors as they worked desperately in a village church in the High Tyrol to save life among the Italian, Austrian, and Hungarian

wounded, using the altar as a couch, the votive candles as illumin-
ation, the communion wine as a stimulant, and the font as a
receptacle for lemonade. 'Je deviens tous les jours plus quaker,'
wrote Georges to his wife, 'et la guerre m'apparait comme le
chef-d'œuvre du mal.' Only later, in an improvised hospital in
Storo, had he opportunity to talk to the wounded and distribute
copies of his little book, reserving a small stock of cigars for the
Hungarians who could understand neither French, Italian, or
German. At the end of the campaign, successful in itself though of
little influence on the outcome of the war, Garibaldi expressed his
admiration for the brigade's work in the letter, still preserved by
the Committee of the International Red Cross, in which he asked
to be regarded as 'pour la vie votre dévoué et reconnaissant
confrère'.

Under the Peace Treaty signed in October 1866, Austria retained the Trentino but ceded Venice to Italy. Back in Florence,
Georges was intending to spend the Christmas vacation quietly
with his family. Instead, he spent it in Venice, helping to conduct
the delicate preliminaries to the foundation of a Reformed Church
there, characteristically finding time to muse on the history of this
City State, note the glories of its architecture, and revel in the
incomparable colour of the Venetian school of painting, however
much he regretted its lack of the ideal and the spiritual. As his
term in Florence drew to a close he was thrown into a painful
state of perplexity as to which of several demands for his service he
should accept. This state was aggravated by grief at the death of
his mother; their relationship had remained exceptionally close
and he had relied on her judgement in all matters of importance.
Finally he decided to return to Naples, this time as pastor of the
Protestant community there. In October 1867 a daughter, named
Caroline after his mother, was born. Shortly afterwards, Georges,
who had long felt that the Neapolitan Protestants lacked adequate
buildings for their corporate life, conceived the ambitious plan of
raising money to build a worthy church, a school, and a hospital.
Consultations on the best means of raising so large a sum led to

Georges's decision to go to America. This mission was to involve his sister-in-law, Henrietta, the tenor of whose life had hitherto been very different from that of her sister.

Eight years younger than Helen and delicate in health, she had grown up thinking of herself as 'poor little Henrietta'. The separation from her sister so soon after the loss of the mother whose declining years she had so closely shared must have made her feel doubly orphaned. 'The longing will often come into my heart', she wrote to her sister when she was twenty-one, 'that I may soon go to those precious treasures who are awaiting us in glory.' Nevertheless, she sought earnestly for 'a sphere of usefulness' on earth and felt it her duty to be a comfort and support to her ageing uncles and aunts. She first went to live with 'poor dear Uncle Samuel' in his retirement in Brixton, where she settled down to doing wool work, reading *John Halifax, Gentleman*, and making friends with his housekeeper, Elizabeth Boyes. A few months later Uncle Samuel died of an apoplectic stroke while out in his carriage. It took Henrietta some weeks in East Coast resorts to recover from this emotional shock. For the next three years she lived with Elizabeth Boyes in Camberwell, where she attended the Baptist Chapel and was also much drawn to the Metropolitan Tabernacle, recently built for the popular preacher Charles Spurgeon with seating for 6,000. Her weekly letters kept Helen fully informed on the health and business concerns of their relatives, whom she assiduously visited.

The move to Hastings in 1864, a curious step on the face of it during the life of Uncle Thomas and Aunt Esther, was presumably for the good of her health. 7 Wellington Square, where she set up house with two members of the Boyes family, still stands at the quiet end of the town, sheltered behind by Castle Hill and immediately opposite the unusually imposing Baptist Chapel. Henrietta still felt she was 'walking in the valley of the shadow of death', for Aunt Esther died in August 1866 and Uncle Thomas eight months later. Thomas left £23,000 in trust to Henrietta, £10,000 to Helen, more modest provision for the children and grandchildren of Nathan, who had died three years previously, and the rest of his fortune to his brother George, the only survivor of his generation.

Helen meanwhile had had no need to search for 'a sphere of usefulness'. The difficulty of providing for the physical well-being of an habitually self-neglectful husband and a growing family of delicate children in a succession of temporary homes in often unhealthy and sometimes hostile places must have been formidable. She had, however, a genius for household management, and with the help of good Vaudois girls she generally succeeded in establishing a routine capable of responding to Georges's impulsive hospitality, containing his alms-giving raids on the larder and the linen cupboard, and maintaining the standard she herself thought proper to the social position of the family. For her children she was a centre of calm, and of strong, undemonstrative affection. As Pasteur Appia's wife she worked unobtrusively, very much the woman of 'silence and duty' he had so early seen in her. When by April 1868 Georges had finally decided on the voyage to America, Helen was anxious that he should not go alone. Not only was his English unpractised, he would be liable to forget his spectacles, forget to eat, and try to do too many things at once. She wrote asking Henrietta if she would be prepared to accompany him on this mission, which was expected to take three months.

There were many Quaker family links with America and the name of Sturge was known in wider circles, for Uncle Joseph had undertaken a personal anti-slavery campaign in the States and had been acclaimed in verse by the poet John Greenleaf Whittier who accompanied him. Though full of doubt as to her physical stamina and her ability to look after Georges, 'as of gentlemen I am a perfect ignoramus', Henrietta rose to the occasion. In the midst of her preparations, however, she was faced with a decision affecting her whole future life. On 28 April she wrote to tell Helen 'of the subject that has well nigh excluded all others from my thoughts since Friday morning, when I received a very straightforward, kind and manly offer from Dr. Daniel Moore'. Her explanations of how she had arranged to discuss this proposal with Uncle George and Aunt Jane before giving her answer were interrupted by the unheralded arrival of Georges, with bookings on the Cunard steamer *Australasia*, sailing from Liverpool the following Saturday. Five days later, having 'had the luxury of being seasick' on the Irish Sea, she sent a brief note to Helen telling of her acceptance of Dr. Daniel's offer: 'All along I have had no ecstasy of feeling, nor any wild rush of joy, but more of a calm, quiet contentment that God has given us to each other.'

With money still needed for repairing the ravages of the Civil War, Georges had not chosen a propitious time for his American mission. Moreover, he had acted with such precipitation once his mind was made up that no itinerary had been planned, nor accommodation arranged. Indeed, on arrival in New York he had to leave Henrietta on board ship while he went to a post office to discover the address of a minister in Brooklyn to whom he had an introduction. Fortunately, this minister not only offered them hospitality, but introduced Georges to leaders of church organizations and helped him to obtain the sponsorship of the American Christian Union. For Henrietta the outstanding event of this exhausting first week was the Sunday service conducted by Henry Ward Beecher, whose sister, the author of *Uncle Tom's Cabin*, had been a close friend of Uncle Joseph. His name as yet untouched by scandal, he was then at the height of his fame, a preacher unrivalled in emotional appeal. Georges could not share his sister-in-law's enthusiasm, evidently finding the histrionic element distasteful, and even she had to admit that some mannerisms were 'distinctly peculiar'. It was in helping Georges phrase his own less rhetorical sermons in idiomatic English that she began to feel she was of real service to him when he embarked on his mission in Boston. Amongst the mail awaiting Georges when they returned to New York was a pencilled note from his sister Louise, telling of his son Jean's death from croup. In his first bitter grief, Georges felt this death must be a judgement on him for deserting his family. Helen, however, with a stoical loyalty, wrote that she would not wish him to leave his mission unaccomplished, and Henrietta, rather against her own inclination, also urged his remaining. After a period of uncertainty and prayer, he decided to carry out his programme.

Even in his depressed state Georges found joy in the sharing of faith and concern, though the door-to-door collecting was always a burden to him. In 'hot and dusty' Philadelphia, both he and Henrietta found comfort in the company of the Cadbury family. They stayed next in 'the smoky Iron City of Pittsburg' and then in Chicago, where many of the popular preachers had left the heat of the city, taking the more affluent members of their congregations with them. This also proved the case in St. Louis, Cleveland, and Buffalo and it was not until they reached Saratoga Springs, after a refreshing sight of Niagara Falls, that Georges again had large congregations—and the especial pleasure of preaching in French to a group of itinerant Canadian Indians. Henrietta, too, had an unexpected privilege, which as a motherless bride-to-be she much appreciated; she attended a course of lectures on 'The Physiology of Women' given by a woman doctor: 'Her refined and chaste manner, her well-chosen language and above all her evidently high Christian principles tended greatly to take away from the prejudice you naturally feel against a woman being a Dr.' From Albany they took the night steamer down the Hudson river, arriving back in New York on the morning of 14 August.

Already they had been away from home for over three months. Georges had only raised half the sum he had hoped for, and was advised by zealous friends to stay on until the end of September. He was again torn by conflicting loyalties. Henrietta, on the other hand, was persuaded by both love and duty that she should take the first convenient ship to England. Apart from her being 'almost knocked up' by the heat, the dust, the bustle, and the incessant travelling, Dr. Daniel was now extremely impatient for her return. He had bought a larger house in Wellington Square as their future home and needed to consult her about the interior arrangements, besides which it had all along been agreed that the wedding should take place in November and she would have a host of things to do beforehand. At the eleventh hour Georges decided to accompany her on the *City of Boston*, which docked in Liverpool on 2 September. He stayed in England long enough to call on the Sturges in Birmingham and London and meet Dr. Daniel and his family in Hastings, and then travelled on to the Vaudois Valleys, where Helen and their three surviving children were staying with his sister Louise.

CHAPTER THREE

&❧&

The Baptist Moores

'FAMILY' was never to the Moores the absorbing interest that it
was to the Sturges and the Appias. What was known to them of
their forebears can be briefly told. During the seventeenth century
a Roger Moore, for reasons believed to be political, fled from
Ireland to the Low Countries; in 1688 he landed at Brixham,
Devon in the train of William of Orange. In Devon he married,
and by the late eighteenth century his descendants were sufficiently
well established for a John Moore to become Clerk of the Thurle-
stone Parish Council. As dispenser to the Plymouth Infirmary, one
of the sons of John Moore began a family tradition in medicine, of
which his son George, born in 1803, was perhaps the most distinguished example.

George Moore studied at St. Bartholomew's Hospital, in
Edinburgh, and in Paris, won the Fothergillian medal for an essay
on puerperal fever, became a member of the Royal Colleges of
Surgeons and Physicians, and a Fellow of several learned societies.
Ill health seems, however, to have interrupted his professional
career and limited its range. In 1838 he gave up his busy practice in
Camberwell and moved first to Tunbridge Wells and then to
Hastings. For a time he was physician to the Hastings Infirmary,
of which he was made a life Governor, but later returned to
private practice, tending, according to his future daughter-in-law,
to collect those patients whom other doctors had given up as
hopeless.

His illnesses did not prevent him from reading widely and
writing prolifically. When he was twenty-three a book of his verse
entitled *A Minstrel's Tale and Other Poems* was published in
London: diffusely written in the conventional poetic diction of the

time, these verses are unlikely to have been a source of inspiration to his poet-grandson. Apart from medical papers, his main subsequent works were motivated by his religious beliefs. He was a Baptist, though not an unquestioning one; indeed *Infant Baptism Reconsidered* (1840) questions a basic tenet; whereas of his counterblast to Darwinism, *The First Man and his Place in Creation* (1866), the *Athenaeum* reviewer wrote '. . . a vigorous argument on the orthodox side. From his own standpoint he has unquestionably done well.' He became most widely known for a series of books in which he considered man and theories about his physiology, psychology, and behaviour in the light of his own religious and medical experience. *The Power of the Soul over the Body* (1845), the first and most popular of these, went into six editions and was published in America and Germany. Drawing on modern and classical literature and philosophy, comparative religion and a fascinating diversity of medical case histories, he expresses his views with force and clarity, but disconcertingly allows of no distinction in kind between the scientifically proven and the divinely revealed. One admirable chapter entitled 'Injudicious Education' he was later to expand and publish in 1872 as *The Training of Young Children on Christian and Natural Principles*. This homely, rambling little book shows a psychological insight not usually associated with its time; it will be mentioned again in connection with the upbringing of the writer's grandchildren.

Information about Dr. Moore's private life is scanty and contradictory. Apparently he married four times, but only had children by his third wife, Hannah Green. Three sons became doctors, the eldest, George, practising in Hartlepool, where he became Mayor, the second going to Madras, probably as a medical missionary, and Daniel, born in 1840, practising in Hastings. The married daughter, Selina George, lived in Upper Norwood and had there got to know Henrietta Sturge before her move to Hastings.

There had consequently for some time been references to the Moore family in Henrietta's letters to her sister. In October 1864 she mentioned the announcement of 'Annie Miller's engagement to Dr. Moore's son Daniel, which is I think in most respects the subject of universal rejoicing'. Daniel's first marriage followed the same sad pattern as Henry Sturge's; it took place in 1865, and Annie died in January 1867, a few weeks after giving birth to a daughter, named after her. Baby Annie was then looked after by her maternal grandparents. So Henrietta, like her mother, was to marry a widower with a daughter. She had not known Daniel as long or as intimately as Lydia had known Henry, as is indicated in this picture she drew of him to satisfy her sister's curiosity at the time of the engagement:

He is very tall and rather slender. . . . His eyes are blue and although short-sighted and obliged almost constantly to wear glasses, he has a habit of looking you thro' and thro' so that from the first moment I saw him I always said I would be very sorry to have anything to hide from him. I think it is this partly that makes him so peculiarly clever in his profession; he is extremely kind and a great favourite with the poor, although he has a great objection to indiscriminate alms-giving; gentle enough to have satisfied our own precious Mama, and yet firm when he feels it his duty to be so. Naturally shy and reserved, yet really sociable and with plenty of good sense and as capable of saying cool and impudent things as ever his father is . . . and from what I have heard, tho' of this I cannot judge for myself, one of the most amiable tempers that can be found.

On her return from America, having approved Dr. Daniel's choice of 3 Wellington Square, Henrietta methodically set about the practical and social preparations for the marriage. In five hours at Hitchcocks in St. Paul's Churchyard, with Selina George's support, she bought 'a quantity of material' which was then delivered to the Office for the Employment of Needlewomen to be made up for her trousseau. She ordered her wedding-cake and selected the ornaments. Then came the most important occasion of all—the introduction of Dr. Daniel to Uncle George and Aunt Jane. She had warned them beforehand, as she did everyone, that her fiancé's extreme shyness might conceal his admirable qualities. However, what with Aunt Jane's sympathetic manner and Uncle

George's interest in medicine, he made, she believed, a favourable impression. The visits to those most closely concerned paid, she left all further arrangements in capable Boyes hands and set off on a pre-nuptial progress lasting the best part of a month. Her 'happy prospects', her recent experiences in America, the photographs of Helen's children she brought with her, all made her the centre of affectionate interest to well over a hundred relations in the Midlands and the West Country. When poor Dr. Daniel came down to fetch her from Bristol, he was introduced on arrival to Aunt Jane's numerous brothers, sisters, nephews, and nieces, and taken to call on eight other families the following morning.

The marriage took place in the Baptist Chapel, Wellington Square, on 26 November 1868, Henrietta then being twenty-nine years old, and Daniel twenty-eight. On the first day of the honeymoon, Henrietta wrote to her sister from Paris:

It is to me a sweetly solemn coincidence that this is the anniversary of the day ten years ago, when dear Mama was buried: and I can scarcely suppress a vain longing that she could have known and loved him who is now so closely connected with poor little Henrietta, as she did your best beloved. And yet when I think of the pathway of trials and tears that I have since had to pass thro' I cannot but be thankful she escaped them.

Ten days later they were with the Appias in Naples. The warmth of welcome there, from a family who could all speak his native tongue, must have melted Daniel's reserve. They then travelled to Rome (where even the sight of the Pope in his carriage aroused no discordant feelings), Florence, Milan, and again Paris, returning to Hastings on 23 December.

Early married life at 3 Wellington Square moved along quiet, comfortable lines. Henrietta was happy to leave to Elizabeth Boyes the main responsibility for running the household and supervising the care of her three-year-old stepdaughter Annie. This left her free to accompany Daniel, who was a great believer in fresh air and exercise, on his morning rounds, read Froude's

Essays on Great Subjects with him in the afternoons, interest herself in chapel affairs and maintain her voluminous correspondence. In August 1869, by which time Henrietta was expecting, they returned from a rather wet and uncomfortable holiday in Scotland to find that Elizabeth had fallen ill. In the agitation of managing without her, Henrietta wrote to her sister, 'I sometimes look a little wistfully forward, and wonder how I shall meet the new cares and responsibilities likely to open upon me . . . . the management of servants and children is the thing of all others from which I have most shrunk back, from the feeling of unfitness. . . .' This continued to be the case. While she could manage money matters and be sympathetic with people set in ways with which she was familiar, unpredictable human behaviour alarmed her. She had no natural gift for 'managing' servants and children, this was a duty forced on her by marriage. It was fortunate for Thomas Sturge, born on 4 March 1870, and all the subsequent children, that Daniel was the man she had married.

A month after Tom's birth Helen had another son, Charles, born in Paris where the Appias had at last settled. They decided that this would be a happy juncture to spend their summer holiday at Hastings, as Henrietta had often urged. Accordingly, by the middle of July, the Appia parents, Henry, now nearly nine years old, Louis, Caroline, baby Charles and Georges's sister Louise, were all installed in lodgings near the front, enjoying the sea and the sand and the company of the Moores. Their enjoyment was rudely interrupted by the outbreak of the Franco-Prussian War. Georges, not questioning for a moment that his place was with his parishioners, immediately returned to Paris. At first he and Helen could exchange letters frequently, but after the Battle of Sedan on 1 September, Paris was encircled and all normal communications broken. During the five months of the siege a few of Georges's letters got through by balloon, but from Helen he received only two brief messages by carrier pigeon. Fascinating as Georges's letters are as a record of life under the privations and bombardment of the siege, it can hardly have relieved Helen's anxiety to hear of his good fortune in sharing a 'gigot de chien', or of his involvement in the expeditions of the ambulance brigades. He was then unaware that behind the Prussian front his brother Louis was directing the work of the Red Cross aides in this first major conflict between co-signatories of the Geneva Convention.

For Helen and Louise the waiting seemed endless as they trailed from lodgings to relations and back to lodgings, unable to make plans, not knowing what was best to do for the children. Helen was back in Hastings for the birth of Henrietta's second son, Daniel Henry, known as Harry, only ten months younger than his brother Tom. Louise, meanwhile, had made arrangements for her eldest nephew's education with friends in London, while she raised money among Quaker circles for the relief of the starving Parisians. Then, at the end of January, Paris surrendered, letters began to arrive, at first through the Dutch diplomatic bag, and at last in mid-February, thinner than ever, Georges reappeared. During his short stay, it was decided that Louise should take Henry to the Claparèdes in Geneva, while Georges returned to make arrangements for Helen and the younger children outside Paris. Rejoicing in this prospect, Helen went for a farewell visit to the Midland Sturges, only to hear from Georges that the outbreak of civil strife in Paris made her return impossible. This second break in all communication, as the fighting intensified and the Commune was proclaimed, almost drove Helen to distraction. Charles was teething and had earache, Louis and Caroline had croupy coughs, and Alice, the nursemaid, a perpetual cold. 'I have had enough of England for a long time to come. I hope you will not feel insulted and will forgive me for being so savage, but I am so altogether discouraged that I don't know what to do,' she wrote. A postscript, unique in character in the correspondence between the sisters, follows: 'I shall have a certain temptation to get drunk between Charlbury and Birmingham. I do so miss my ale here, I wish I had thought of bringing a bottle of wine with me to drink on the sly.' It was not until April, by which time Helen was with good friends called Mayo in Hampstead, that she and

Georges were together again. After much 'considering, recon-
sidering and unconsidering', they crossed the Channel on 17
April, Helen then taking the children to Fontainebleau and
Georges returning to Paris.

Henrietta's domestic problems were of a different order. After
Harry's birth the house seemed cramped and the comings and
goings of a doctor's surgery more disturbing than before. All
Moore babies were breastfed, for Dr. George Moore strongly dis-
approved of wet-nurses except for compelling medical reasons.
This made it awkward for Henrietta to visit Uncle George and
Aunt Jane as often as she wished. Nathan's sons were still abroad
and all his surviving daughters under some form of guardianship,
so that she was the only near relative able to give the old man some
companionship in his retirement at Woodthorpe on Sydenham
Hill, Upper Norwood. There can be little doubt that the decision
to leave Hastings was inspired by Henrietta, just as it was she who
financed the leasing from the Governors of Dulwich College of a
new red-brick house, with three oak trees in the garden, in
Victoria Road, Dulwich Wood Park, Upper Norwood. Hastings
Lodge, as they named it, was only a few minutes' walk from
Woodthorpe, near to Selina George and her husband, a mile
from Dulwich College, and immediately opposite the fabulous
grounds of the Crystal Palace. They moved there in the autumn
of 1871.

From this address over the next seven years, Daniel announced
in brief, brisk notes to his sister-in-law the births of three daughters and two more sons. Over the same period, the Appias lost
their son Charles from meningitis, and of two daughters born to
them one died in infancy, so that Marie, born 8 June 1872, became
the youngest member of the family by five years. While Helen's
more robust constitution sustained her through the birth of eight
children and the death of four, Henrietta's rapid succession of
pregnancies further undermined her vitality. She grew thin and
sharp-featured, and became more and more of an invalid. The
children were all too often a source of irritation.

The move from Hastings had virtually made Daniel a doctor without patients. He was not a man to compete in a neighbourhood already well supplied with practitioners, and Henrietta's health precluded, in her eyes at least, a more distant practice. 'Daniel is often tired of waiting for patients,' she wrote in 1875, 'but I can be so little with the children that if they had not a Papa who plays with them so much and is in every way so good and watchful over them I am afraid they would suffer in many ways.' There was no lack of the usual nursery help; if nursemaids came and went, there was always Nana Padgeham. She was a positive influence on all the little Moores, most of whom remained warmly attached to her for the whole of her long life. Tom later recalled how, if any of them happened to fart, she would march round the room brandishing a smouldering roll of brown paper, while they all danced behind her, chanting, 'Let's get rid of the nasty smell!' Nevertheless, it was Daniel who to a degree that must have been uncommon at that time assumed much of the maternal role, without, however, usurping his wife's place as mother in the eyes of the children. It was he, for instance, who took three-year-old Tom into London, 'to get him a knickerbocker suit, so that he now leaves off his frocks and becomes a young man, of which he is very proud'.

In this task of bringing up his young family, Daniel had his father's opportunely published book as a guide. Except in his reticence in regard to excretion and sexual development, Dr. George Moore evidently bore little resemblance to our stereotype of the Victorian Parent. His advice on the upbringing of children is based on three main convictions: physical constitution, intelligence, and character are largely determined in early childhood; development should be guided through affection and trust, never through fear, whether of corporal punishment, hell-fire or the withdrawal of love; children should be respected as the individuals they are and so grow to respect themselves. 'Our natural endowments may be used or abused, but to suppress them is directly to fight against their Giver .... To fail in properly encouraging childhood to express itself as best it can is to turn all its nature awry.' His sense of the harmony between Christian and Natural Principles is also, though differently, apparent in this: 'Play is the serious business of child-life. Children go about it too with a solemn brightness in their eyes which we can imagine angels to have when most intent upon their blessed work.' The practical advice he gives is always positive. Plenty of outlets for physical and creative energy should be provided, including the freedom to make mistakes; when accidents occur children should not be over-comforted, nor over-rebuked, nor taught to blame the furniture. 'Strong temper is not necessarily bad temper, but rather is usually conjoined with warm affections and a will', and should, he believed, be controlled through these affections rather than by commands or correction. 'Divert rather than deny,' is one of his frequent recommendations, as is 'Expect well', while not expecting perfection. In education he maintained that enjoyment was essential and attention should never be forced. He vehemently attacked the method of making children learn by rote strings of facts unconnected with their experience. 'Attempts at education with mere verbal lessons, without illustration, merely stupefy children. ... A child should be told but little ... it should be induced to discover facts and principles for itself.'

Brought up on these enlightened principles himself, Daniel would probably anyhow have applied them to his children. It is known that he introduced them all to the piano at the age of three, and for at least half of them music became a lasting pleasure; if however, like Tom, they were not enthralled, the lessons were not continued. As they grew older, Daniel taught them reading, writing, arithmetic, geography, and English history, and encouraged them to garden and, bringing his microscope early into play, to study natural history. It was, no doubt, also he who grounded them firmly and imaginatively in Bible stories, and decided when they were ready to accompany the rest of the family to the Baptist Chapel in Upper Norwood, where the minister, Dr. Tipple, was, according to the third son George Edward's recollec-

Henry and Lydia Sturge, *c.* 1840

Georges Appia and the Sturge sisters, Henrietta (*left*) and Helen, December 1858

tion of him, 'exceptionally unorthodox, broad-minded, gentle and refined'. This was a place of worship congenial to Daniel, who was, like his father, an inquiring believer. In 1875 he had given his wife Matthew Arnold's *Literature and Dogma* as a birthday present, he read T. H. Huxley calmly, and he certainly discussed and argued religious questions, as most others, with his children later on.

Of all the children it was probably Tom who gave his parents most anxiety in his boyhood. A dreamy small child, allowing the more forward Harry to take his toys away from him, he was frequently unwell. A tendency to left-handedness had to be checked, according to current belief, by tying the offending hand to his chair. He was slow in learning to read and spell; it is probable that he was mildly dyslexic. When in September 1879 he and Harry started as day-boys at Dulwich College, it was the elder of the two brothers who lost his appetite and suffered sleepless nights. Throughout his school career, without being positively unhappy, he never seems to have related in any significant way to the life of this reputable, many-sided school. He was to tell his own children that the only occasion on which he distinguished himself there was on a hot sultry afternoon when all the class was drowsy; the master interrupted his lesson, lined the boys up in a row and fired questions at them. 'What', he asked, 'is better on an afternoon like this than a ripe and juicy plum?' Tom, tenth in the row, replied, 'Two ripe and juicy plums' and was fleetingly promoted top of the class.

In contrast to his lack of response at school, he remembered the keen pleasure of a summer holiday when he was about twelve. Usually the whole family, retainers, and baggage, travelled by special saloon railway coach to Hastings for the month of August, but on this occasion the children went without their parents to stay with the Boyes sisters in Reigate. A Miss McHedrow was there. She aroused in Tom a sense of such ease and confidence that from her he felt he could have learnt anything. His first letters home date from this period.

My dear Mama,
   I hope you are quite well.
   Yesterday morning we went to Mr. Ardennies Chapell a Mr. Hill I
did not care for him. In the evening we went to Red Hill and heard a
very nice Gentleman who preached on the XIX chap of the 1st Kings
and the 2, 3, 4 verses he was a very enerjetic man I know you would
like him he was Curate of the Church and acted as Curate as well as
Minister. I am reading the Victory of the Vanquished it is a very nice
book one of Schonberg Cotta Series a tale of the 1st Century I suppose
you have read it I am beggining to learn Needlework I am going to
dress a doll I take lessons from Annie when the girls do their work I
can hem pretty well for a begginer but I always go off into sowing I
can gather turn down and so end my accomplishments I made a petti-
cote yesterday this letter is not going today it is going tomorrow I
must stop for the present the little ones want me to teach them dress-
making
I must now say good-by as the paper is running [out] I send my love
and sprig of heather Your affectionate and loving son
                         T. S. Moore

Pressed flowers, varnished butterflies, and sketches in pen-and-ink
and water-colour often helped him to fill up the notepaper. A
knight in armour with a plumed helmet and a mysteriously em-
blazoned shield takes up half a page of this note:

My dear Mama
I hope you are quite well.
I have got a peakcock out It is drying its wings I have very little to
say so I shall ornament as much as possible but I received your letter
I am very sorry Miss McHedrow is gone

There follows a tiny sketch of a timid-looking lady and gentleman
carrying lamps as they are ushered from a large grey cave into a
smaller darker one by a figure in black. Under this is printed in
tipsy ornamental lettering,

                         I have tried
                           in vain
                         Riegate caves
                           to explain

However artistically embellished, such letters from her eldest son must have caused some dismay to Henrietta, who had herself from an early age written correctly in two languages, and she was probably less likely than Daniel to have appreciated their humorous gusto. Neither parent is likely to have been made uneasy by Tom's sudden enthusiasm for dressing dolls, which was, in fact, a ploy for remaining in Miss McHedrow's ambit; he had always been a sharer in the younger children's enjoyments, never, at this stage, giving himself elder-brotherly airs. His sister Hettie remembered him initiating games and enlivening mealtimes with his jokes. When he first went into long trousers he came and danced round the nursery to display them to her and Nellie, and then rolled them up to reveal his long woollen pants, so arousing envious admiration in their hearts. Not that he did not also share in activities more usual to his age. In the castle grounds at Reigate, he enacted Fenimore Cooper's *The Last of the Mohicans*, using the crooked handle of his butterfly net with low cunning. Playing Red Indians in a rocky dell in the grounds of the Crystal Palace was part of the activities of the exclusive Boomerang Club, of which the members were himself, his brother George and their school-friends, the two Paton brothers. They organized athletic contests, played two-a-side football, produced a monthly magazine of prose and verse, and gave recitals of music and poetry.

Tom missed much schooling through illness, so that by 1883 he was well below the class standard for a thirteen year old—a backwardness made the more noticeable by the scholastic progress of his school-age brothers and sisters. Annie had so distinguished herself at Dulwich High School that Henrietta, imbued with the Quaker concern for women's education, provided the money for her to read classics at Newnham College, Cambridge, two years later. Harry had early won a scholarship on the Science Side of Dulwich College; when a little later, Sanderson, the future headmaster of Oundle, was appointed head of this Side and set up the engineering workshops, Harry was one of his most brilliant pupils. This scientific bent, incidentally, possibly accounts for

Harry's non-membership of the Boomerang Club; his hobby was photography. Besides her all-round academic ability, eleven-year-old Hettie was showing uncommon musical talent. Most impressive of all was young George's progress. The early evidence of his powerful intellect must have been something of an embarrassment to his teachers; always top of the form, winning all the prizes, at the age of ten he had to be promoted to the Lower Sixth. Had Tom returned to school after recovering from a severe attack of scarlet fever, he would have been in a lower class than two younger brothers. Daniel, probably recognizing that the natural endowments of this son needed a different kind of nourishment, decided that his education should be continued at home for the time being.

During this year at home there were some formal lessons, but it seems that Daniel mainly guided and discussed Tom's widely ranging reading of literature, encouraged him to draw and paint, and introduced him to Ruskin's works. Henrietta gave him lessons in French, to which his lack of ear, perhaps, made him resistant. Annie attempted to teach him Euclid, but he could see little point in proving things that often seemed to him self-evident. For part of this time Hettie, who was suffering from eye-strain, was also being taught at home. In the afternoons they went for walks together, usually in the grounds of the Crystal Palace, for which all the children were fortunate in having season tickets. The Great Exhibition building in its setting of wooded parkland on the top of Sydenham Hill was then a world of wonders. The Palace itself was a centre for music, from brass bands to classical concerts and the great Handel Festivals; it had statues and classical friezes (whose contours, Tom noted, were becoming blurred by annual coats of whitewash); it contained a huge tropical house of flowers and trees, a parrot house, a monkey house, and an aquarium. The prehistoric animals had not yet invaded the lake which was the home of gulls and other water fowl: seals had a pool of their own. For a time that year a bear was chained to a stake in a gravel enclosure in which it paced up and down until its feet were sore, stopped to lick them, and then resumed its pacing. This, like much else on these walks, sank deep in Tom's mind, and was later to appear as a simile in his verse-play *Absalom*. As Hettie was then not allowed to read, he told her stories of his own invention or about the books he himself was reading, and as he was reading Ruskin this often led them to the Old Masters in the Dulwich Art Gallery. Hettie admired him immensely at this time; the strong attachment then formed was to last throughout their lives.

While the Moore children enjoyed and generated a full and stimulating life, that of their parents was circumscribed by Henrietta's invalidism and Daniel's reserve. They sometimes attended concerts at the Palace together, and occasionally Henrietta accompanied her husband to London—to the Landseer Exhibition or the Royal Academy. She did not accompany him to hear the revivalist preachers, Moody and Sankey, because, as she wrote to Helen, 'I question very much whether my Christian character would not have been more thorough and strong if I had not indulged in this sort of religious excitement in past years.' Their social intercourse was almost entirely confined to the circle of their close relatives. Not long before his death in 1880 Dr. George Moore stayed for two nights; 'so kind gentle and interesting . . . so really able to enjoy himself', he went to the British Museum, to see the Doré pictures, and to the Crystal Palace 'to view the fireworks and the Sultan of Zanzibar'. After Aunt Jane's premature death from diabetes in 1883, Henrietta made every effort to visit Uncle George daily. He was eighty-six and partially paralysed, but mentally alert. Partly to relieve himself of the burden of considering the appeals for money which came by nearly every post, he now made a Settlement of Funds, amounting to £350,000 in trust. Under the larger section of this, one hundred charities received donations; while the main beneficiaries were hospitals and Nonconformist Missionary Societies, many small welfare, educational, and penal establishments were included, Homes for Seamen rightly not being forgotten considering how this fortune was amassed. The smaller section provided life annuities for fifty relatives, including Henrietta's children.

In the spring of 1885 Helen arrived with her daughters Caroline and Marie, now aged eighteen and thirteen respectively, for a fortnight's stay. Marie was at first somewhat over-awed by the size of the Moore household; when at morning prayers after the Bible reading the assembled family, nursery and domestic staff fell to their knees, she was quite stunned. Her natural vivacity soon reasserted itself in the company of her cousins, who were intrigued by this foreign girl and happy to introduce her to the wonders of the Crystal Palace. Their elders meanwhile decided that Tom should join the Appias for their summer holidays, which they now regularly and joyfully spent in the Vaudois Valleys. Marie may well have whetted his interest by describing their house there. Just above La Tour, on the south-westerly foothill of Mont Vandalin, her parents had bought the land known for centuries as the Airals Blancs, because of its white farmhouse with a paved threshing-floor. On to this farm they had built a tall, roomy house with two roofed balconies, the lower of which ran right along the front of both buildings. Only a hedge separated the courtyard and garden of the house from the tenant farmer's yard; his cattle grazed the orchards and steep meadows below, and on the lowest slopes he grew grapes and maize. In a little oak wood there was an iron summer-house, and nearer the house were two shady arbours of sweet chestnut, each with a stone table.

At the end of June, an excited, slightly apprehensive Tom, inwardly convinced that nothing on the Continent could be as good as in England, was taken as far as Paris by his father. A few days later the advance party of Aunt Helen, Caroline, Marie, and himself set off on the long, dirty, never-forgotten train journey to Turin. In an early autobiographical poem, Tom recalled the faint dawn over the lake at Culoz, Marie's excited chattering as the train climbed into the mountains, and then,

> Modane, we are out on the platform,
> The torrent, with thunder below,
> Shakes a sun-filled vivacity that warm
> Is all as fresh as snow.

Oh the peaks! Oh the pines so tiny
That over the shoulders crowd
In countless millions, all shiny
From combing the hair of a cloud!

I saw them and staggered dumbfounded;
Their beauty breathed power through me.
All my energies keen hunger hounded,
I drank enough coffee for three.

From Turin a local train trundled them on across the plain, past the great rock of Cavour, to La Tour; with Chitta the donkey drawing their luggage, they walked up to the Airals Blancs.

At first Tom accompanied his aunt and cousins on leisurely expeditions, either on foot or in the donkey-cart. He was enthralled by the mountain rivers; on the other side of their Mont Vandalin foothill the Angrogne rushed down in ragged waterfalls and pools, whereas the Pellice entered La Tour as a broad, glittering stream. In the town they went to the market and paid calls. Many streets were named after Vaudois heroes and martyrs, and one after an English benefactor, the one-legged veteran of Waterloo, General Beckwith, who had endowed all the Vaudois settlements with schools. Tom was shown the old, yellow-washed church of the Coppiers where his uncle Appia had been consecrated, and the presbytery that he had converted into a training school for girls in 1856, the year the grape harvest failed. His uncle's exertions during that year of famine thirty years before were part of the collective memory of the peasants; he had raised money to buy food and set up small workshops for basket-making and weaving: throughout the bitter winter he had brought spiritual consolation and material help to the mountain farmsteads, often giving the clothes off his back and, on one occasion at least, the boots off his feet.

Soon Uncle Appia arrived with his two grown-up sons, Henry, already a pastor, and Louis, just completing his theological studies. Uncle Appia, one of whose simple maxims was 'Il faut savoir tout', took Tom for long walks. During these a stream

41

of information on the flora, fauna, geology, husbandry and history of the Vaudois Valleys poured from him, however steep the gradient. He seems to have found especial pleasure in thus increasing the knowledge of this young nephew from England who knew so little. One day he took him up the winding Angrogne valley of hanging wooded cliffs and showed him the narrow cave, best entered on hands and knees, used as a church in times of persecution, and the smaller caves, some only accessible by ladders, where the Barbes had lived. The following day all the family were to have gone into La Tour. 'Everything was ready,' Tom wrote to his mother; 'just at the last minute Uncle Appia decided to take me a course with him and let the others go down alone, so off we went. I think you would not like Papa to do that.' Uncle Louis of Geneva stayed for a few days, but Tom saw little of him; he was now the senior member of the Committee of the International Red Cross and seems to have been in need of quiet and rest.

Then Tante Louise joined them and preparations were made for the ascent to the Uverts, her holiday retreat, lodged on a natural terrace at the head of the Rora valley. This was built of stone on the model of an old mountain farm. The ground floor, instead of housing cows, goats, and pigs, had been designed for human use; steps led up to a balcony on to which the bedrooms opened; the low-pitched roof was of huge slabs of stone. From the front one could see the rocky ridges of the Valleys dwindling down into the vast plain of the River Po. A short scramble up the flowery pasture and scrub behind led to a ridge with a view over range after range of mountains to the snowy peaks of the High Alps. Firewood had to be collected, water fetched from a spring and, though quantities of provisions had been brought up from the Airals Blancs for the three-week stay, milk, butter, cheese, and eggs were fetched from the only other building, a farm belonging to true 'aristocrats of the Valleys', an ancient family of Vaudois peasants. By this time Tom had been fitted with proper mountain boots, 'coming half a yard too high up my legs, but a very nice pair'. So equipped, he undertook quite strenuous climbs, usually under the guidance of his kind and gentle cousin Louis. From the Col la Croix they climbed Mont Palavas, from whose summit, thanks to a perfect day, they saw Mont Viso, the Gran Paradiso, Mont Rosa, the Matterhorn, and Mont Blanc. Tom's quick sketches in his letters home convey more vividly than his words the struggle and exhilaration of such climbs.

Apart from carefully planned expeditions, Uncle Appia believed in improving every shining hour, so that back at the Airals Blancs Tom, like Marie, had a basic daily programme:

I am called at seven, breakfast half past, prayers at eight. My French lesson [with Caroline] lasts about an hour then I read history, then I catch butterflies, read for my own pleasure or something of the sort till dinner at half past 12. After dinner I draw and we have a reading aloud or such things till four afternoon tea, then we go for a walk till supper ... after supper I do something or other until it is dark enough to catch moths, and so on with a great many alterations practically every day.

On butterflies Tom was already an authority. For the benefit of his brother George, he recorded the capture of Clouded Saffron, Marbled White, Alpine Argus, Camberwell Beauty, Small Tiger, and Large Oak Sugar Moths, and posted him an unusual green beetle. Of his progress in French, about which his mother often inquired, he could only report after some weeks, 'I can now manage to make the cook understand what I like which is an improvement.' Marie's fluency in English may have been one reason for this unremarkable advance, for as the only children in the party they naturally spent much time together.

Had she given the matter a thought Marie might well have been surprised that a boy cousin two years her senior should have been so ready a companion in her chosen activities, but she was quicker in response than he and the difference in age caused no barrier. He had some reservations, it is true, about the small menagerie she had adopted by various means: rabbits, guinea pigs, a tortoise, a lamb, a cock and hen, two orphan jays, and an ailing woodpecker. When the woodpecker finally died, Tom was much embarrassed by her uncontrolled sobs. Her pet lamb, Minablanc, he always referred to as 'that 'orrible moutong'; it tried to go everywhere that she went, lay gazing at her through the French windows of the salon while she practised her music, bleated stridently whenever she was out of sight and altogether took up too much of her time and attention. Not that Marie did not appreciate Tom's company too. In retrospect she decided that because of it that summer holiday was the best she had ever had. Never before had helping with the grape harvest been such fun; never before had she taken off her shoes and stockings to paddle in the Pellice—and caught little fish and *écrevisses*.

'It was rather queer,' Tom had written after attending his first church service in La Tour, 'during the sermon $\frac{1}{4}$ of the congregation were asleep, and $\frac{1}{8}$ were gigling and wispering to one another, another an $\frac{1}{8}$ were staring around them and the rest were listening. The men are divided from the women.' This was certainly unlike Dr. Tipple's chapel in Upper Norwood. After he had spent a month with the Appia family, he must have revised his impression of the Vaudois attitude to religion. Here was an unquestioning evangelist fervour, an exaltation of faith, an involvement in works he had not encountered at home. Only Aunt Helen, quietly providing domestic comfort and unlimited hospitality, had little time for active evangelism. Tom heard his uncle and cousin Henry preach, he met all the neighbouring pastors, the candidates for ordination, and cousin Caroline's Sunday school class. He helped Louis distribute clothing to the poor and Marie sell lottery tickets for the Missions. A climax of activity was reached during the Annual Synod of the Vaudois Churches in August, when the foreign delegates stayed at the Airals Blancs and numbers were entertained in the evenings. Although Tom was fired with enthusiasm for the history of the Vaudois people and inevitably impressed by the personality of his uncle, he seems on the whole to have remained a detached observer. Uncle Appia was the man whose character he grew to love and admire more perhaps than any other, but not the man who was to influence him most profoundly.

He returned from his three-month holiday so invigorated, so in every way enlarged, that he seemed like a new person to his family. When in September he started as a student at the Croydon School of Art, his head was still crowded with memories, not so much of his Uncle Appia or his Gallic cousin Marie, as of the Alpine air and sun, the mountains and the torrents.

CHAPTER FOUR

❦❦❦

Art Student

HAD it not been for the presence of a 23-year-old part-time teacher of engraving at the Croydon School of Art, Tom might have found little more inspiration there than he had at Dulwich College. Charles Haslewood Shannon had been apprenticed to one of the last engraving firms to specialize in book illustration; while there he had made friends with the slightly younger Charles Ricketts. They had both progressed to the Lambeth School of Art and were still attending classes there. Shannon was an athletic, handsome young man, quiet in manner and with an ironically jocular way of talking to which Tom readily responded. He proved, indeed, to be Shannon's most responsive and promising pupil. With this teacher's help, Tom had by 1887 persuaded his parents to allow him to transfer to the Lambeth School, where he was enrolled in the modelling class. Here he first met Ricketts, the man whom Shannon had admiringly described as always able 'to evolve good compositions, to pick out good work and to remember everything he had seen'. Tom was astonished by the appearance of

a short ramshackle youth in a cloud of extremely fine tow-coloured hair which stood round his head like a dandelion puff. At 11.0 a.m. he had just turned out of bed and had no collar, no socks and but just enough on to enable him to cross the 200 yards from their rooms to the school. When he entered he was imitating an orchestra with gestures as well as sounds, a life-long mode of progression from room to room. Someone began describing a picture of young girls with hay rakes; he pretended to be shocked, 'What, young girls with rakes!' and danced about, hiding his face in his hands, and laughed even more than we did. He looked and behaved as little like my preconceived Ricketts as creature well could.

46

Like Tom, Ricketts had received little formal education. Until he was left an orphan in his middle teens, much of his childhood had been spent on the Continent, for his mother, a gifted amateur musician, was a Frenchwoman. Back in England with grandparents, too delicate in health to attend school regularly, his swift intelligence and exceptionally acute sensory perception found their own sustenance and direction, so that he early acquired aesthetic purpose and authority. In the shabby rooms in the Kennington Road he now shared with Shannon, the hideous wallpaper was hidden by reproductions of Old Masters and the moderns they most admired: Rossetti, Watts, Puvis de Chavannes, Gustave Moreau, Rodin. . . . Here Tom 'trembled lest the minutes were going too fast' as he first listened to Ricketts's talk or watched the scrupulous care they both gave to the 'hack' illustration with which they then supplemented their extremely meagre incomes. The following year, 1888, they moved to The Vale, then a cul-de-sac of four low, balconied eighteenth-century houses, where, at different times, Whistler, Walter Sickert, and William de Morgan lived. At Number 1 they inherited Whistler's decor of daffodil-yellow walls and panelled dadoes of apple-green in the finely proportioned downstair rooms. This house was to give them a fitting atmosphere to work, and more space for the art treasures which, by skimping on food, they gradually acquired. At first, however, they could not afford the rent unaided, so two upstairs rooms were let as 'work rooms' to Tom and another student.

To Tom, immature for his seventeen years, groping towards self-awareness and expression, his glimpses of Ricketts's and Shannon's total dedication to creative artistic activity, the mastery of different media, the study of past masters, were a revelation of the ideal life. The Vale, not the Lambeth School of Art, was, in fact, to give him his artistic education and form his aesthetic philosophy. Ricketts was the eloquently dominant partner. The energy and rapidity of his mind, his savage fastidiousness and his brilliant talk excited in Tom feelings not this side of idolatry. While his own intellectual and creative powers received great stimulus from this

47

association, they were directed and moulded by his veneration for Ricketts, whose views on art, on literature, and (or so he then thought) on life he accepted absolutely.

Unlike Ricketts and Shannon at his age, however, he was still, and was for years to remain, firmly rooted in his home and family. At Hastings Lodge he shared a bedroom with Harry and George. After the light was out he told them a serial story of which the hero was a red-haired criminal called Rabbits, a character based on Mr. Roberts, the blameless station master at Upper Norwood. Years later, George, always one for a good story, still marvelled at the ingenuity of the escapades in which night after night Rabbits and his pal defeated 'the guardian angels of the law'. During the day Tom, who was now composing as well as reading poetry, took to reciting in his bedroom, so loudly that on one occasion a small boy passing along the street was moved to knock on the door and report, 'There's a man upstairs—preaching.' He was also given to wandering about the house murmuring, 'Now more than ever seems it rich to die . . .', partly one suspects for the pleasure of hearing his mother say, 'Oh, Tom, *don't* say that!' She had no doubt forgotten that at his age she had expressed not altogether dissimilar sentiments.

The noise and turmoil created by her growing children in the restricted space of the house had indeed for some time adversely affected Henrietta's nerves. Annie, always quiet and predictable in her ways, had now graduated and was set for a teaching career, but her brothers and sisters were not particularly quiet or predictable in their behaviour. Harry, president of the school Science and Photographic Societies and about to win a scholarship to Trinity College, Cambridge, needed space for equipment and experiments and found a great deal to argue about with Tom and George. Indeed they all talked and argued all the time and enjoyed a wealth of family jokes, often sparked off by Hettie's keen eye for the absurd. Only the youngest brother, gentle, diffident Bertie, seems to have inherited his mother's unalloyed earnestness, while the baby of the family, Sarah, was precocious in jokes. Both these younger children were musical, as was George, who had a clear singing voice, so that it was not only through Hettie that the piano was in constant demand. To meet the conflicting needs of his children and his wife Daniel was planning to build on to Hastings Lodge when in April 1888 Uncle George Sturge died.

He was ninety years old and had settled his affairs with true Quaker care. 'I make the dispositions hereinafter contained', he had written in his will two months previously, 'under I trust some sense of gratitude for many mercies received, and with a desire not to forget those who may be considered my poorer neighbours in the widest sense of these words. I request that my funeral may be plainly conducted and free from all pomp and parade.' Eighty further charitable bodies received legacies, as did over a hundred relatives, friends, and retainers. His personal possessions were individually allocated down to the last butter knife, which, together with £50, went to 'Annie, daughter of Daniel Moore by his first wife'. Henrietta, the residual legatee, inherited Woodthorpe, with 'gas fittings blinds carpets carriages horses garden tools stock alive and dead', and a share of the furniture. The old man had become increasingly reluctant to spend money on anything connected with his own comfort so that the house was in bad repair and proved a considerable worry to Daniel. However, by the end of the year the family were able to move into this far roomier home with a large garden and land for a few cows and poultry.

Even after the move Henrietta would not agree to Hettie's making music her career, the prospect of a perpetually practising daughter still being more than she could bear. There were perhaps other reasons too; in spite of her shrewdly critical eye and tongue, Hettie was, as Tom was to say, 'the most motherly of sisters', sensitive, kind, and clear-headed. The early ambition of her younger sister Nellie to study medicine was, on the other hand, encouraged by both her parents. Tom now had a room of his own at the top of the house and, though chilly, it was a sanctum, a little annexe to 1 The Vale, where he could work, compose verse of his own, and

49

recite undisturbed and undisturbing. In the autobiographical chapter that George later wrote by way of introduction to a book on his own work published in America, another aspect of Tom at this time emerges. Of the five people George mentions as influencing his early intellectual development, four were masters at Dulwich College and the fifth was his eldest brother, 'a far readier talker than I and far more fertile of ideas ... his conversation, including conversations he sometimes had with my father at meal times, had a great deal of influence on the formation of my opinions'. He amplifies this by describing how during a summer holiday at Hastings he became so deeply involved with an 'ultra evangelical' group that, much against the grain, he was impelled to distribute tracts to holiday-makers on the beach. The falling away of these intense religious feelings and his becoming an agnostic by the time he left school he attributed largely to this brother's influence. Tom's own views on religion during this time were undoubtedly inspired mainly by Matthew Arnold; his mother's copy of *Literature and Dogma* remained for many years his Bible. These views were soon to be enlarged by his reading of Ernest Renan's *Vie de Jésus*.

Uncle Appia's interest in English Nonconformist movements was by this time bringing him over to attend conferences every spring. From 1887 onwards Tom returned to Paris with him to spend his Easter holiday visiting the Salons and studying the permanent art collections. The Appia home by the Luxembourg Gardens in the rue d'Assas was a world as different from Woodthorpe as that was from 1 The Vale. A perpetual ferment of activity sprang from his uncle's ministry and its ramifications. Since 1879 Georges had been one of the four pastors appointed to the large Protestant parish in the centre of Paris. Their church, the Rédemption near the boulevard des Italiens, had been simply and impressively constructed inside the former Toll House, by panelling one half of this huge hall to three-quarters of its height, the light coming from windows in the bare masonry of the arched roof above. Its congregation was drawn from a wide area. Georges's tall, spare figure, proceeding rapidly at a characteristic forward angle, was a familiar sight in the streets of the city. He had close ties with parishes where he had worked previously, particularly with the Maison des Diaconesses in the rue de Reuilly. This was a sister house to that of the Protestant nuns in Kaiserswerth, where Florence Nightingale had studied sick nursing in 1851, and like it had a school for novices, an orphanage, a home for old people, and a hospital. Georges had been chaplain-cum-teacher there in 1857, his mother had died there, and in the Maison's barrack-like buildings, set in a peaceful, wandering garden, he and his family still sought recovery from sickness or exhaustion. Relief of material distress in the parish was carried on in Georges's usual impulsive, somewhat unco-ordinated way, though one evening a week was theoretically set aside for applicants. These ranged from intellectual *émigrés*, many from Alsace, to an old prostitute who banged on the door in the middle of the night, bawling, 'Où est Georges? Je veux Georges!'

Parochial duties alone could not of course satisfy Georges's energetic evangelist spirit. He was Vice-President of the Association of Sunday Schools and of the Protestant Missionary Society. He was on the Council of the Paris Christian Union and meetings of the Y.W.C.A. were held in his home. Inspired by the Scotswoman Miss Howard, he pioneered an early version of the Student Christian Movement amongst undergraduates of all faculties. Josephine Butler recorded how when she came to Paris to win support for her moral crusade in 1875, 'it was he who first held out his hand when our mission was very little understood and to a group of friends gathered in his home interpreted our message with a clarity and eloquence that my husband and I have never forgotten'. The name of 'la chaine humaine' that Georges gave to this crusade in France came from a whaling story told him by Thomas Sturge. During an island landing, one of the whaler's crew was knocked into the water by a wounded sea-lion; the other seamen formed a chain by linking hands and so rescued him before he was swept irrevocably out to sea. Louise Appia, shaken to the depth of her being by Mrs. Butler's revelations concerning prostitution, decided to dedicate herself to rescue work and since 1876 had been in charge of a Refuge for Young Women opened by the Diaconesses.

While Georges would in principle have subscribed to Dr. George Moore's theories on the upbringing of children, his own fervent religious convictions and his encyclopaedic knowledge made him willy-nilly something of an exacting parent. When Henry was just two, he had written to his wife, '. . . il est fort capable de s'intéresser aux autres, ne crains pas de lui faire *donner*, *donner* à ces camarades, *donner* aux pauvres . . . Il faut qu'on le tienne et qu'on ne lui passe rien'. As he was helping the doctor wash his new-born daughter Caroline, he had said, 'Qui sait si, un jour, cette enfant ne prendra pas le chemin de l'Orient pour être missionnaire en Perse, en Chine ou aux Indes?' Although he would not have deliberately influenced them in their choice of career, it is not surprising that both sons followed in his footsteps. By the time Tom's visits began, Henry was pastor of 'l'église missionaire belge' in a working-class suburb of Liège; in 1886 he had married Thérèse Rey, a sculptress who had studied under Rodin and Mercie. Louis was assisting his father in Paris.

The two daughters had first been educated at home, by their parents and governesses. Caroline had suffered much illness, possibly rheumatic fever. A warmly affectionate girl, intelligent and creatively gifted, her conscientious effort to fulfil her father's expectations may have caused strain; when her younger brother Charles and her baby sister died within ten months of each other, she was old enough at ten to feel she ought to comfort her mother as well as cope with her own grief as her father enjoined. Whatever the cause, she tended as she grew older to be easily thrown into a state of emotional agitation and to feel the need to justify her actions and motives. She became progressively engaged in work in Sunday schools and the Christian Union. Her creative gifts also found outlet in the elaborate celebration of anniversaries that the family so immensely enjoyed. Marie had not experienced the same pressures; her father's outlook had mellowed, Paris had always been her stable home, and she had a natural gaiety of disposition, a quickness of sympathy, a readiness to admit she was at fault, that endeared her generally. When in 1889 she was given the exceptional opportunity of entering the Lycée at Versailles she embraced her studies with confidence and a spontaneous delight in learning. Both girls had been brought up sharing in their mother's household responsibilities. The apartment in the rue d'Assas, though small, was always hospitable: to *déjeuner* came a variegated stream of parishioners, European colleagues, professors, students, Quaker cousins, foreign missionaries; to soirées, with music and guided discussion, the more intimate circle of friends and relations.

During his early visits to the rue d'Assas, Tom experienced a malaise which he did not hesitate to confide in letters to his mother written in the sarcastic vein he then affected:

The Appias are now, as ever, in the midst of a whirlwind, out of which from time to time looms one of their excited faces to say a few words to me sitting in a corner apart, soon again to be lost in the hurricane of unfinished sentences and incomplete ideas in which they live. The most astonishing thing of all is that they seem never to lose their tempers ... the reason is I suppose that for them out of the darkness shines a light.

He dutifully attended the services at the Rédemption, where the dark wood-panelling gave a suggestion of opulence to the plain interior and the only focus for attention was the elegant canopied pulpit. As he listened to sermons from his uncle and the other preachers, all men he respected, it was gradually borne in on him that by them he must logically be regarded as a lost soul destined for hell-fire. He was hurt and indignant. 'At home these sort of thoughts are merely a mental recreation, but here one meets them face to face every day and they become anything but recreative. . . . Yesterday I had the pleasure of hearing Uncle Georges call Renan bad names and make faces over la Vie de Jésus. . . . I of course sat very good and said nothing.' Among the bewildering welter of

Appia relations, however, he was relieved to discover some near to him in age who shared his scepticism. Ernest Guy, a lively young man of unfixed ideas, and his medical student cousin, Raymond Penel, indulged indeed in uninhibited mockery, hilariously recounting, for instance, how Tante Louise, on having the theme of Daudet's *Sappho* explained to her by a nephew, had asked with grave incredulity, 'Mais, dis moi, est ce qu'ils vivaient dans le péché?'

If the Appias' exclusive religious creed alienated Tom by its narrowness, the Protestant community to which they belonged was more scholarly, cultivated, and cosmopolitan than his own home circle. From the first he benefited from his uncle's portfolios of reproductions of Old Masters and his comprehensive knowledge of the art treasures of Paris. As his grasp of the language slowly improved he devoured French literature. Initially, however, he felt himself to be slow-witted, lethargic, and gauchely English in comparison with most members of the family. They were so learned, so accomplished, so ardent, and wore their hearts so naturally on their sleeves. Even from his former playmate, Marie, he was in some ways distanced. Her confirmation in 1888 heightened a solemn inner certainty he could not share. The instinctive social *savoir faire* she already showed made him more conscious of his own awkwardness. His habit of 'sitting good and saying nothing' because as yet he lacked the confidence to voice differences of opinion in the presence of his aunt and uncle, misled them as to the nature of his thoughts. To them he appeared a shy, meditative youth, wholly dedicated to the contemplation of art. His aunt appreciated the way in which he always returned punctually, if breathless, at meal times.

Nothing indeed could detract from his delight in what was the main purpose of these visits. He spent days in the Louvre, the Luxembourg, the Musée des Arts Decoratifs, and visited all the exhibitions. In his letters home the emphasis is on recent and contemporary work—the Societé des Pastellistes, 'that great desert the Salon', the Beaux Arts. Rodin's *John the Baptist* at the

Luxembourg which Caroline and Marie 'think simply horribly ugly' to him 'is full of movement and expression and stands out among the other statuary with the force of a Titan among the lesser gods—the simile is very bad, but it must pass'. An exhibition of the animal bronzes of Barye made him envious of his mother who had attended Barye's lectures in her youth—'he invented animals in sculpture and I don't think anyone has gone beyond him since'. 'Imagine only,' he writes of an exhibition of Japanese prints, 'there are considerably over 100 works by that old man who was so in love with making pictures, including the best part of the 36 views of Fujiyama, than the best of which there are no more beautiful landscapes in the world—unsigned by Turner.' Puvis de Chavannes' *Poor Fisherman* and *Execution of John the Baptist* and Gustave Moreau's *Orpheus* aroused especial enthusiasm. He spoke so earnestly to Madame Lecadre in her art photography shop of the admiration for Moreau's work among English art students that she persuaded Moreau to allow more of his work to be photographed. This led Tom to plead with his father for an extension of his stay in Paris so that he might have a chance of seeing the originals in her studio, 'which will be more useful to me than a week of school work'. Many of his preferences reflect the influence of Ricketts, as perhaps does his dismissal of Monet's *Studies of Haystacks* 'from a variety of points of view and in various effects of light' as 'food for asses' (an opinion he was later to revise). Ricketts and Shannon were traditionalists; in their own work they aimed at applying the techniques of the Old Masters within established conceptions of composition and they were resistant to innovation.

In 1889 these two impecunious young men launched a brave venture—*The Dial: an occasional publication*—whose 'sole aim' was 'to gain sympathy for its views'. The first number of this folio, fastidiously printed on handmade paper, was composed mainly of their own work: lithographs, etchings, wood-engravings, short stories of a legendary Pre-Raphaelite character, an article on Puvis de Chavannes by Ricketts. John Gray, who shared their admiration for the French Symbolists, was the other significant contributor. This friend, who later became a Roman Catholic priest, was then at once a civil servant, a scholarly poet, and 'a dandy about town'; he was to be named by the *Star* as the original of Oscar Wilde's Dorian Gray, a journalistic indiscretion for which the paper apologized when threatened with action for libel. Both he and Reginald Savage, another Lambeth student admitted to the Vale circle, remained constant contributors.

It was in the second number, not published until 1892, that the 22-year-old Tom first appeared in print; so substantial was his contribution of ten short poems, an article on Maurice de Guérin, and a short story that, to his unconcealed delight, it became known as 'Moore's number'. In the three further numbers, which included work by Lucien Pissarro, Michael Field, and Laurence Housman, his first woodcuts appeared, showing the range of technical skill he had learnt, mainly from Ricketts and Shannon, and a robust quality entirely his own.

A briefly kept journal opened in July 1891 was, like that of his grandmother Lydia, a form of self-disciplining, though with an object very different from hers. 'Here no secrets of soul or felt lack of soul; this little book shall be a record rather, with such power of precision as I may, of those things noted by the eyes which might never have a second passage through the mind through memory's fault.' The first entry is a lovingly careful description of Whistler's portrait of Miss Alexander: '. . . against the black dado is a chair with a mantle of green, the green of sliced cucumber without the glister'. After a second viewing, he added, 'What complicated, mysterious simplicity! With what dextrous hazard the great grey, white and black tones are interrupted by beryl and gold gleams.' Subsequent entries are not, in fact, confined to the visual; an impression of a fellow student: 'How strange this young man, physically splendid, with the brain of a hen, picking about for crumbs of scandal, cackling with endless small talk'; a ribald story told him by Ricketts, redounding to the credit of Arthur Symons; impressions as he walked in the rain from Cambridge station to

Trinity College, carrying a sodden box of Woodthorpe eggs to Harry; reflections, after a visit to Ely Cathedral, on 'what makes all modern restoration ineffectual. The absence of that seriousness induced by the presence of the devil?' After two months the journal lapses, to be resumed a year later. 'These old pages show me other than now; the gap between is a period of transition. A greed of sight and noticing then to a thirst for aspects, atmospheres, "les ensembles"; changing not changed, for one has to begin again as it were for this new result, stammer, blunder up a new technical stair, top is out of sight.' The closing entry of the second series is a description of a day spent with his mother in Bristol, where, after he has been formally appointed a trustee of her marriage settlement, they visited the home of elderly Quaker relatives, 'the inside revealing a comfort evidently costly; the two small-bodied old maids with an immense cat more or less form a sameness of hue and texture, dark and silky, unnoticeable among the crowded cosy furniture'.

Another exercise in observation which must date from about this time is a study, scribbled in a notebook, of Miss L.N.S., a girl model in the life class. He first describes her appearance, and how her initial concern to hide her private parts when posing 'soon vanished as she became certain of us and must have been mere prudence. She never behaved other than modestly, though without the least reserve, as frankly as any girl when clothed'. From her chatter between sittings, he then pieces together her background: her earlier experiences as a ballet girl; her rowdy home life, punctuated with violent quarrels with her sisters; her various 'fellahs' and 'mashers'; her brief flirtations with the Salvation Army and the Band of Hope. She claimed to have been a model for eight years, and to have sat for Mr. Watts, draped, for Mr. Ricketts as an angel with wings, for Mr. Burne-Jones, in his always unheated studio, both draped and in the nude, for Mr. Tadema, who kept slippers at the door for models to change into because he couldn't bear boots, and in classical drapery for Mr. Ruskin, who always asked what the sermon was about on Sunday, as did Mr. de

Morgan. She is effectively and objectively brought to life; but this was not the genre, and Miss L.N.S. was not the kind of subject, that Tom was to pursue.

At this stage in his life he began using his second name, Sturge, as part of his surname. This was doubtless partly to avoid confusion with the Irish songster, but it also denoted the assumption of a persona appropriate to his aspirations. He grew a beard, not then usual among young men. His scrawly writing was transformed into a beautiful, even, yet quite unmannered hand. Amongst his fellow students he spoke with authority and now had disciples of his own.

Harry Mileham, a natural protégé being a younger former Dulwich College boy, left an account of how his education was taken in hand by Tom. On Sundays they often had tea together in their respective homes, not, however, mixing with the families. At Woodthorpe Tom would read poetry, particularly Browning and Keats, aloud to him, and at his home Mileham would produce his own work for inspection and receive advice and encouragement. Then they would set out on long walks, allowing no one to overtake them, during which Tom discoursed on Walter Pater, Matthew Arnold, or Flaubert. Alternatively, they took the train to Victoria and walked rapidly to the South Kensington Museum, where Tom showed him the work of the Old Masters most likely to be helpful to him. Another disciple, and one for life, was the much older A. Hugh Fisher, who had thrown up a clerkship in an insurance office to study etching at the Lambeth School. With Henry Poole, the sculptor, the relationship seems to have been on a more equal footing, though both he and John Tweed, whose monumental achievements are conspicuous in London, deferred to Tom's judgement and expressed gratitude for his encouragement.

While his opinions were thus sought by a number of his fellow students, some doggerel verses addressed to 'Our Brother Tom' show that a tendency to play Sir Oracle at home was not appreciated. The first verse is an uncomplimentary description of his appearance, 'Tall, thin and lanky, weak at the joints ...', the second is devoted to his beard 'a most trifling affair ...':

> In the morning and evening with eloquence rare
> We hear him address this beloved tuft of hair.
>
> Within his large head there dwells a large brain,
> Vasty and deep as the mighty main.
> He speaks; we all listen. Oh! woe to the person
> Who, trivially minded, shall make an assertion.
> 'You! Who are you?' ejaculates he,
> 'Poor thing, do you really suppose you can see?'
>
> Ah, well, he's a great and a solitary being,
> This mortal uniquely gifted with seeing.
> Our own foolish thoughts we seldom declare
> So generally nobody knows they are there.
> But, afterwards, when he is no longer by
> We say unpleasant things about his big eye.
>
> Wishing you a very happy Xmas from Hettie.

None of the older brothers and sisters could, of course, really have been so crushed into silence—least of all George, Captain of Dulwich College for two years, and President of its Debating Society. In 1892, having won a major scholarship in Classics, he followed Harry to Trinity College, Cambridge. During the August before he embarked on what was to be a lifelong university career, he and Tom went on a walking-tour—down to the Sussex coast, along to the New Forest and back from Salisbury by train. They spent the first night in Haslemere, where 'Our bill for two meals, sandwiches for today and the nights beds is 7s. .... so every prospect pleases, not even man is vile.' On the walk from Midhurst they became engaged in an argument so heated that they took different routes through Arundel Park, relented and turned back, missed each other and were only finally reunited in Arundel after anxious inquiries on Tom's part. Later they were dogged by violent thunderstorms, but nothing deterred 'the infatuated George' from bathing—in stormy seas, muddy lakes, and shallow nettle-edged streams. Whereas, Tom wrote, 'My chief longing is

for streams like those in the Valleys. We have come across one or
two drinkable and more that were garrulous, but only like old
men, never with the childish buoyancy of chatter and breezy
raciness of Alpine torrents, and tasting always of the salt of experience.' Although they squandered 1*s*. 6*d*. a head on a meal in a
Fish Palace in Littlehampton, they often lunched off bread and
blackberries, 'for which we go with an intentness that reminds me
of the thrushes on the yew berries outside my window at home'.

In view of the customary gusto with which Tom recounted
their strenuous progress a letter from his father received *en route*
comes as a surprise:

Mamma who has gone off with Bert and Sarah to the Zoological
Gardens desires me to write to you. She thinks you do not eat enough
and often enough and says that you cannot carry a heavy meal about
inside you as George can, so that you need to eat oftener. I quite agree
with her and hope you will be careful both in this respect and about
over-walking. George intent on any object is not overburdened with
consideration for others, doubtless he will improve in time, but meanwhile you must take care of yourself and not be led away by him, or we
shall have you returning from your outing the worse rather than the
better for it. . . . We were very pleased to get your letter and appreciated its style. . . . There is a leader in the Daily News of today on
M. de Maupassant which I forward to you. . . . George did not put the
map he did not want into my guide so we have not been able to follow
your movements as closely as we could wish. News from Annie, Harry
and the Appias is satisfactory. We write in much love and look forward
to seeing you back sunburnt and flourishing.

Besides giving a clue to a constitutional weakness which remained
with Tom throughout his life, this letter shows the continuing
parental concern embracing all the Moore children.

When Uncle Appia came over the following spring he was
accompanied by Aunt Helen and Marie, who had now left her
Lycée. They stayed at Woodthorpe, so that Tom was in the new
and delightful position of playing host to Appias on his home
ground and had more opportunity for uninterrupted conversation

with Marie than had ever been possible in Paris. He took her to see the pictures at Dulwich and had long discussions with her on art and literature. As a result, a plan for the improvement of her knowledge of English literature and his of the French language was mutually agreed. He would translate carefully selected English poems into French, and she, having studied the originals, would return his translations with her corrections and comments. Marie stayed on in England to visit other relations and her godmother, Miss Mayo, whose friendship had supported her mother during the Siege of Paris. Tom and Aunt Helen returned to France together. In the train to Paris, while his aunt was sleeping off the effects of the sea-crossing, Tom composed a sonnet to Marie, in which she, 'a woman young and softly clothed', offered him a suit of armour and a sword. This was the first of some 150 poems he wrote over the next four years to Marie, who had quite suddenly become a source of inspiration and an unattainable object of love. A few of these poems were later revised and published, but the great majority remain as they were written, a running record of thoughts and feelings confided only to the pages of a secret notebook.

CHAPTER FIVE

French Translations and Secret Poems

As an art student of twenty-three with no independent income except his annuity from Uncle George Sturge and nothing but a few voluntarily contributed poems as evidence of future capacity to earn, it is understandable that Tom should not have considered himself an eligible suitor. Moreover, his mother, who probably attributed her poor health to her own parentage, is said to have expressed disapproval of marriage between first cousins. Such practical and worldly considerations are not, however, reflected in the secret poems. What might have been considered the most insuperable barrier of all, his agnosticism, is touched on occasionally, but not with great intensity. In one poem he pictures Marie kneeling to say her prayers at the open window of her bedroom at the Airals Blancs

> Are you filled with desire
> Alone for what the heavens hold
> And nothing nigher?
> Ah! the mountains stand
> So thick about you on every hand,
> The snow on their tops is, oh, so cold!
>
> My passion cannot pass
> Or hope to melt your heart,
> And huger mountains mass
> About your soul to part
> Us, dear; to me it seems
> You centre there a waste of old-world dreams.

The gulf between them is a recurrent theme up to 1896, but he clearly did not see his rejection of a formal religious creed as the primary cause of this. Marie's superiority in his eyes lay rather in the way she lived her faith, while he failed miserably to act according to his equally valid ideals. An inner sense of unworthiness and unspecified sin, not expressed in any of his letters, pervades many of the verses. When he asks,

> Should I not lift and love you?
> Should I not kiss?

the answer is always conditional,

> Could you but stoop and cherish
> Cleanse me of mud . . .
>
> Were they but plumed and straightened
> These crumpled wings
> Could lift . . .

When he writes, 'To hope to win you were to love you less', there is another ingredient, made more explicit in the lines,

> I could not but be crowned by plucking them
> The flowers that scent thy peace . . .
> But pillaged thus, thou might'st scorn my best
> Finding such love too fierce.

This fear of bending 'to himself a joy' and the burden of his unworthiness are both looked at more philosophically in the sonnet:

> Finding I still return to my old sin
> (Which resolutions soon repentant shun)
> That vice is night and virtue like the sun
> I fear to think, yet feel much truth therein.
> Must light lead darkness like a loving twin? . . .
> Ah, I do hope to grow, though I confess
> Often mine efforts seem to leave me less.
> Someday, a summer big with leafy trees,
> I would receive thee, shelter thee from showers,
> Lift leaves to show how black the soil, while bees
> Dinned in thine ears how very sweet the flowers.

Sometimes there is an undertow of rebellion against his passive attitude. Memory, in one poem, cheats him by leading up

> ... good fortune to equal desire;
> Courage deserts me, I am not deluded;
> Ne'er will a woman requite him who loves her
> Speechless, subjected by cruel compulsion,
> Slave of her welfare, neglecting advantage,
> Headlong to sacrifice e'en her possession
> May he but bless her, but flatter her heartsease.

So he veers between hope, waiting for a sign from her, and resignation, in which his not merely rhetorical consolation is that

> Love is its own exceeding great reward ...
> Do I not love? Am I not wealthy then?
> Pursy with gains your life must needs afford,
> They make my leisure like a miser's hoard,
> She wakes—she walks—she sleeps—how, where and when.

Every morsel of information about her 'how, where and when' was hungrily received and embodied in imagination. She is at the Airals Blancs; he sees her sitting in the garden in tranquil conversation with her mother, and in several short poems invests recollections of the summer of 1885 with present emotion. She is going to Genoa; he walks beside her along the Mediterranean shore and asks whether 'nothing in the air' of the Palazzo where Breughel's picture of the Temptation of St. Antony inspired Flaubert, 'brought me on visits to your heart!' At Lyon she is staying with a sick cousin and having difficulty in persuading her little goddaughter Geneviève to go to sleep; with tender insight he imagines the child, excited by Marie's presence, wishing to prolong it, bouncing about in bed, begging for one more story, and then writes for her the lullaby beginning,

> Laugh, Laugh,
> Laugh, gently though,
> For leaves do so
> When the great boughs to and fro

> Cradle the birds in the tops of the trees,
> Gently they laugh for the love of these.

In Paris she has been playing duets with Caroline:

> Thy head of hair seems cloud heaped on the heights,
> Thy finger tips, like splashing rain, wake notes . . .

Her hair, which was dark and fine, and after an attack of typhoid had gone crinkly, haunted his dreams and day-dreams even more than her dark, expressive eyes and full pale face:

> Come with me, dearest, tonight I feel
> That the maddest of dreams must needs be real,
> Come; you are close with all your hair—
> More, far more than your usual wear,
> Thick as the fleece of a bold black ram
> Slain by a tartar in Kurdistan— . . .

News of her reached him through the correspondence between their mothers, but above all he longed for her own letters. When these came the first page or so was habitually full of apologies for her tardiness in writing. This was not for want of will, but as she explained to Tom in a letter written in English in September, 1893, because 'the little businesses that are the caterpillars of women's lives have gnawed all my days and I have had little time to read and write'. Her devotion to her family had made her accept with a good grace that she was needed at home, in the parish, and in domestic crises elsewhere. Yet, when she had successfully completed her studies at the Lycée with distinction in mathematics and ancient literature, she would dearly have liked to go on to university like her 'clever Monod cousins', and she attended courses at the Sorbonne whenever this was practicable. So she applied herself to Tom's translations methodically and with evident pleasure. What he sent her first was not a poem but an essay of his own on Rembrandt, against whom he had been shocked to discover she had some sort of prejudice. This was followed by a series of lyrics, including the song, 'Give her but a least excuse to love me!' from

Pippa Passes, and then, for Browning particularly possessed his mind at this time, by 'Artemis Prologizes', a tough assignment for both of them. The corrected manuscripts have disappeared, only some of Marie's covering letters and appended notes surviving. Her alternative versions are always suggested tentatively. This does not prevent Tom from almost jubilantly pointing out that some of them reveal a misunderstanding of the original text; even on this ground and in this relationship, he was now the teacher. The covering letters suggest a comfortably established friendship. They sign themselves 'Your affectionate cousin', and there is no indication, on either side, of a wish for a greater intimacy.

There is hardly a mention of Marie in Tom's letters home during his Paris visit in May 1894. They have a slightly jaundiced tone. 'Owing to something imprudent in your letters I have to eat two eggs every morning. Oncle says it is better to have Paris eggs au miroir than à la coque, as they are not very certain and the little dose of pepper on top partially hides the defect.' Oncle had also taken pleasure in infuriating his daughters and Tom by reading aloud passages from *Dégénérescence* by Max Nordau, demonstrating that modern works of art from the Pre-Raphaelites to Wagner 'are nothing but increasing and intensifying manifestations of insanity'. Ernest Guy was staying, 'so I have someone to get into interminable disputes with'. He encouraged Ernest to read Rossetti's poetry, and talked with him 'about railway engines which he regards as things of beauty'. A secret sonnet suggests that the very intensity of his expectations of seeing Marie again led to disappointment; he was left, 'hurt that I felt lonely at thy side, Lamed from our meeting not enough alone . . .'.

In August, when the Appias were in the Valleys, Tom was again in Paris, at the outset of a three weeks' walking-tour with Harry Mileham, who had now transferred to the Royal Academy School. They went south through Fontainebleau to Auxerre, then west to Orléans and the surrounding forests and back to Paris through Chartres. Gothic architecture, sculpture, and stained-glass was

Dr George Moore

Dr Daniel Moore

Henrietta with baby Tom

Tom with the Appia family at the Airals Blancs in 1885: (*from left to right*)
Caroline, a friend, Henry, Tom, Marie with pet lamb, Louis, Georges, Helen,
and Tante Louise, both seated

The Moore family, *c.* 1884: (*from left to right*) Hettie, Harry, Nellie, Daniel,
Bertie, Annie, Henrietta, Sarah, George, Tom

their especial quest, in out-of-the-way little churches as well as renowned places. Often they were the first Englishmen ever seen in the villages. No one believed they could be walking for pleasure, they must be looking for work, or, possibly, wanting to buy Percheron horses. Trusting in Baedeker's assurance that English gold sovereigns were everywhere current, they arrived one afternoon in the small town of Villethiery with nothing but these and two and a half francs. No one there would have any truck with gold sovereigns. Eventually, the proprietress of an inn accepted the francs and the promise that the balance would be sent when they reached Sens. Their meal was roughly interrupted by the entry of a huge black-bearded gendarme, who demanded to see their passports. Again misled by Baedeker, they had no passports. All they could produce by way of identification was Mileham's 'bone', the ivory disc issued to all R.A. students. It bore the date 1768 and, if anything, aggravated the gendarme's suspicions that they were avoiding conscription, fleeing justice or, in view of their sketch-books, spying for some foreign power. Tom became so indignant that he asked the gendarme by what right he cross-examined peaceable English travellers. This so enraged the man that an arrest was only averted by the arrival of a superior officer of the gendarmerie, who calmed his subordinate, satisfied himself that these were innocent young men, and benevolently advised them to procure passports as soon as possible. They then thankfully retired to their bedroom, to find 'a feather bed each, by each bedside, on a silver salver, hot water, sugar and cognac and on each pillow a handsome red woollen night cap'.

Intermittently throughout this walking-tour Tom was composing in his head:

> I traversed late tall avenues that spread
> O'er highways in your France—above my head
> A highway of fair sky, there your feet walked;
> On either hand a million mad leaves talked
> Where your and my ways forked.

'A mile ahead,' I cried, 'there shall we meet!'
But I then learned, although our fields be sweet,
They never have been kissed, e'en on hill tops,
By the fair sky, though when she weeps the drops
Are precious to our crops.

So, should the future find you sorrows, I
Perhaps might make an honest fortune by
Your tears; till, rich, to you I joy might give,
As the earth moisture for the winds to weave
Raiment sky queens it with.

Mileham was certainly entirely unaware of what occupied his companion's thoughts when he was silent. The same probably applied to all his friends, his brothers and sisters, and his watchful parents.

Tom had recently made a new friend. Since George, with whom he had more in common than with Harry, had been up at Cambridge, he had visited there frequently and so become aquainted with this younger brother's circle. This included Robert C. Trevelyan, who at this time had reluctantly abandoned Classics to read Law in his final year. He recorded his first impressions of Tom:

He was so completely unlike all my Cambridge friends, both intellectually and in appearance. He was tall and slender, with refined features and hands; and he had a thin rather straggly light brown beard. . . . He was the first poet and artist that I had ever met. I myself had written no poems as yet; but I had long had a passion for poetry; and as he had not only shown me his own poems (many of them masterly in form and style), but was ready to talk all day about literature and art, we soon became friends, and looked forward to meeting again later on in London. What impressed me most was not so much his wide knowledge of English and French literature—far wider than my own—but the maturity of his critical judgement.

In London, where he shared a house in Chelsea with Roger Fry, Trevelyan was at first an uneasy pupil in the chambers of the barrister T. E. Scrutton. Then he was advised to take a holiday for the good of his health, and during two months on his own in southern Italy he resolved to break with law, to disappoint the expectations of his family, and to follow his own inclination, which was to become a poet. In this course he was naturally encouraged by Tom, 'whose devoted, but not uncritical, admirer and disciple I then was'. Their friendship thus became close, and lasting. The unfamiliar social background of the distinguished, Liberal, landed Trevelyan family—grouse shooting and all— caused Tom some astonishment, but none of the awkwardness he might have suffered had Bob (or Trevy) been a less spontaneously unconventional person. His letters suggest a man of uncomplicated nature and buoyant good humour, ruffled only, and then often explosively, by any aspersion on his friends. He took the privileges to which he was born for granted and shared them with an entirely unself-conscious generosity.

The correspondence into which they entered reveals a mutually invigorating working relationship. When Bob was in London Tom suggested meetings for translation,

so as to keep one up to that pitch of excitement about technicalities which is the condition of good work. You are the only fellow really interested in arranging words that I know. And it is very difficult to be always spurring one's own flanks, and one so soon falls off into an amiable amble ridiculous in view of the goal that I believe a mutual admiration and damnation meeting every now and then would do us both good. I propose translation as it is not so much a matter of opinion and therefore would not so easily result in deadlock.

In their general interchange most of the 'damnation' came from Tom; he conscientiously dissected Bob's verses and often returned them radically rewritten, a treatment he was to apply to other poets, alive and dead. Bob's amendments were usually rejected initially, though sometimes adopted later. Bob, however, fed Tom's insatiable desire for 'classical subjects', putting him on to the best available translations and himself enthusiastically translating lyrics and whole dramas for him. More than his brother George, who was interested primarily in ideas, it was Bob Trevelyan who furnished the material for an imaginative vision which made later readers of his work unable to believe that Tom had read no Latin or Greek in the original and never been to Greece.

The publication of *The Dial* had meanwhile made the work of Ricketts and Shannon more widely known. William Morris reserved his judgement on the first issue, but was to give whole-hearted praise to a later publishing venture. Sir Edward Burne-Jones and Sir Frederick Leighton gave tangible proof of their admiration. Oscar Wilde came in person to congratulate them; he thought Shannon like a marigold and Ricketts an orchid. He became a quite frequent visitor, declaring that theirs was 'the only house in London where one is never bored' and even tolerating 'dishes of London eggs washed down with the cheapest of drinks' for the sake of their company. 'I wondered', wrote that ubiquitous observer, William Rothenstein, 'whether he knew how gross, how soiled by the world, he appeared, sitting in one of the white scrubbed kitchen chairs next to Ricketts and Shannon and Sturge Moore.' Tom, in fact, only met Wilde on one occasion and was then too absorbed a listener to draw any such comparison. He was aware chiefly of the affection his friends felt for the man and their gratitude for patronage of the most constructive kind. Apart from *Salomé*, illustrated by Aubrey Beardsley, all his books for illustration were placed in their hands; he also paid for the publication of a collection of John Gray's poems, entitled *Silver Points*, to Ricketts's design and binding. None the less, Tom later recorded, 'I can see his [Ricketts's] face crimson as he tore out the fly-leaf Wilde had inscribed from the copy of *The Sphynx* sent to him. "Vulgar beast!" he cried, for the signature ended in a straight lined Z scrawled right across the leaf, an outrage to the exquisite niceties of the artist's book-building, in blatant contrast also with the modesty of his insect-like autograph.'

The encouragement from Wilde, a legacy of £500 from his grandfather, and the appearance on the scene of a wealthy patron of the arts, Llewellyn Hacon, all contributed to the realization of a cherished dream of Ricketts's—the setting up of a press of his own.

He longed to create books in which, as in William Morris's Kelmscott Press, every ingredient—the paper, the print, the text, the engraved illustration and ornament, the layout of the pages, the binding—were fashioned into a harmonious whole. In the autumn of 1894, Hacon took over the lease of 1 The Vale and Ricketts and Shannon moved into 31 Beaufort Street, where preparations for what was to be known as the Vale Press began. Tom spent most of September and October helping with the transfer of their possessions, also moving his own belongings from the 'work room' into a studio in the new house.

For the New Year he sent Marie, from whom no letter had come for a long time, Henry Vaughan's 'Beyond the Veil', copied in his fairest hand:

I add no translation this time, simply some brief explanatory notes to save you trouble in understanding the idioms of an earlier period. These lines were chosen because I believe you will be in sympathy with their subject, and their beauty, like the delicacy of their senti-ment seems to me peculiarly suiting to you.... You will perhaps laugh at the notes, as I laugh at those of les Messieurs de l'Académie Française in the works of Molière, which are almost always as useless as holding a candle to the sun.

She responded immediately, with appreciation of the poem and of his magnanimity in overlooking her failure to return his transla-tion of 'Artemis Prologizes', due to 'la vie vagabonde' she had been leading in France and Italy. Shortly, she was to leave Paris again, for a long visit to Germany.

> Further from me, my Love, and toward the East
> You fare heroic in thick winter wraps ...

are the light opening lines of a sonnet which ends, however, on a sombre note. Tom had a premonition, which continued to haunt him, that she would there fall in love with someone else:

> ... must I learn his name, debarred amends,
> Forever outcast—useless in a word,
> And pray such prayers I could not wish them heard?

71

They exchanged letters when she was in her father's birthplace, Frankfurt, staying 'à 5 minutes de la maison au toit pointu, aux fenêtres antiques, à l'aspect confortable et presque imposant où Goethe est né'. After seeing the Rembrandt portraits in Cassel, she had learnt, he was gratified to hear, 'à aimer, à admirer avec passion le "Maître"'. He advised her on her reading in Goethe and Heine, and recommended that she should shelve his French translation to absorb the German view.

When he visited Paris in May, this time accompanied by his friend Henry Poole, the sculptor, Marie was still in Germany. There was for him an exquisite compensation for her absence:

> I have slept, Sweet, in your bed,
> On your pillow laid my head;
> Dreamed beneath your curtains too
> Twixt your white sheets thought of you.
> Such my luck beyond compare,
> Though, alas, you were not there!
> Gone the dull despairing mood,
> Gone the bitter turn to jest,
> Gone all sloth and come new zest.
> For a fortnight was my rest
> Perfect in your haunted nest.

He searched the mirror for her face, examined the books for her thoughts and noticed that in her much-marked Bible the passage in John 20, 'Jesus saith unto her, Mary!' was underlined. Sitting on her bed with the book in his hand, he pondered on the story of Mary Magdalene and wondered whether Marie, 'in naive humility' thought she were equally in need of forgiveness. Then, in a sudden flight of fancy, he imagined himself following Marie up to Heaven, where she is crowned and he becomes a Believer through love:

> Help me, lead me, love me, Dear,
> Pray for me who am so vile
> That having owned your crown is clear
> I cannot yet forbear a smile.

A kind of knockabout exuberance is apparent in the letters to his mother during this fortnight. He guided Poole through the Paris galleries, took him to Chartres and to a play by Alexandre Dumas, fils, at the Comédie Française, where they arrived late and left early: 'it seemed stupid and stale and to have all the modern idiocies about marriage and the lack of it mixed up with all the old conventional frivolities dear to the heart of a Frenchman on the subject of *the sex*'. They also visited Rodin, whose genius Tom irreverently suggested had been affected by his over-eating. 'I thought the work he is now doing hardly up to his mark, but he was very nice and we are to go again on Saturday, to see the big studio and the "Gates".' For the first time he met the whole Monod family and 'talked to M. Monod, le père . . . you would have been surprised to hear me enunciating views as to the various denominations of English dissenters, such as the good little old man swallowed with apparent satisfaction. . . . I went yesterday to the "Fête de la Jeunesse", good old sport that I am. I was separated from Caroline and the young people behind me behaved as only Christians would dream of behaving in a place of worship . . . so I went out and walked about the streets till Caroline came out enthusiastic for so beautiful a réunion, etc.'

On his return to England, an uprooting of the Moore family was imminent. Daniel and Henrietta had decided to sell Woodthorpe and retire to Cheriton, a house in the village of Cockington near Torquay. All their children had now left school except Sarah, who was preparing for Newnham entrance at the Quaker boarding-school in Southport. Annie was teaching Classics in Clifton. Harry, after a double First in Natural Sciences, had been elected a Fellow of Trinity College the previous year, and then, somewhat to the consternation of both his parents and his Faculty, had announced his intention of taking Holy Orders in the Anglican Church. George, now reading Moral Sciences after a First in Part I of the Classical Tripos, and a member of the élite band of Cambridge Apostles, showed no sign of swerving from the academic path. For Nellie and Bertie, however, a home in the

London area was still needed; Nellie, the only one to carry on the Moore tradition in medicine, was to study at the London Hospital for Women and University College, and Bertie, who had shown artistic and musical rather than scholastic talents at school, at the Slade School of Art. It had been decided that Tom, with Hettie as housekeeper, should preside over an establishment which would also provide a London base for other members of the family.

Although this plan must have been thoroughly discussed with Tom beforehand, it seems to have been put into operation most abruptly. The first indication of it in the correspondence is a letter written by Tom on 1 August 1895 from 39 Southgrove, Highgate, to Hugh Fisher, holidaying in Wiltshire with his wife:

No doubt you wondered why I did not look you up on coming home from Paris but I was almost at once beset by a flood of cares of this world and so could not. Now at last I am stranded like Noah's Ark a little out of repair on the top of Highgate Hill. Having left for good and all both 31, Beaufort St and my old home Woodthorpe . . . I am now a householder and head of a family and feel the mediocrity of these characters already making way in my mind. Two sisters, myself and a younger brother form the household with a servant who has varicose veins in her leg and finds the stairs woefully too many.

He asked, as a matter of urgency, if any of Fisher's relatives could help him find 'a strong, sensible, trustworthy and otherwise ideal general servant' to replace the one on loan from Woodthorpe, before he and Hettie set off on a Cook's tour of Germany on 11 August. 'I have bought How to speak German in no time without a Master, 1/6 net, also a Baedeker, and shall do everything in a hurry as cheap and nasty as possible.' He complained that he had not been able to read for weeks, had 'gone over from Culture to Anarchy and only sometimes "Je me souviens des cieux". But you now among cows and haystacks, "self-schooled, self-scanned, self-honoured, self-secure . . . go round with trees and stocks and stones", keeping the stars at a becoming distance and much too content to be happy.'

That August the Moore family dispersed for their summer holidays. Nellie and Bertie stayed with their parents in Babbacombe exploring their future home county, Sarah went to school friends in Sunderland, Harry, now a theological student at Bishop Auckland in the Durham diocese, paid his first visit to the Appias in the Valleys, and George joined Tom and Hettie for part of their tour. Although not without its share of misleading information from Cook's, closed picture galleries, and attacks of diarrhoea, this breathless trip enabled them to see something of Antwerp, Brussels, Aix la Chapelle, Cologne, Heidelberg, Munich, Nuremberg, and Regensburg, and on the way home the itinerary was broken for special visits, in Marie's footsteps, to Frankfurt and Cassel. Tom returned outraged by the German habit of exhibiting pictures 'as though they were collections of butterflies', but overflowing with enthusiasm for the work of Albrecht Dürer and his then little-known contemporary, Altdorfer. Some three weeks later, however, all enthusiasm in him was extinguished by news in a letter from his parents. After one month in the Valleys, Harry had become engaged to Marie.

'Ah, this is worse than what I dreamed would be,' he wrote on 1 October. Even in those first anguished days it was not the fulfilment of his premonition in a particularly wounding way to which he was referring, but to his own abject reaction. Marie had made her choice; whether she would come to regret it was not for him to ask. Instead of surmounting the loss of his hopes he had fallen into a 'listless, limp despair', was behaving like a dog without a bone, hunting 'always nothing everywhere', and writing 'moaning verse'. For years he had allowed Reason to smother 'Instinct, misnamed the brute'. Now his only salvation lay in rejoicing in Marie's happiness, so gaining 'strength to love on anyway'.

Despair was to him a disreputable state and jealousy a despicable emotion; marriage was, ideally, a binding union and for Marie he wanted nothing less than the ideal. The struggle towards a stoic acceptance of a future of platonic love was fought, and directed the writing of the verses that followed. In one sonnet, he considered the English and French names for their future relationship:

Sister-in-law, the term is of the north,
Severe and stringent to force home the fact.
Beautiful Sister, southern, sweet with tact
To call the homage due to honour forth.
O, help me bind my love with these two thoughts . . .

and later he formulated a statement of belief for his support,

Not on mere personal hope and dreaméd bliss
Can the maturing spirit long subsist.
Beyond the beauty that glad lips may kiss
It lifts to where relations pure exist
And worships nobler character, nor deems
That bodies are more real than other dreams.

On the day that Harry stayed with them at Highgate on his return
from the Valleys, he was able to write,

An emanation seems to come
With those who have been near thee,
And, though my hopes are dead and dumb,
In seeing them I hear thee.

Thou art close by.
Thus from the sky
The angels see us close,
Two specks not far apart,
Your joys my pains and woes,
Two complements and each a heart
So like the sad the gay
That which is which they cannot say,
They cannot from such distance say.

Though in myself I always know
How far Love must decree thee,
My heart leaps fast that did beat slow
And hearing of I see thee.

His letter of felicitation to Marie was not preserved. In her
reply she returned his translation of 'Artemis Prologizes', corrected and lucidly annotated, with many apologies and a reference
to the mountain of unanswered letters on her writing-desk:

Allow me to say a tardy thank-you once more, but a very warm one, for your fraternal welcome. As you say so prettily, 'transports actuels' are those that predominate. But as I have the intention of finding, from today, more and more the fulfilling and the complement of all good things which went before, I hasten to assure you that I have not lost interest in these and that all your communications will always be welcome.

She then again gratefully refers to how he has opened her eyes to Rembrandt, hopes she will soon hear his impressions of Germany, and asks his views on Claude Lorraine and Nicolas Poussin. This promise, however fragile, of a continuing sympathetic interchange must have alleviated his sense of isolation as other members of his family gathered in the rue d'Assas during November and December. The Moore parents, who hoped to gain in health and strength for the move to Devonshire by wintering on the Mediterranean, arrived with Sarah early in November. Sarah stayed on for two months and wrote regularly to Tom of her doings. She had French lessons with Uncle Appia and then, more fruitfully, with his great-nephew Paul Vallette; Marie took her to the Louvre and the Panthéon; she attended lectures at the Sorbonne with Marie; she looked at all the pictures Tom had advised and rebelliously refused to admire Puvis de Chavannes; Ernest Guy sent him messages. Then Annie arrived, armed with books on French history recommended by Tom. Hettie joined them not long before Christmas. Finally, Harry came to celebrate both Noël and his engagement to Marie in the heart of the Appia circle.

❦

CHAPTER SIX

A Breach in Relations

JUST before Harry's departure, Uncle Appia suffered a severe attack of influenza; this was followed by shingles, which reduced him to a weak and emaciated condition. Convalescence in the mild Mediterranean climate was advised, so, on 14 February 1896, Aunt Helen took him to the Hotel de Genève et d'Angleterre in Cannes, a resort where there was a Vaudois community and they had many friends. She wrote a detailed daily report on his progress to their three children in the rue d'Assas, at the same time giving advice on household matters to Caroline, while Georges wrote frequently on parish affairs to Louis. Because these letters have been preserved, the devastating development of the next few weeks is seen through the eyes of the Appia parents.

On 18 February Marie received a letter from Harry in which he raised obscurely defined doubts about the rightness of a marriage between them. A further letter reaffirmed these doubts without making the reasons for them any clearer. Marie asked that *no one* should be told until the dreadful uncertainty of her situation had been resolved. On receiving this news, the Appia parents were not only profoundly shocked, they were utterly bewildered. What could have induced their nephew, a well-brought-up young man destined for the Church, who had so recently celebrated his solemn engagement under their own roof, to behave so cruelly and dishonourably towards their cherished daughter? At first they clutched at the supposition that after five months of engagement Harry had belatedly become afflicted by scruples concerning marriage between cousins. In writing to Paris, Georges blamed himself for having given no guidance to the young couple and for not having got to know Harry more intimately, but maintained, as always, that if they all put their trust in God some blessing would accrue, even though through the crucible of suffering. Helen's faith, on the other hand, was not so steadfast under this trial. 'It was not, therefore, for nothing', she wrote to Caroline, 'that I found it so difficult to accept the engagement at the beginning, and all through the winter I felt a pinch at my heart every time I was congratulated. ... I don't know what to do; at every moment I have the horrible temptation not to believe in the governance of G.— oh pray for me, Louis and you.'

Georges, who believed that Harry's doubts might be overcome if only they could be expressed and discussed, had immediately written to him for an explanation, but there had been no time for a reply before the situation was most painfully complicated by the arrival in Cannes of the Moore parents. They had originally intended to spend a week in Paris on their way back to England, but on account of Georges's illness had altered their plans to include three days in Cannes, a brief visit to the Valleys, and a final night in Paris with their future daughter-in-law. It was at once clear that they were entirely unaware of Harry's change of mind, or heart. After two days of unimaginable strain, and still no letter from Harry, the Appias decided that Marie's request did not justify their continuing in so false a relationship and they told the Moores of the dreadful enigma. That they would be appalled was expected, but Georges was not prepared for the violence of Daniel's reaction. Usually so calm and moderate, at this revelation he was angered beyond measure, as much, it seemed to Georges, by Harry's having kept the matter from his parents as by the wrong done to Marie. Stung as he must have been by Harry's apparent lack of openness, this was certainly not the main cause of his indignation. 'Women are helpless in such situations,' he later wrote to Tom, 'and it appears to me all the more dishonourable to ask and receive their love and then leave them in the lurch.' At the time, he quite alarmed his brother-in-law by citing the English law on breach of promise. Georges was puzzled by this legalistic approach to a personal problem; he remained primarily concerned to discover Harry's motives so that a clear understanding of some kind could be reached, and greatly hoped that Henrietta would exert a softening influence on her husband's attitude. On the following day, 22 February, the Moores, now entirely preoccupied by this trouble which could not yet be shared with their other children, left for Turin.

Three days later, Marie, unable any longer to endure the strain of her normal life in Paris, and shrinking from a meeting with the Moores, joined her parents. On hearing that the Moores had been told, and learning something of their reaction, she explained that after receiving Harry's first letter she had asked him not to let even his parents know of his uncertainties. This information was immediately passed on to the rue d'Assas by Helen, so that in this respect at least Harry could be absolved from blame in his parents' eyes. In this letter to Caroline, written at a time when her distress and anxiety had been intensified by the arrival of her stricken daughter, Helen did not forget her concern for meticulous household standards. The Moores were to sleep in the Appia parents' bedroom. 'I hope that Catherine [the maid] has not only washed the marble of our washing-table and the mantelpiece with soap and water, but also used sand or mineral soap, it was *so* dirty, and also that my carpet has been treated with tea-leaves. I also hope that Catherine has properly cleaned my foot-warmer so that there's *no more black* even on the bottom.' A shirt lost in the laundry is relentlessly chased in letters throughout this period of emotional crisis.

Every day Marie asked the courier if there was a letter from England. But by 1 March no letter from England had come. Isolated up in Bishop Auckland, locked in some inner struggle, Harry was rendered incapable of replying to two urgent appeals from his uncle or of writing again to Marie. Baffled by this inexplicable silence, increasingly concerned by its affect on Marie, unfit to leave Cannes himself, Georges gratefully accepted Louis's offer to go to London as his representative if Harry would agree to an interview there. Much searching and anxious consultation went into preparing Louis for his mission and in the course of this Marie consented to show her parents the two letters that previously she had found it too painful to expose. Of these, Helen wrote to Caroline,

nothing is made much clearer, but it is absolutely revolting, the way he interlards his letters with texts, as though, thus, he could console the heart he has broken with unpardonable levity . . . I cannot stand it, God has not yet granted me the power to take from Him this bitter cup. I am in the deepest darkness, I cannot even glimpse any joy on earth when I think of the collapse of all the hopes of my darling child, who was worthy of a loyal and ardent heart, who had a heart made to make a husband as happy as possible, to be the light of a rich and warm home—this is cruel to the last degree, it is unimaginable bitterness. I want for love of *her*, as you say, to ask for the strength to believe that G. did not *wish* it. He *allowed* it to happen . . . but can I ever forgive? Oh mystery of sorrow which burrows day by day more deeply into the heart seeing such irreparable misfortune.

On 4 March, the courier at last brought a letter from Harry to his uncle. He accepted the proposed interview with Louis and suggested the following Sunday (which further damned him in Helen's eyes, since Louis was undertaking his father's parish work as well as his own). Beyond this, he expressed regrets in a manner the Appias considered most perfunctory, and added by way of explanation that he was convinced he would not be able to make Marie happy. A telegram was sent to the Moore parents, who arranged to come up to London from Torquay that Sunday. On 6 March a letter from Harry to Louis cancelled the interview. The same day, however, a letter from Caroline to her parents threw a new light on the mystery for Georges. She had remembered that during Harry's visit to Paris at Christmas there had been discussions with Marie on questions of Christian doctrine, in which certain differences of opinion had emerged. Here was something that Georges could understand. With that agility of response so characteristic of him he instantly wrote a long letter to Louis in which he endeavoured to put himself in his nephew's position. Harry was a recent convert to the Anglican Church; he had sacrificed a brilliant academic career to prepare himself for ordination in that Church; only during the Paris visit had he become aware that his chosen helpmate was a Dissenter, holding views so at variance with his own, so unorthodox, as to present a threat to a fully harmonious relationship between them and an embarrassment to him in his vocation. The moral dilemma in which he was placed should be respected, and his difficulty in explaining it to his pastor uncle understood; they should therefore not attempt to *impose* an immediate interview on him. This humane analysis of the situation lost some of its cogency when further news came from Henrietta on 9 March. In a letter to his parents Harry had written 'that he was convinced that they were thoroughly unsuited to each other' but 'that nothing was settled yet and he could not write further about it till it was, he had to write again to Marie'. For Marie, this was another turn on the rack; she declared she never wanted to hear from Harry again and asked her father to forbid him to write to her. To Georges, too, this seemed evidence of an irresolution so self-centred that a reconciliation was no longer to be desired.

Before the breaking-off of the engagement could be officially announced it was still essential to the Appias to know Harry's reasons for withdrawing from it. Georges therefore now sent him a sorrowful ultimatum, requiring him at once to clear Marie's name by explaining, either by letter to him or in an interview with Louis, why he wished to break his solemn engagement to her. In sending a copy of this letter to Louis, he expressed his intention of writing to Harry's bishop if there were further procrastination; in a postscript he added that this could only be a last resort, as Harry might regard it as revengeful, and the bishop as outside his competence. This drastic step was fortunately not needed. Harry, now also appealed to by his father, who would certainly have urged candour, responded promptly and fully in letters to his uncle, Louis, and Marie. All letters from Harry appear to have been destroyed, but it can be inferred that he asked to be released from his engagement on the grounds that he had entered into it too hastily and had subsequently realized that he was unable to return Marie's love worthily as she was too good for him. At the same time he expressed a remorse, which his uncle, at least, felt showed some appreciation of the gravity of the suffering he had inflicted.

The Moore parents were now free to tell their children. On 16 March Henrietta wrote to 39 Southgrove:

Dear Sons and Daughters,

The three enclosed letters will tell their own sad tale and shew why Papa and I have been so troubled since our return to England. [The enclosures have disappeared. Henrietta then recounts the sequence of events up to Harry's first letter to them.] Papa answered entreating him for an explanation, and he only had an answer last Friday evening in which H. says that he did not love Marie as she loved him.

There is no shadow of doubt, I think, that Harry is at present quite unconscious of the great wrong he has done, but if he could have had a sight, as we have had, of the misery in the faces of Marie's loved ones, he might perhaps awake to the awful truth. Marie herself, as you know, we did not see, but this is Aunt Helen's description of her state, speaking of Harry's action she says 'Whatever the motives may be, the stern fact remains that our Marie's life is clouded, her brightness gone, and that she must now give up all hope of a happy home of her own, with a faithful loving heart by her side, for it is very unlikely that she will ever love again as she has loved, she believed in Harry's true love and responded to it with all the strength and depth of her affectionate and loving heart.'

All comment on these things seems to me unnecessary; but I think all of us must deeply feel the disgrace entailed in Harry's conduct, and that the only excuse to be urged on his behalf is his ignorance of what true love is.

Papa and I write in much love to you all,

Your affectionate Mother, H. Moore.

Later Tom was to say that Harry had disclosed certain doubts to him when he stayed at 39 Southgrove on his way back from Paris, but his mother's letter seems to have been as much of a shock to him as it was to his brother and sisters, though a shock with different vibrations. In a long, Wordsworthian poem written on 18 March he describes how Marie had grown through childhood to womanhood surrounded, guided, and inspired by the loving concern of her family. Then Harry, who 'had not watched, not he, The slow-evolving tune of that sweet soul' had come to 'seize her in rude grasp she thought embrace'. She had responded in absolute trust and with all the ardour of her nature, her friends had regarded him as the worthy recipient of such riches and he had then

> Stopped like a thief half blind with lightning might,
> And turned about, protesting to repent,
> And left her drooping and half-rooted up,
> Flying far off from all her stricken friends
> To plead he had not read his heart aright
> When he had thought he wanted her so much.
> 'She was too good for him! He could not love
> As she loved!' Why, who dreamed he could so love?
> And we, her friends who loved her, we must ache
> To watch now whether she will live or die. . . .

Nevertheless, with the possible exception of the spontaneously charitable Sarah, who had been in Paris throughout Harry's visit, Tom appears to have been the only member of the family to have shown a sympathetic understanding of the humiliating predicament in which his evidently still emotionally immature brother had placed himself. Gratitude for this sympathy is expressed in a letter from Harry dated 24 March, in which he writes, 'I was very glad to see that you felt so clearly about it, for it doesn't all seem so clear to me. But on the whole you see I did come to the conclusion you agree with me in.'

In a letter to his father, Harry implied that Marie had 'understood the matter'. He was wrong; she never understood and she never forgave. She could indeed hardly have been expected to understand why Harry had so rapidly fallen out of love with her, if that were the case; nor, if her father were right, could she have been expected to understand, as he did, that doctrinal differences between the established Church and Nonconformism in England could create a barrier between two devout Protestants. As it was, the whole framework of mutual trust she had hitherto inhabited had been fractured, her confidence in herself dangerously undermined. Consequently, she was in no state at all to follow the sound advice given to the whole family by her father. 'We must give no further substance to regrets and pass on to another period, a new chapter of duty and labour, new occupations and new hopes, for which we shall need new strength, when we have broken the sterile habit of looking backwards.'

When he was well enough to return to Paris, Marie could not face returning with her parents, nor could she well stay on in Cannes alone. This problem much exercised her mother, who finally arranged for her to take shelter for a period, which lengthened into months, in a Maison des Diaconesses at Livron on the Rhône, where the Sœur Bontemps was an old and close friend of the family. Here, Marie composed the letters announcing the end of her engagement. Through her parents she let it be known that she wished for no direct communication with any member of the Moore family.

Tom had already written Louis a brief note of sympathy 'over this dreadful affair', in which the only consolation he could see was that Harry had discovered his inadequacies in time. He then turned to Tante Louise, close to, but not actually of, the family, to voice a conviction he was most desperately anxious should be heard. Writing from the standpoint of the only person who knew both Harry and Marie well, he blamed the former for acting in a way which 'was very giddy and wrong', but felt that Marie, too, had acted with wilful impetuosity.

And then, of course, all the others did their best to help them both deceive themselves. How rash an engagement, so public, after only four weeks of holiday time, when absolutely nobody there had any really serious knowledge of Harry at all! And now, too, I am afraid they do not wholly see their mistake, but are tending to make matters worse, both Aunt Helen and Caroline, without seeing that Marie, also, did not love Harry; it is true that she did love, whereas he did not, but she did not love *him*, because she did not know him. And though these bereavements of people who never really had existence are at first the most cruel, they are not the most hopeless, surely? Yet Aunt Helen and Caroline seem to feel so strongly that Marie can never get over it. But natures like hers, so rich and varied . . . are just those which have most resources, who can rise again and again, and each time better and nobler. And I so feel that they, with their great love and too fond sympathy, will perhaps be inclined to deepen in her the sense of her wrongs and losses. My dear Aunt, it seems to me that there is no one like you, who could, waiting the right moment, lead her out of the circle of overworn emotions into the exercise of those many powers in her, which it is quite certain can have been very little called into play by Harry. Let her be drawn to study Shakespeare, whom she so loved, and to think of things that will not bring Harry's image into her mind, you will guess best what they are. Let her, too, be led to view the whole affair from as great a distance as possible, as impersonally as possible, not looking on what she felt but on what she actually *did*. My dear Aunt, I hope you will not think it presumptuous of me to write thus, but I have felt so horribly how incumbent it was upon us to do howsoever little it might be towards retrieving what our brother has so weakly done.

There is no trace of a reply from Tante Louise, who was, in fact, reputed to have been foremost in encouraging the engagement.

'My heart aches for thee in thy widowed state' and 'I gave no light nor leading to thine eyes' are the opening lines of two sonnets reflecting the undercurrent of yearning, grief, and self-reproach in Tom's life during these months. 'The impulse that would fly' to Marie has been petrified by cruel circumstance:

> And instead of changing sky,
> One grey eternity—
> Instead of lands and seas,
> Impalpable distances—
> Instead of fields and woods,
> Blank wastes of barren moods—
> Instead of friends, one foe,
> An incommunicable woe— . . .

As Marie's twenty-fourth birthday approached, he was overwhelmed by the desire to be of some comfort to her, and with anxious solicitude composed a birthday letter in French, of which this is perhaps the final draft.

My dear Marie,

It is in some fear of being ill-advised that I write to you. Well, if it pains you to see my writing, even to think of my name, put the whole contents of this envelope into the fire, or in a drawer, without reading a word more and forget about it and me and all of us for as long as you please. . . . You are constantly in my thoughts and I am very unhappy at not being able to help you in any way; so the possibility of adding to your sorrow almost decided me to let this day pass in silence, yet to have done so might have seemed still more unsympathetic.

Enclosed is a little poem by Wordsworth which I have copied because it is extremely beautiful, and beauty is a great consolation. The sonnet is by Matthew Arnold and I am sure it will please you. We should all bathe in seas and blue skies. Wide horizons are as fortifying as deep wells; they give us more light and make us aware of the true proportion between ourselves and the whole.

You asked me my opinion of Claude Lorraine, and I replied without showing much appreciation of him. Well, I have been punished. For I have since seen a remarkable picture by him; it is a Sermon on the Mount. Although I had always recognized that his sketches and designs were distinguished, I would not have believed him capable of painting it. Perhaps it was Goethe's opinion of him that made you interested? Certainly I must now agree with that great man, whose artistic evaluations are often very difficult for me to follow and, I believe, are sometimes as perverse as many of his scientific theories. But I talk at random. That two years have passed since we saw one another seems strange to me in view of the distinctness with which you have occupied my mind recently. However far out my thoughts of you may be, believe that they are entirely sympathetic.

It may interest you to know that I have just come back from Torquay, where I have seen my parents and the new home. I hope that the countryside round you is as beautiful as Devonshire. It does us all much good to see the sunlit hills and to feel how the resources of nature are inexhaustible. My poor Mother appears to me to look upon the move with very little enthusiasm, the immediate past seeming to her so dismal that even Sarah's gaiety fails to give her confidence in the future. And is this, perhaps, what you lack too? I think we should not search our own personal pasts, but the great past. We all live in our own heads and I don't know whether you will understand what I am trying to say to you, but believe me that I remain more than ever

Your affectionate cousin,

Tom Moore.

The poems, Wordsworth's 'The Solitary Reaper' and Matthew Arnold's 'Quiet Work', are written with a very fine nib on small rectangles of paper fastened together with a tiny brass paper-clip. Almost certainly he also enclosed a birthday poem of his own, as had been his custom for several years.

Marie did not reply to this letter, but through her mother she sent a message of thanks to Sarah and Tom for their letters, adding that she was much touched by the poems in Tom's. Then, early in July, Uncle Appia came to London for various meetings and dined at 39 Southgrove. 'We were so unfortunate as to see hardly anything of uncle,' Tom wrote to his mother,

but what we did see was quite as inspiring and refreshing as he always is. . . . He said that all in Paris were well and that Marie seemed to be really getting the better of her trouble, though she didn't see any one yet and left church before the end of the service so as not to have to meet people . . . after dinner I went to the station with him, but when we got there we found that the train did not start for another hour, although he had the time written down on a piece of paper, so he took me to Exeter Hall, where M. Coillard was going to speak, and uncle was asked to open the meeting by a prayer, which he did. We had to come away before M. Coillard's turn arrived, but when I saw him into the train he made me promise to go back to hear M. Col. Which I did . . .

During this typically Appian helter-skelter, his uncle evidently told Tom something else:

> Thy father said three times that thou hadst aid,
> Hadst solace of a letter sent by me . . .

The mood of elation engendered by this success was clouded by an extract from a letter from Aunt Helen sent to him by his mother on 27 August, exactly a year, as she pointed out, since Harry's arrival in the Valleys. The Appias, with their son Henry and his family, were again in the Valleys and Marie had come from Livron to join them.

She is very energetic and will not let her trouble weigh on those around her, and she is constantly occupying herself with the children, who are almost exclusively under her care and oversight just now, at least the 2 or 3 elder ones. The return here was extremely trying to her, and when Caroline and I met her at the station . . . her pale looks and the expression of her face was distressing to see. I think our stay in the mountains did her good, but she has lost that exuberance of life and buoyancy of spirit that characterized her, and her sociability has quite abandoned her; she goes away whenever callers come. . . . With *us* she tries to be lively and join in the conversation, but when her face is at rest or no one is observing her she has a sad expression. Of course we never, any of us, mention the subject to her.

'Is there not on both sides risk, cost, pain?' Tom asked himself,

> For unbeloved, deserted, sick thou art;
> Yet, knowing of such love as mine, thy heart
> Were surely rent by fears and hopes in twain;
> So generous to respond and yet again
> So true to all thy past, thy faith, thy friends—
> So little doubtful of a Father's ends,
> How couldst thou happiness through mine attain? . . .
> Ah, lurks no true consenting in the beat
> Of our two acheing hearts, so rich, so poor?

These questionings continue through several sonnets. Was there a then unimagined truth in the conceit in the last stanza of that poem written two years before; had Marie's sorrows in some sense indeed made him rich enough to give her joy? Certainly, his understanding of her desperate need had shifted the emphasis away from thoughts of his own sinful unworthiness to a maturer assessment of what he had to give. In spite of the obstacles, he began to have an obstinate core of faith in his power to bring about 'a true consenting', though how and when remained obscure.

A note received from Caroline in October brought home to him with unintended brutality that the time had not yet come. She had heard that he was planning a journey to Italy.

This is not a letter, just a message it is my duty to send. . . . I do not know which is your itinerary, but I dare say it leads through Paris, perhaps you will stop there and desire to see my father. I come to ask you not to call at our home, which as you know is a new one. [They had recently moved to 119 bis, rue Notre Dame des Champs.] If I tell you my sister has just returned there to keep the household for my father and brother you will understand why. Please send a word to Louis and he will tell you where and when you could meet my father. All this is very strange, although hardly anything can now to me seem strange after what we have been through.

That Marie was well enough to rejoin the mainstream of her life was a matter for rejoicing, which should not have led to any expectation that a brother of Harry's would be a welcome visitor. Yet this note of Caroline's was like a prison sentence, shutting him out from Marie, shutting him in on himself for a further indefinite term of silence and inaction.

CHAPTER SEVEN

Highgate Hill and the Vale Press

DURING these painful months, Tom was outwardly well and zestfully occupied. His position as head of the household at 39 Southgrove was in itself no sinecure. Hettie and he each received an annual allowance of £50 from their parents in recognition of the extra work and expense entailed in running this London family home. £16 a quarter was allowed them for the board of Nellie and of Bertie and they were supposed to charge other brothers and sisters who stayed a proportionate sum. Besides entertaining their own friends, and Nellie had acquired a large number during her time at University College, they gave hospitality to Aunt Selina and Uncle Edward from Norwood, their paternal Uncle George on visits to England from his retirement in Jersey, various Sturge and other cousins passing through London and, of course, whenever possible to Uncle Appia. Although so firmly cast in the role of housekeeper, Hettie had no natural gift for the practical side of domesticity; Tom entered fully into her various initial problems, which usually caused them both as much hilarity as frustration. He wrote to his mother for advice on such matters, for instance, as what to do about their first servant Lizzie's request for a rise in wages on the grounds that she was a *cook*-general, though she didn't know how to cook, and about the butcher who persisted in delivering 'awkward shaped joints', impossible to carve properly, even with the help of Nellie's knowledge of anatomy. When the kitchen stove broke down, it was he who chose an up-to-date kitchener, 'as I am to have ... the entire supervision of this addition to our comfort'. The weekly letter home on which the parents set so much store was written on a rota, but as Tom filled in any gaps life at 39 Southgrove is well documented from his point of view.

The study where he did his literary work and designed his wood-engravings was upstairs, insulated from household noises. Hettie was taking music lessons and practised regularly on her small piano; once the household routine was well established she also undertook rent collecting under Octavia Hill's plan for the management of working-class housing. Nellie took her medical studies 'very jollily', according to Tom, combining them with membership of a dramatic society, helping to run a Girls' Club, and much sociability. She was perhaps the one who combined the Moore brains with the Sturge resolute social concern most consistently; she had determined to become a medical missionary. There were some clashes and coolnesses between her and Tom on the subject of religion. Their differences were no doubt aired in the serious readings aloud, a family tradition, which took place in the evenings—the Bible, Plato, and Emerson are mentioned. Young Bertie, the most eager, painstaking, and conforming of art students, could only have been confused had his eldest brother voiced the iconoclastic views on art schools in general that he shared with Ricketts. A protective attitude towards this least self-assertive member of the family seems, however, to have prevailed, and much interest was taken in his progress and activities. It was he who decorated the front of the house with three flags and six lanterns for Queen Victoria's Diamond Jubilee, and stationed himself at five o'clock in the morning against the Green Park railings, from where, crushed, perspiring, and jubilant, he watched the long imperial procession pass down Piccadilly.

One of their most frequent and welcome visitors was former Nana Padgeham, now Mrs. White and living nearby. She always appeared at moments of domestic crisis; she also came to all birthday parties, and it seems to have been she who suggested that a visit to the Drury Lane pantomime would make a nice birthday treat. As he wrote to Fisher, Tom 'found Dan Leno quite Shakespearean. He made a speech about an egg in the character of a

Provision Storekeeper which would not have disgraced Launce or Touchstone.' He was fascinated by the whole world of panto-mime, the rightness of its wrongness. He later recounted an argument, in which 'I thought it was philosophy that made the donkeys take to thistles and so had reason on my side and the laugh against me, like Dan Leno when his face was black and he didn't know it'. They were all already devotees of Gilbert and Sullivan. Bob Trevelyan now tried to convert him to Wagner. 'What a splendid commencement it has,' Tom wrote after a per-formance of *The Flying Dutchman*. 'Why cannot we begin a poem with repeated sounds that mean nothing, but prepare the soul? That is the trouble with literature, that every word means some-thing, often has an offensive history.' Both Bob and Hettie per-suaded him to concerts conducted by Hans Richter, but he was little able to appreciate music as such and it was the opportunities for theatre-going proper which he embraced with a highly critical fervour. Grand productions of Shakespeare, such as *Henry IV* with Beerbohm Tree and *Cymbeline* with Ellen Terry, failed to satisfy him, though an *As You Like It* with Julia Nielsen led him to write a hurried postcard to Fisher, '. . . mind and notice the way the folds of her tunic float over the unstayed torso of the beautiful Julia'. Although critical of the acting, he was impressed by the simplicity of some of the productions of the Elizabethan Stage Society, particularly *The Tempest*, accompanied by 'the twangling music of Mr. Dolmetsch'. *Little Eyolf* was his introduction to Ibsen. He went twice to this, and missed no other performances of his plays. 'Nobody laughs at Ibsen,' he commented regretfully to Trevelyan, 'and he laughs with nobody.'

Neither visits to the theatre nor to Ricketts and Shannon at 31 Beaufort Street were made easy by the situation of 39 Southgrove, which Roger Fry was to describe as 'further from anywhere than anywhere else'. Early in 1896 Tom began to learn to cycle on Henry Poole's machine. The chorus of dismay that greeted this news, accompanied as it was by the announcement that he and Poole intended cycling to Florence in the autumn, suggests that

Tom was still regarded as exceptionally vulnerable physically. His mother begged him not to venture into the heavy traffic of London and enclosed newspaper cuttings of cycling accidents, Uncle Appia sent messages warning of the dangers of the roads in France, even Uncle George in Jersey, a cyclist himself, wrote urging extreme caution. His father, on the other hand, while finding difficulty in imaginining him 'careering through the land on wheels', wished him well and offered a loan for the purchase of a thoroughly reliable machine. Off this reliable machine Tom somehow managed to pull the handlebars; he had earlier injured his knee severely falling off Poole's. Nevertheless, he persevered, saved himself a great deal of time on local journeys and, though the trip to Florence was abandoned, became a hardy long-distance cyclist. Hettie and Sarah meanwhile had quietly learnt to ride during their summer holiday at Torquay; this led to a bantering correspondence between Tom and Sarah, who then signed themselves Twintom and Twinsal.

His first long ride took him on a visit to Harry. It is probable that Harry had suffered more acutely as a result of the disastrous engagement than his parents ever appreciated. After becoming convinced that his vocation was to act as a spiritual guide to others, to have lost his own bearings so injuriously, so disgracefully, to use his mother's word, must have been a crippling shock to his confidence and self-esteem. It was years before he brought himself to see his parents again. His letters to Tom, who seems at this time to have been his main link with the rest of the family, are baldly factual and reveal little of his state of mind. In the long vacation of 1896 he came to Oxford for a period of study and stayed with the Reverend Chavasse, then Principal of Wycliffe Hall and later Bishop of Liverpool. Tom responded to the suggestion that he would find much to interest him in the Taylorian Institute and should see Holman Hunt's *The Light of the World* at Keble College, and spent several days with him. There is no record of what was done or said on this occasion, but afterwards it evidently gave Harry satisfaction to convey a cordial invitation to stay with the Chavasses again if ever he were in Oxford, 'if they are not too Philistine for you!'

For his disciples Harry Mileham and Hugh Fisher, both much dependent on his advice, Tom also felt concern. Mileham had won the R.A. Gold Medal for painting and was spending a year in Italy. '. . . he has got as far as Capri and stuck,' Tom reported to his parents in June. 'Disgraceful I think. He was to have seen a lot of North Italy by now and instead there he is bathing and basking in the sun and painting peasant children's heads for Xmas cards.' In fact the poor young man had been prostrated for several weeks with dysentry. Once recovered, he raced through the churches and galleries of northern and central Italy, relying on the rendezvous with Tom in Florence to steady his mind before starting on the composition of the design and cartoon required by the Academy. As this rendezvous never materialized, he fell back on sending his preliminary sketches to Tom for comment and finally posted him the finished works for decision on whether they were worth framing. Fisher's problems were mainly financial. 'He is so terribly virtuous (being far the most virtuous person I have ever fallen in with) that if he does not get on the reputation of Providence will be severely damaged in my eyes. He is indefatigable and a wonder of candour and good temper into the bargain, and has never had a fair chance of showing if he really has anything artistically valuable in him as he has been continually harassed by getting a living . . .' As a married man studying full time at the South Kensington Institute on a scholarship of twenty-seven shillings a week, Fisher had to take any hack-work he could get. Even his attempts during summer holidays to explore his talent in the peace and rural austerity of West Wiltshire had to be interrupted if the chance of earning by, for example, drawing a wedding-cake for a pastry-cook's advertisement presented itself. Henry Poole, by contrast, was working steadily on his first public commission—four caryatids for a public building in Rotherhythe.

These friends, and Bob Trevelyan, all came to 39 Southgrove

95

and were, more or less, part of the Moore family circle. 31 Beaufort Street remained a sphere apart. At this stage all Tom's creative work found its outlet in the ventures of Ricketts and Shannon. Apart from the main undertaking of the Vale Press, they were simultaneously engaged in no less than three periodicals. The last two numbers of *The Dial* came out in 1896 and 1897. In January 1896 *The Pageant* was launched, a substantial periodical with a cloth binding designed by Ricketts, endpapers by Lucien Pissarro, a title-page by Selwyn Image. Shannon, the Art Editor, reinforced the work of the *Dial* artists mainly by reproductions of the work of such well-established men as Whistler, Millais, and Burne-Jones, while the Literary Editor J. W. Gleeson White ranged more widely in the introduction of younger talents. 'I am glad "The Pageant" has gone off well,' wrote Daniel to his son, 'I hope it may bring you in something besides honour and glory, public appreciation in the shape of money helps one to bear the honour more comfortably.' The second and last number appeared the following year. Before then, *The Dome: A Quarterly containing Examples of All the Arts* was in circulation; a smaller review, more modest in format, this ran as a quarterly into 1899 and continued as a monthly for a further two years. It was edited anonymously, and probably variously. Among the 'Notes and Reviews' in the second number is a review of *The Dome* itself in which one hears the voice of Ricketts, the Ricketts who addressed his letters to the President of the Royal Academy 'opposite Fortnum and Masons, London':

As there are already quite twice as many magazines in existence as there ought to be, we are a little sorry that the Editor of the latest addition to their number has not condescended to spare half-a-dozen pages for an account of his Aims. He probably imagines that the very unwieldy sub-title tells the public quite enough; indeed in one sense it tells them too much, for, while promising Examples of All the Arts, there is not so much as a reference to Sculpture, Poker-Work or Self-Defence; and to make the sub-title good, something should surely be said about Amateur Bent Ironwork (Revived Young Ladies' Victorian).

The first of the Vale Press books appeared in the autumn of 1896. Among them was *The Passionate Pilgrim and the Songs from Shakespeare's Plays* edited by Tom. His brother George had given him considerable help with this—in the choice of readings, the punctuation, and when to spell 'O' with an 'h'. Indeed, over the next couple of years he made no secret of his reliance on a younger brother to correct his own spelling and punctuation. Two further commissions were a selection of Wordsworth's poems and the translation of Maurice de Guérin's *La Bacchante*, to be printed together with his earlier translation of *Le Centaure*; for both these volumes he was to design and engrave the illustrations. He had also to rework his long poem *Danaë*, published in its first version in the 1893 *Dial*, for its appearance in book form with illustrations by Ricketts. At the same time he had willingly been drawn into collaboration with Lucien Pissarro.

Disappointed by the lack of interest among French publishers in his wood-engravings for children's tales, Pissarro had come to England; a letter of introduction that Félix Fénéon had given him to John Gray brought him to Ricketts just at the time ideas for the Vale Press were germinating. His fresh, sturdy woodcuts were very different in character from the work of Ricketts or Shannon, but they and he were welcomed with generous warmth and he, in turn, was inspired by Ricketts's conception of the printed book. Whereas, however, the Vale books were to be actually printed by the firm of Ballantyne, Pissarro decided that he would like to make his own books from start to finish. He bought a hand press; Ricketts allowed him to use his Vale type (one of the three founts he designed in all); together, he and his wife Esther mastered the craft of printing. He then experimented in printing in colour, often using five different blocks for his illustrations. And so were produced the little books of the Eragny Press, named after the Normandy village where he had lived and worked with his father, Camille. Tom was touched and delighted to be presented, in January 1897, with a copy of the first of these, Laforgue's *Moralités légendaires*, and honoured when Pissarro asked him to design and engrave illustrations for Charles Perrault's *Histoire de Peau d'Ane*. When later the Vale type was withdrawn from use and Pissarro designed his own Brook type, the first book printed in it was *A Brief Account of the Origin of the Eragny Press and A Note on the Relation of the Printed Book as a Work of Art to Life*, written by Tom. Although this did not appear until 1903, these two short quotations from it illustrate an already well-established aesthetic creed:

It is no longer necessary to defend the beautiful printed book, because the price is established and the collector appreciates its rarity. But it may not be altogether vain to say something of the ends that should be attained by reclaiming the book for beauty, and making it a work of art. Haste and hurry are the mortal foes of delicacy, discrimination, contemplation and refinement. In an age of motors Art has untold enemies; the circumstances of life are hostile to beauty; we are robbed right and left, but have not time to realize our losses . . .

and this from a passage linking discrimination in reading with book design:

For effectiveness there is no human creation to compare with a good habit. . . . To occupy the mind with the same thoughts every day is as wise as is for an artist the daily use of his implements; skill and character are effects of precisely parallel disciplines.

Ricketts and Shannon opened a small shop off Regent Street for the sale of the books of both Presses, where alternative bindings designed by Ricketts in pig-skin and morocco were also on display. The binders could not keep pace with the demand; the books, all in limited editions, rapidly sold out. They were fortunate in hitting upon the young Oxford graduate, Charles J. Holmes, to manage this shop and then take over the business side of the Vale Press, together with much proof-reading and some editing. For Holmes, too, the association was a fortunate one. Although his hobbies were golf, angling, and boxing, he had always wanted to be an artist. Having, however, a widowed mother to support, he had first gone into publishing, and after some unfortunate experiences in this field had landed up as book-keeper at Ballantyne's Press at the time *The Dial* was being printed there. He was invited to 1 The

MY heart leaps up when I behold
A rainbow in the sky

I HEARD a thousand blended notes
While in a grove I sat reclined

Two wood-engravings for the Vale Press *Wordsworth*

'Peau d'Ane bathing':
a wood-engraving for the Eragny Press

Vale. There, he was entranced by Ricketts's talk, encouraged to draw and paint and taught to etch. Later he hunted through the art sales-rooms every week for Ricketts and Shannon, bidding on his own behalf when he could afford to do so. He was, in fact, set on the path which eventually led to the Directorship of the National Gallery, a post Ricketts himself was to refuse.

In the excitement of this successful enterprise Ricketts and Shannon did not neglect other activities, nor did they forget their friends. They were instrumental in setting up a committee to raise money to buy a picture by Alphonse Legros for the nation: 'Old Watts has promised £50 alone and they have already reached £130. They think he is very much bullied at home by his wife and children because he no longer makes money and that this will make them think more of him.' During 1897 Ricketts was elected a member of the Arts and Crafts Exhibition Society 'without in any way soliciting the honour', and Shannon and Burne-Jones were the two English painters awarded Gold Medals at the Munich International Exhibition, 'which is very fortunate for the former, as he might have got it with all sorts of small fry, or even not got it at all as this is his first exhibition in oils . . .'. The medal-winning picture was a portrait, entitled alternatively 'The Man with a Yellow Glove' or 'Sturge Moore as Poet'. The bearded figure is seated at a table, the eyes cast down in thought, a spray of bay leaves lying by the right hand. Of this painting Shannon had written in his working diary, 'Found great difficulty, finally despaired and turned it upside-down . . . the whole picture was handicapped by the large accumulation of paint on and off for 2 years.' When it was returned from Munich in the New Year, he added, 'rather too black, seems darker than when it went. This is the picture that ravished old Legros so much. An admirable portrait of Moore as he will be next year.' On the following day his entry is, 'Moore's little woodcuts returned from Munich, where they made some impression. [They were reproduced in a magazine called *Jugend*.] Very racy and charming little things and looked delightful when seen together. I suppose he will have to wait for about 10 years.' It was not only by sitting frequently to Shannon, in other characters besides his own, that Tom forwarded his friends' work. As a matter of course he gave hours to helping with the lithography and etching. When they were both away he acted as 'house dog'. Although most of his own work was done at home, he was at the same time an integral part of life at 31 Beaufort Street.

There was, however, a concealed discord in this relationship that was so precious to him:

> I joined in mocking laugh when it was said
> That such-an-one would marry, 'Ah, poor fool!'
> They said; . . .
> 'Poor fool,' I said, and meant myself instead . . .

Ricketts, with his penchant for extravagant expression, was fond of saying among his intimates that all creative artists should be forbidden marriage by law. He was himself clearly so constituted as to find marriage no temptation, and on one occasion certainly he effectively obstructed Shannon's desire to commit wedlock. Whether theirs was physically a homosexual relationship remains an open question, of no great importance here. Their partnership was an enduring one. Tom may have been right in regarding them, as he always did, as married to Beauty in a monastic sense—as a brotherhood, of which he too was then assumed to be a member. So important to him was Ricketts's approval that he dared not disillusion him. This deception, a denial of his own nature, a disloyalty, as he saw it, to his love for Marie, caused him moments of shame. For a man so essentially honest, to continue for years in this pretence indicates the negative, restrictive side of the influence Ricketts exercised over him.

In May 1897 Uncle Appia was in London again, this time as the French Protestant representative to an International Congress called by Church leaders as a result of the latest massacre of Armenians by the Turks. Tom attended the meetings at St. Martin's Town Hall on both days of the Congress; Nellie, anxious to consult her uncle about work in the mission field, and Bertie came for part of the second day, and Marie's godmother, Miss Mayo, was also there. Tom was introduced by his uncle to several of the moving spirits, taken by him to the Armenian Aid Office and to an at-home at the Hotel Metropole, 'where Uncle was installed in an armchair of seniority [he was seventy] and was both the most reticent and most attentive . . . of all those present'. As a result of conversations he then had, Tom formed the opinion that an element of factual distortion and hypocrisy had gone to the working up of popular feeling on behalf of the suffering Armenians. This scepticism was reinforced by several of the speakers, particularly by 'Canon Gore, utterly without restraint in word or action, trembling about from one leg to another. . . . To me he seemed utterly depraved by emotionalism, but was applauded like the hero of a melodrama.' Uncle Appia was 'the briefest of all the speakers, insisting chiefly on the bond of fellowship that charity made' in time of disaster. Immediately after making his own speech, Uncle Appia acted as interpreter to that of the German delegate.

During both evenings he made time for talk with his nephew. Never before had Tom so warmly appreciated the searching energy of his spirit: 'I recall his walking up and down the room, grinding his teeth, saying Renan lived as the beasts that perish and looking at Ernest Guy's copy of Vie de Jésus as though he would not like to touch it with the tongs'. Yet now he referred the Diaconesses' novices to Renan and quoted him in his sermons.

What a different road this indicates to that which English theology appears to be taking, how much more uphill and an old man too . . . And when he found that I was not indifferent but felt altogether opposed to Christianity, he rejoiced and said, 'Celui qui resiste, apprend' and quoted Michelet against the extravagance of religious sentiment and won my heart entirely. He is, after Ricketts, far away the most wonderful man I have ever come across, and he is very like Ricketts in some respects, though so opposite in others.'

The news Uncle Appia brought of his own family was not cheering. Aunt Helen had been suffering from migraine, Tante

Louise was visibly getting older, and Caroline he described as 'worn and weary for her sister's sake'. Of Marie's condition 'he had nothing very comforting to say', yet was confident she would recover in time; no doubt he remembered that the depression he had suffered at about the same age had lasted for two years. The whole family had been in great anxiety over a serious illness of the eldest grandson, Théodore. On hearing that Marie was then nursing this boy, Tom recalled his own sickly childhood and nourished the forlorn hope that she might share in the special quality of child convalescence:

> Which, thoughtless, has no need of thought,
> For contentment is its essence. . . .
> Conscious of a perfect right
> To take its own time day or night,
> Never anxious or in haste,
> Sure such sweet hours are not waste,
> Brooding on its better self
> While truant strength comes back by stealth,
> Till at length with half-hurt cry—
> Earth distinguishing from sky—
> It wakes surprised by perfect health.

Within a few days of this meeting with his uncle, and not impossibly because of the talk they had together, Tom took an important step. On 1 June he wrote to inform his father that he had consulted a doctor in Harley Street: 'I did this having been addicted to masturbation since I first went to school, and wishing to know if there were no way of getting a total mastery over the habit'. The doctor had recommended circumcision, had put him in touch with a surgeon, and the date for the operation had been fixed. In his reply, after warning his son that the mental habit also needed determined resistance, Daniel wrote, 'I shall have you much in mind and with constant prayer that your efforts may be crowned with complete success. And now I am sure that they will.' Tom then evidently wrote for advice on the practical arrangements for the operation, and at the same time asked why the subject of masturbation was not more openly discussed with children. On the latter point Daniel answered with less than his usual conviction: 'I do not think there is any intention to deceive in talk about the subject, but it is not easily approached and with some natures the mention of the subject has produced the very end the warning was intended to guard against. Schoolmasters and Parents are difficultly placed, for secrecy and self-indulgence are hard to combat.' He then advised Tom to tell Nellie in advance that he was to have a slight operation about which their father knew: she would be responsible for the household arrangements and carrying out any instructions the doctor might give, and might be alarmed unless prepared beforehand. 'I have merely told Mamma what I recommend you to tell Nell and Hett: and Bert or anyone else. All will be well with you I feel sure, and you will be emancipated.'

In fact, Tom had already been emancipated. The consultations with the doctor and surgeon had in themselves released him. For this was 'the sin' referred to in the secret poems, a sin surrounded by punitive superstitions. He had believed his virility might be affected. Freed from this fear, he was able to write to Marie on her birthday a letter he could not have allowed himself to write before.

This declaration is introduced by a sonnet, written in the field behind Woodthorpe on her birthday two years previously; it expresses, in a mood inspired by the fitting beauty of that June day, his realization that love

> . . . is a prayer
> Wholely of silence, hushing all who ask,
> Till, quieted, their souls become aware
> That wants prove selfishness—that love must give
> And only takes to help another live.

Marie, that was written knowing that I was not a Christian, that even as a man I was unworthy of you and that I had next to no material prospects; so that it seemed *then* and had for long before then, that my chief duty was to brace myself never to tell you that I loved you. Very little has altered in my position but my love for you has grown more not less. At the very first I had looked about for a way to convert you into a sceptic, and if I never attempted to do so, the reason lay in the sentiment that it would mean rooting you up out of your life and connections, and I had too much reverence for what you already were to really desire that. And now I recognize much more fully that my duty must be to act as anxiously for your conscience as you yourself could.

... I thought then that the religious question, added to the knowledge of my prospects and character, laid an absolute veto on my proposing marriage. I have been slowly convinced that I was wrong. There seems a horrible waste of suffering on both sides; which has hindered me in my work, and you might have been saved how much misery! Yet there has been this much good, that whether you feel able to accept my love or bound to reject it, I feel confident that you will continue to work for good in me and that I shall continue to advance in either case. So I hold you absolutely free to reject my offer. My love constitutes no claim. ...

Should you feel that you could let me begin to try to help you (however that help may later stop short of what I desire), I would first write you one more letter, which I should feel bound to in that case, to confess the sum of evil about myself; then, if you did not forbid me, I would come to Paris, or if you did not wish me to do so at once, would try by writing to win your heart to view the future as bravely as loved lovers only dare. And always I would limit myself by your slightest hint, my object being not to conquer but to help you, which, even if not to try be the only way you can allow me, I will embrace. But chiefly, Marie, I wish to urge you to believe in your great worth, for my sake believe it, and for all our sakes who love you, all who truly know you. You are a real revelation of wonderful promise, do not impair it, or allow it to be impaired in you!

To be so taken up with you has often seemed a kind of crime and I have fought against it, yet you would wonder if you could know how you have haunted me every day, and especially this last year you have been always there as soon as I was alone. Oh, Marie, I am not what I was, I have learnt a great deal and worked, constantly thinking of what you would say of my achievement, and I have done better and still better work. Yet an union between us, if not impossible would be immensely difficult; not at first only but afterwards; we should be constantly prompted to mistranslate each the other by our several pasts and habits of mind. I do not ask you 'Are you ready to make compromises?' but 'Could you with me face difficulties which are usually met with compromises doing without them to the utmost of our strength?' We each have a field of work irrevocably chosen for us, yet, working side by side, the mere fact of such diversity might keep our minds open and our hearts alive to things beyond our own personal interests in a way that few, even of those who succeed in life, achieve. If we were true to one another's good, if we renounced all petty jealous attempts to dominate or overlord each others consciences it would be so; then, too, whatever truth we have either of us had revealed to us must, by degrees, become a mutual possession. That is all I dare urge; what such success would demand on both sides of toil and pain I do not wish to disguise. I still know myself to be unworthy as well as unsuitable, but I have doubted if one has a right to pronounce absolute judgements even on oneself. Though my love, demanding the best possible for you, condemned and condemns me, it may still be that in me lie the best aids actually offered to you, and that I have done you great wrong in holding them back. Yet it is so hard not to be selfish in thinking of such immensities of good fortune that I am still horribly frightened lest my offered aid be only the most hateworthy begging.

Do not be in a hurry to answer this, and do not think you are asked for more than you feel free to grant, neither feel bound to accept what you do not desire! I can never prove to you how much I am in your debt already! So do not let any pity work with you; to need is not to deserve, to mean well is not to do well and has no necessary value beyond one's own soul. Leave me out of the question and examine whether such an affection as I confess mine to be could make a wholesome condition of your life, even under the narrowest circumstances that might arise. Then, if it can, may it not be best to leave to the future our education in the how-complete and how-restricted a field such a relation shall claim between us? I believe you may trust me never to urge false claims or take advantage of any generosity in an unfair way; for my love is rooted in the faith that the only desirable relationship between us is the really true one. I have tried to be just in weighing every word I have used, but of course there are many, many other points to be considered, and those too of the greatest importance, yet perhaps they had better wait. If I have not said enough to make you feel that I mean wholeheartedly, there can be no more to say.

I have ventured to send you a book for the editing of which I am responsible, but that is its least interest. Plastically it is the work of my friend Ricketts who has already won a distinguished position and will I believe go on to very great things. He has designed type and all; his energy and his enterprise have alone made its publishing a possibility. Perhaps 'The Passionate Pilgrim' is not worth your perusal but the 'Songs', if I have succeeded ought to make the loveliest sequence of pages. I am enclosing some written elucidations, also the copy of two incomparable sonnets [Milton's 'To a Virtuous Young Lady' and Wordsworth's 'To Toussaint L'Ouverture'], one of which, Milton's, you may feel able to appreciate in a deeper sense than any possible for me; but I know that this must be so very often, and want to learn of you if you dare be so kind as to teach me. The woodcut ['The Centaur's First Love'] is to be published as an illustration to a translation that I have made from de Guérin's 'Centaur'. Do not think from what I have said that I expect to be always penniless, only I can't be sure of making money. But I shall try now, before I never have done so.

I should have liked to have written sweet things to you but have no right to do so yet.

I hope Aunt Hélène and Caroline have lost their colds. Has little Théodore quite recovered? and you, are you regaining strength? I immensely enjoyed Uncle's too short visit and was sorry to learn he caught cold going back. Now with love to him and Aunt Hélène, Aunt Louise, Caroline, Louis and you know how much to yourself, believe me to be always, in every case,

Your most affectionate cousin,

Tom

P.S. There is or has been an Exhibition at the Palais des Beaux Arts where among others some Reynolds and Gainsboroughs and other pictures by the English school have taken by surprise the French artists, who, as a rule, know next to nothing of our English work. I hope that you may also have or have had the pleasure of finding among them fresh claims for your admiration. There is a good deal of translation after Browning which has waited to be sent to you for more than 2 years: perhaps you might like to make it an excuse for us to begin where we left off and leave it to Nature to lead us into the Future. Yet, Marie, if you feel either reluctance or lack of enterprise to entertain the proposals of my letter, as well you may feel after all that you have had to suffer, in that case do not worry: do not dwell on them: let the matter rest! I can wait or ought to be ashamed of myself by now. It would be misery for me to suspect that I had added to your pain or hurried you into undertaking what lay beyond your inclination. Yet I hope that to know that you are and have been loved quite simply for what you are may work good for you, even though you cannot yet-awhile respond. Your best interests must also be mine or I really have none in you; remember that, and don't be afraid to wait. Marie, it is 3 years since I saw you, and such years!! I have been slow to understand. Forgive me. T.S.M.

As this letter was on its way, Tom recorded his trembling hopes and apprehensions as to the effect his declaration of love might have, hedged about with solicitude though it was. He likened it to a rain cloud approaching Marie, with the power either to bruise or to revive:

> Be silvered falling rain
> That she not fear thee;
> And yet she must—and yet she need not, being loved again.

Although he reiterated his recognition and acceptance of a gradual response being the most desirable outcome possible, the poem ends with the line,

> So not at once—and yet at once if best it is.

The secret having now been revealed, this is the last line written in the notebook.

CHAPTER EIGHT

꧁꧂

Bridges across the Channel

By a strange coincidence a voluminous letter from Caroline, embarked upon in April, crossed with Tom's declaration to Marie and reached him on 8 June. After her note the previous October telling him he must not call if he came to Paris, Tom had evidently written to her twice, begging to be kept informed of Marie's progress and repeating the view he had earlier urged in his letter to Tante Louise. By this time he must have given up expecting any answer, let alone so circumstantial an unburdening. She first explained how she had repeatedly attempted to reply to his letters, 'mais toujours le temps, le courage, la tranquillité d'esprit, d'âme et de circonstance' had been wanting. 'The future', she continued,

cannot be what the past was, but the nobility of our mothers has kept up a link where otherwise an uncrossable abyss might have opened. I would like you to know, that as far as you are personally concerned, a profound regret will always remain in our hearts. . . . I don't think I can give you better proof of the place you had made there in former times than the letter I am writing you today, in spite of all that it has cost me to stir up this past.

In response to Tom's wish to be informed of Marie's state, she quoted words her sister had once written: 'Je ne demande à personne de soulever le voile qui cache la dévastation de mon cœur.' 'It is certainly not for me to raise that veil before you. There are wounds that one conceals with pride, particularly perhaps those inflicted by a base betrayal.' She then echoed, and amplified, the sentiments already expressed by her mother on Harry's conduct, the irreparable damage it had caused and the near impossibility of accepting such wrongs in a spirit of Christian forgiveness. In her view, Marie had shown 'le triomphe de l'âme la plus vaillante, de l'énergie la plus indomptable, le triomphe de l'esprit sur le cœur naturel'; nevertheless, it was only superficial wounds that healed without trace, and her emotional and spiritual suffering had naturally affected her physical state.

Appreciative as he may have been of Caroline's protracted struggle to discharge a cousinly obligation towards him, Tom was shocked to find that well over a year after the breaking of the engagement both she and her mother were apparently still frozen in their original attitudes of accusatory and fatalistic lamentation. Hoping to bring about a frame of mind more conducive to Marie's recovery, he therefore devoted the greater part of his reply to an attempt to put the whole affair into what he considered its proper perspective. The principal blame, he argued, should be thrown 'not on a person, but on the circumstances of the parties and the ideas that ruled them'. Harry, he maintained, had already been given somewhat exalted notions of his worth by the acclaim with which his conversion to Anglicanism had been greeted in Cambridge; for the same reason the entire Appia family had tended to idolize him. He had probably decided that, as a clergyman, a wife would be 'a good help to have by his side', and, from what he had heard of Marie, might have already thought of her as a candidate for this role. The warmth of his welcome, Marie's frank and radiant nature, the exhilarating air of the Valleys had done the rest. 'While Marie, with her wonderful generosity, scarcely conceived or dreamed how easy it is for a young man to imagine himself in love, but felt it would be unworthy of her to doubt his word and so gave herself entirely up to the study of how to love him.' At quite an early stage, however, as he had intimated to Tom on his return from the Valleys, Harry had become aware of disconcerting traits in Marie's personality, but confident that 'he would be able to school her into a model after his own heart' he had continued to profess a love he neither felt nor understood. Before his Christmas visit to Paris, Tom had begged him, for Marie's sake, to be careful, but he had only laughed. 'When he was

III

alone once more, he came to his senses and did all he could do—which was to break her heart.' The fortitude with which Caroline had described Marie suffering this experience was not what Tom meant by 'triumphing'. She would, he knew, not only recover from it wholly but be strengthened by it; to think otherwise was a blasphemy.

Only a few days after the dispatch of this letter, Marie's answer came, ominously soon. Unaccountably, considering how everything she ever wrote was treasured, it has disappeared. Its main purport is, however, made clear in Tom's reply, the one further letter he had allowed himself whatever Marie's decision might be.

My dear Marie,

Your letter is very good and kind. Believe me that for my own sake I would never have thrust in on you, and that it was only the fear of depriving you of a help, however small, that was yours by right that led me to discover myself. I do not understand why you reject me; perhaps it is for every reason, or perhaps only on the religious ground; but no doubt you would not have withheld your reason unless you deemed it right to do so.

You say that it is my duty to try to detach myself from love of you; that I cannot in the least understand, nor why it should be yours to efface yourself. . . . That you never surmised my passion may, however, be your surety of my power, as I must beg you to accept my word for my will, never again to refer by word or deed to my love for you; unless indeed you should give me clear permission to do so. . . . Yet do not think I rely on your changing your mind; I should feel it *treachery* to do so. . . . That you are right in what you do I do not question; if I felt I had been deceived in you, then I could have seen my duty where you point it out, but I have made no mistake. You are what you have always been to me. There, your letter is my comfort, since it shews you do not view the future so blankly as I have been led to fear. . . .

To go back on any good thing has always seemed to me an impiety, so that I hope you will not insist that the very limited interchange of good will between us be broken off. When Christmas comes, let me feel free to send, if not a letter, yet whatever token I have to hand. I will take silence as my permission. . . . Thank you then again and again for what you say of friendship, which I shall hope to deserve and in no least point violate when you feel free to renew it outwardly. I will hope to see things a little more from your point of view and will strive for more light. The *best* remains most real for me as for you. Only things that never really were cease. . . . I shall look for news that you do gain in freedom, of which your suffering has stinted you, and will make it my own strength, believe me, as also that I am always

Your most affectionate cousin

Tom Moore.

That the restrained tone of this letter was not easily achieved is shown by several false starts and rough drafts of letters subsequently written to Caroline. Marie had evidently told Tom that to her sister alone his proposal had been confided. To Caroline, therefore, he turned in a turmoil of rebellion, especially against certain sentences in Marie's letter. Of his proffered love she had written, 'Je ne puis et je ne pourrai jamais l'accepter.' He could not refrain from pointing out that whereas it had taken him five devoted years to make his proposal, she had given fewer days to rejecting it absolutely than she had to accepting Harry's. Since she had alluded kindly to their former friendship, he could only assume that religious prejudice against him had led to so hasty and unconsidered a conclusion. 'I have understood that suffering and the death of my hopes ought in no way to detract from the beauty and greatness of whatever task God may give me perform.' Why did she, in the present context, speak of the death of her hopes? And why did it not even occur to her that he, Tom, might form part of a God-given task? 'It is difficult for me to speak to you of the help that comes to me from above this earth; however much I may wish to do so, you would not at present understand me.' The assumption that because he was not a professing churchman he must be incapable of any spiritual understanding wounded and angered him; it was contrary to the true spirit of Christianity, it was foreign to Marie's nature and had been imposed on her by an arrogant sectarianism. He did not ask Caroline to plead his cause with Marie, who could, he acknowledged, be right in rejecting

113

him on other grounds, but hoped she might feel able to persuade her to reconsider the religious objection. In any case, he again begged her to send him news of Marie from time to time.

Marie's decision to make Caroline her sole confidante in a family so affectionately interlocked must have already added to her sister's chronic sense of stress. Then, in rapid succession, she received these two letters from Tom, both calculated to agitate her extremely, more particularly the second, placing her as it did in the position of a go-between. For, genuine as her expression of her family's regard and esteem for Tom no doubt was, it is unlikely that she then regarded him at all favourably in the guise of a future husband for her sister. Nevertheless, by early August, in the comparative calm of the Valleys, she had composed her feelings and thoughts sufficiently to write to him again. This letter never reached him. The result of this miscarriage was a silence of several months between them, during which both came to believe they had seriously offended the other.

Tom meanwhile was trying to immerse himself in work. He had finished the first draft of a verse-drama on the Phaedra theme, eventually published as *Aphrodite against Artemis*, and was looking about for another dramatic subject before going back again to Phaedra. Early in July he wrote to Bob Trevelyan, first apologizing for having been uncommunicative:

I have been in the doctor's hands, and down in the mouth too. . . . I am now in a speedy way of recovery as there proved to be nothing much the matter with me. This moment I have finished reading *Mariamne* [Herod's wife] in Josephus. It is unimaginably beautiful . . . I can't sit still. One needs a god to pray to and praise. How I shall ever be able to content myself I do not know. It is a virgin land, but the oldest countries are not so rich in voices that tell tales to the brooding soul. It is a chance such as few men have had granted to them. Unworthy me, alas!

Trevelyan, thoughtful for his friend's health as well as eager to exchange poetic inspirations, immediately invited him to stay in his country home near Haslemere. 'I am in clover here,' Tom wrote to Fisher, 'with the Sussex Weald out of the window and books from the London Library loading the table; it is only I am vile and still full short of the capacity to enjoy things.'

In August, Poole suggested a cycling tour of French cathedrals, 'to cost not more than £5 a head and last not more than a week'. This tour revived Tom's zest. He described to Fisher how they crossed overnight to Dieppe and then set off for Amiens:

We passed through the forest of Eu in fine feather with Puvis de Chavannes opening out on either hand ... on we went and soon came to the most wonderful place we were to see—Rambures, an old village stretching some half mile along a cross road with houses on one side of the way only; immense woods immediately behind it and in front; the church alone faced the other buildings and stood in a wilderness of half gilded, half rusted iron crosses, to which hung white glass wreaths etc. Everything was just as one would desire it and a few yards further on the trees opened up on one side and through some park gates we caught a glimpse of a chateau. Four solid Norman towers of red brick planted so close together there hardly seemed room for any- thing between them. However, out of this massive calix there rose a little Mont St Michel of pointed roofs and turret chimneys, the four pepper-box Norman towers being quite dominated by its flowerlike elegance. The whole stood like an elephant in the water with a Queen's houdah on its back. ...

In Amiens our host was a big man with red hair and the longest moustaches I have ever seen, these when he ate or worked he wound round his ears. We climbed all over the Cathedral, where the concierge remembered Ruskin who always complained of being ill yet was always working hard. ... The rose windows are like sea weeds spread out under a still sea to a perfect circle. The choir stalls are unimaginably rich, the whole Bible in little wooden figures trying to struggle out of seats and panoplies. Of course there is cause to curse. There is such a glory in the choir as makes one sick at heart; 17th century cherubs and thunder clouds with shafts of gold thicker than any weaver's beam piercing them, and all sprawled in stucco right across the absidal arches. ...

'Beauvais is all in height,' as the concierge said in its disparage- ment. ... But we climbed all over it, and incomplete and faulty though it is there is something huger in the beauty of it than one can well describe.... In the moonlight it was a perfect vision.... From Beauvais almost to Rouen in rain till the bykes were creaking and night closing in, so we stopped at a little roadside inn, whose copper and brass pans and old chest and small, dried, aged but motherly hostess you would like to draw, and the potage au lait more than made up for the *living* water we found in the ewer and which gave one unpleasant sensations when washing. Rouen is electric trams etc. We went to Croisset and saw Flaubert's lime walk ... his house is gone and his tulip tree, but there is still the little winding walk up the cliff and the little look-out summer house.... We also saw the Hotel Dieu of Rouen where he lived as a child and to whose lowest windows he and his sister used to climb up by the vines to watch his father dissecting, and the same flies which settled on the corpses came buzzing out and settled on them and the flowers.... We rode up and down the rue Flaubert, and in the Cathedral saw the St Julien window.... We were short of cash [in Dieppe] so went to a very queer grub shop and got a rather strange glimpse of *low* life. Then we watched a Roundabout ... quite altogether the Emperor of Roundabouts and in its way as decorated as a Cathedral, and French women in large skirts which filled out reminded one of Velasquez' Equestrian Queens....

Battling through the rain towards Rouen, Tom had thought of Jacob wrestling with the angel; that evening he scribbled down the first draft of his poem 'At Bethel'.

For several weeks after his return to 39 Southgrove he was often alone. Bertie and the sisters were at Torquay. Poole was engrossed in a new commission—a statue of the Earl of Wemys. Bob was in Northumberland. Harry Mileham was with his parents in the Isle of Wight, worrying about his current painting of Joan of Arc. Fisher had just transferred himself, his somewhat reluctant wife, and his furniture to a tiny, primitive cottage in the remote Wiltshire village of Imber; by living frugally he hoped to work there uninterruptedly at least until the spring, making studies of rural life in a wintry landscape. While Ricketts and Shannon were on the Continent, Tom house-dogged at 31 Beaufort Street for a week, taking his engraving tools with him. The creative atmosphere of their home, their collection of beautiful treasures, should have inspired him, but 'the vein did not flow', he could not concentrate. In his last letter to Caroline he had promised not to be importunate, not to write further until he heard from her. But that was in June. By October he could no longer endure this banishment into outer darkness and he appealed to her again, in terms which can only be guessed at from the interim reply she wrote in English on 18 October She wished to answer him fully while she was still in La Tour, 'away from my sister and Parisian agitated and interrupted life', yet, 'if on one hand I intensely desire helping you to see things in a truer light, on the other I feel I can hardly do this without speaking more explicitly or saying more than Marie thought it right to say. . . . And really it seems that you nearly put me in an unbearable position, asking me as it were to open my sister's heart to you.' She assured Tom that she had never judged him hardly, she had, in fact, 'at times thought you judged yourself more hardly than others'; she was painfully aware of his suffering and of how hard it was for him to have to turn to her and 'try to feel entire confidence'. If she could be sure he had received what she had written in August, it would be easier for her to write now; as it was, 'your letter has agitated me much, and though I read it over and over, and thought it over all day long, I do not yet see clearly what I ought to say'.

The correspondence that followed at first contained recriminations. Certain pages of Caroline's letters still quiver with a burning indignation that Tom's new light on the broken engagement had only fuelled, and she asked why, since he had foreseen the likely dénouement, he had sent no word of warning. He blamed her parents for the imprudent haste with which they had sanctioned the engagement, and she expressed their 'stupefaction' at his parents' failure to induce their son to show even a common humanity in its closing stages. From the fragmentary drafts of Tom's letters it is, however, clear that his main and dogged endeavour was to gain Caroline's confidence in him as an *ally* in what was their common concern—Marie's well-being. She conceded that his June letter, though premature, had helped Marie, not, she was careful to stress, in the way he had hoped, but simply by enabling her to speak the name of Moore again, and, perhaps too, by making her aware that life might still hold surprises. Rebutting a reproach implied by Tom, she maintained that Marie, like a climbing plant that had been dashed to the ground, could only gradually, discreetly, and tenderly be supported back to an upright posture. For this reason, she had not, by December, spoken to Marie of the points raised in his letters, but promised to do so as soon as she judged the right moment had come. The arrival before Christmas of a fat envelope addressed to Marie in Tom's hand therefore threw her into a state of perturbation lest impatience had driven him to another direct approach. She need not have feared. The envelope contained Shelley's 'Spirit of Delight' and Wordsworth's sonnet 'The world is too much with us . . .' copied out for Marie, and some of his own recent woodcuts as Christmas cards to the family.

The exchange of Christmas wishes between Tom and his uncle led to a correspondence on religious questions. In the only surviving fragment of Tom's part in this he does not mince his words:

It seems to me undeniable that Christianity has always, and does still, oppose progress. As the baggage of dogmas has never been in perfect intellectual harmony, every advance seems to threaten it and therefore they have always opposed as long as they could things which now the majority of them accept. They are always afraid of losing their power over the multitude if they give the right hand of fellowship to the children of light. I know there is much to be set against this; the importance of solidarity, the truculent face often put upon innovations, the real importance and beauty of the Christian life. Nevertheless I cannot help thinking that Christianity will never succeed until as a body, in its policy as well as in individual cases, it imitates its master by laying down its life for its adversaries. I mean by making no dogma essential and by considering everybody whose life does not absolutely forbid it as a Christian whether they call themselves so or not. . . . The arguments for Christian morality are so solid, they can be practically tested every day; those for its dogmas seem to me so worthless. When I say 'morality' I mean, more, 'life'.

While naturally challenging many of Tom's arguments, his uncle recognized and welcomed a common ground between them. He cited a Japanese who had finally said to his would-be converter, 'Comment voulez-vous que je puisse aimer Dieu; c'est un paquet de lois'. He asked for the loan of some of Matthew Arnold's writings and much wished that he could again talk with his nephew 'bouche à bouche'.

In January the whole Appia family fell ill, with high temperatures and varying persistent symptoms, all described as 'la grippe'. 'It is horrible about all the Appias being in bed again,' Tom wrote to his mother. 'It must be drains or water one would think, as for several of them it is the second attack. I'm afraid they are very obstinate and wrong-headed about taking precautions. Couldn't Father supply some awful examples? ... or they will get typhus or something fatal. The worst of it is they all think we have got drains on the brain.' It was with more than just relief that on 20 January Tom received a postcard from Marie. As her father was still very weak and had been ordered to Cannes for convalescence, she would be sending Tom his 'Noël', a miscellany produced every year for the parish; to this both his daughters had contributed, she herself having written the short life of Jeanne d'Albret, the steadfastly Calvinist Queen of Navarre. Scrupulously, Tom replied on a postcard, commiserating with her on the family's illnesses and adding, 'My uncle has always struck me as having very markedly the "sentiment historique", not exactly in the sense that Renan gives to these words, but like our own Carlyle's—the little glimpses into the past, those vivid portraits of folk long since dead and gone, that he would give us sometimes at mealtimes are among my most delightful reminiscences. I hope you will have the same gift, and believe you have.'

By an unexpected turn of events, Fisher was now in Paris. An uncle of Mrs. Fisher's, dismayed by the snow-bound prospect for his niece on Salisbury Plain and concerned by her husband's inability to provide for her more comfortably, had offered to advance him the money for six months' study in Paris. The Imber cottage had been shut up, Mrs. Fisher had gone to her uncle's family in Liverpool, and since October Fisher had been 'grinding away at Julien's', and copying pictures in the Louvre. His letters to Tom described the Paris scene, then troubled by the Dreyfus riots, and asked advice on how best to use his windfall opportunity. Advice, general and particular, Tom willingly gave, including a long dissertation on the 'Nature Superstition', which Ricketts held to be the undoing of the Impressionists; then he turned to his own difficulties with the *Peau d'Ane* illustrations:

I believe this is the true problem presented to modern art. That is to say the element that is condemned as 'fin de siècle', 'la curiosité du diable' must be harmonized with health and refinement. This sounds dangerously theoretical, but my method is very safe if only I am strong enough to carry it out—i.e. like the Princess of Tyre who, contemplating an almond bough in full flower, became pregnant and was delivered of Atys; an organic whole, opposite to nature in being simple, impassioned and individual, for nature is always indetermined, confined and incapable of producing a united impression . . .

Later, he apologized for this 'ghastly jabber', and was embarrassed when Fisher replied, 'Your letters are one of the joys of my life.'

In February, Tom sent Fisher the Appias' address, explaining that he had thought it best to wait before doing so until peace had been re-established after 'a family disturbance about a brother of mine'. 'They are all wonderful and dear, and my uncle has a finer head than I have seen on another living man. My aunt is a dear old lady, with an expression about her mouth which strikingly recalls Gustave Moreau's Jeune Fille avec la Tête d'Orphé. My cousins are very intelligent and *vivacious*, not like me. . . . They are very, very, very Christian, so don't indulge in blasphemy or anything approaching it.' Fisher called at 119 bis on the day the family had learnt of the death of Dr. Louis Appia. Nevertheless, he was warmly welcomed into Georges's study, where his eye was immediately caught by the sketches hanging on its walls. 'But really great as his landscapes are, it is the man himself impresses one most—calm, dignified and with a face showing at the same time such power and such tenderness. . . . His manner somewhat reminded me of Mr. Gladstone whom I was once able to watch for some time . . . and he seemed to me more rugged and less refined than Appia.' Later Fisher was asked to dine and met the other members of the family, about whom, however, he made no comment. In his way this industrious, appreciative friend of Tom's was another bridge across what Caroline continued to refer to as an abyss between the families.

But by now Marie had sent Tom a birthday present, with a covering note in which she alluded to the letters he had written to Caroline. While she trusted that her sister had disabused him of certain misconceptions, she could not, at the moment, enter fully into this subject:

Today I cannot write more—I only wish to send you an affectionate message for the fourth of March, which I did not forget when I remained silent on it. I thought that you would like to read this new Mistral poem. . . . I remember that you were a great admirer of his 'Mireille'. You will have learnt of the passing of our Uncle Louis. He has at last reached the haven—his fine face, so peaceful, showed it well, Aunt Louise wrote to us, after a life full of storms and ferment. Soon a long missive, today it's only 'Happy Birthday'.

This time Tom replied, not with a note but at length, hoping thereby to clear the ground for the promised 'longue missive'. He confessed to being thoroughly ashamed of himself for having been so upset by her June letter that he had written to Caroline in bitterness. He had never meant to imply that Marie was un-Christian, but, on the hypothesis that her rejection of him was on religious grounds, had felt bound to challenge the validity of the ideas that might have influenced her. But all that was in the past. What he now urged was that they should work to discover their true relationship with one another. Neither of them should take up a fixed position; it would be no more sensible for her to say she

could never come to love him than it would be for him to say that
never, under any circumstances, could he come to love someone
else. Both should therefore adopt 'what Huxley calls that most
wholesome of frames of mind "a *suspended* judgment". . . . And all
I ask is that you will be your natural self, that you will do your
duty towards me; for is it not our duty to adjust our relationships
with others until they are truly balanced and work freely?' He
added a postscript:

I feel I have not thanked you enough for your kindness in sending to
me as you have, not only did I not expect it, I did not deserve it and
am indeed most grateful and have not felt so happy for a long time;
and if I seem obstinate and persistent it is not that I would not resign
for myself, cost what it might, but for your sake too, ought I not to
persevere? It may be that the best that you were meant to be depends
on my being brave to hope against hope?

There are signs that even Marie's January postcard had lifted
Tom's spirits appreciably. In February he had written with immense enthusiasm to his mother of his discovery in the British
Museum of the early version of Flaubert's *La Tentation de St.
Antoine*. 'Flaubert's corrections are a wonderful sermon on what
hard work joined to the power to bide the right time can effect.
"Quel fin nez j'avais de ne pas publier quand j'étais jeune" he used
to say, and he was right.' During the same month Shannon's
portrait of him was exhibited at the Medallists, immediately sold
for £100 and then exhibited again at the New English Gallery.
'Het thought it very like but too sad; however it was painted when
such was my chief feeling, so this ought not to detract from it,
besides being highly poetic.' Mileham, however, was disrespectful,
describing it as 'Moore as a dream, dreamed by the mummied past,
or a mixture of coal and egg. It is not my idea of a good portrait,
that is a likeness. . . . I have always laboured under the delusion
that there were beautiful gold bristles in your beard; must study it
through a glass darkly.'

Early in March, Tom spent a weekend in Cambridge and had,

he wrote to Fisher, 'a very jolly time. They live in unbelievable luxury and leisure, but I should say it was a good thing to have lived there.' The main purpose of this visit was to run through his translation of the *Bacchante* with George, but with Sarah now up at Newnham and Harry also there as a visiting Fellow, it at times took the form of a lively Moore quartet. They all breakfasted and lunched together in George's or Harry's rooms and had tea and a conducted tour of her college with Sarah. On the Saturday Tom spent the evening listening to Harry and his friends talking about the Christian Social Union and the proposed Roman Catholic College in Cambridge. On Sunday, George had Desmond MacCarthy and Charles Sanger to lunch; the conversation, mostly about the theatre and acting, was animated and agreeable, and after the meal George sang German *Lieder*. Later, Tom attended the evening service at Trinity College Chapel, 'sitting close beside Harry in a velvet cushioned desk and hearing George read the First Lesson'. Between whiles he spent time in the Fitzwilliam and Archaeological Museums.

Caroline now wrote to Tom on a straightforward practical matter. As she was to spend a much-needed holiday with her god-mother in Naples, visiting Rome and Florence *en route*, she asked his help in obtaining certain highly recommended English guides to these cities. This seemed to Tom a further indication that he was back on his former footing with the Appia family. He knew his uncle was eager to see him again. April was the month that had always taken him to Paris in the past. In the covering letter he sent with Caroline's books he asked whether a visit from him to the family would be acceptable to Marie. In her reply, profuse in expressions of gratitude for the dispatch with which he had dealt with her request, Caroline expressed a wish to postpone an answer to this query. Put out by what seemed to him an evasive response, Tom wrote directly to his aunt, suggesting a visit while his friend Fisher was still in Paris, if this would be convenient to them. He then cycled off to Stratford-upon-Avon, to stay with Bob Trevelyan at Welcombe Abbey, which he described to

Fisher as 'a big house in the style of Mr. Spark's zenith of influence, hideous and uncomfortable, a white elephant to its owners. Yet it is set in lovely grounds in as pleasant a position as the heart could desire. We two are alone with four servants, a man and three women, to wait on us.' Again, he had a very jolly time. They cycled to Warwick and Kenilworth, read their recent compositions aloud to one another, and Tom modelled a portrait medallion of Bob in profile, which Poole later cast for him.

Two letters from Paris arrived shortly after his return home. Caroline, writing reproachfully from a sick bed, explained why she had delayed replying to his inquiry. She could not do so without consulting Marie, and as she knew that at that very moment Marie was preparing to write her long letter to Tom, she did not wish in any way to distract or agitate her thoughts. Tom's letter to her mother had then greatly aggravated the difficulties of her position. On the morning that Marie finished her letter to Tom, Caroline herself had undergone 'une affreuse opération dentaire'—six teeth extracted under chloroform. Although hardly capable of speech when she came round, she had nevertheless forced herself to fulfil her duty to Tom by discussing his proposal with Marie the same afternoon. She had then collapsed, and had only now regained the strength to convey the outcome of this discussion. It was this: if when he came to Paris he stayed in their home, Marie would not be there; if he stayed in a hotel, he would, of course, frequently be invited to meals and meet Marie as a member of the family. Her father hoped Tom would stay with them. Marie, regretfully aware that for sometime she had been preventing the others from enjoying Tom's company, hoped the choice now presented would not be distressing to him.

In her letter, written on 4 April in ignorance of Tom's proposed visit, Marie set out to explain '*pourquoi* je vous écrivais ainsi en Juin et *pourquoi* j'agis *maintenant* si différemment . . .'. Caroline had already told him how it was that his June letter, instead of assuaging her suffering, had aggravated it:

I could not say all that in June, first because it was still too burning and then because if I had confidence in the *friend* whom I had known for many long years, how could I be free of all mistrust towards the *man*, whoever he might be, who said what you said to me? ... So you found me vague and you sought in my refusal a religious reason and you believed that I was moved by opinions or ideas or prejudices coming from outside myself. Believe me, it was my sentiments and not my ideas which caused me to act. And if I rejected your offer immediately, without even discussing it, it was because it hurt me and was in absolute opposition to my desires, decided as I was henceforward never to seek nor accept the realization of the dream glimpsed by all women.

Since then my sentiments have not much changed. But I have learnt not to be pre-occupied about the future and to leave it entirely in the hands of God, without stubbornness, whilst continuing to desire and to believe that I would accomplish my task *alone*. I know that you find this 'never' very pretentious, but it expresses my conviction. That is why my answer was so categorical. I should have found it disloyal to give you the slightest hope when I saw no possibility. ... Whilst fully understanding that your sentiments were not superficial I was nevertheless persuaded that you held many illusions about me; that you only knew the artistic side of my nature, and that alone had attracted you towards me, and that you gave it a much greater importance than it really has. I therefore dared to hope that it would be possible for you to detach yourself from me, and anyway I wanted to do all in my power to achieve this. That's why I thought that it would be better for me to keep quiet and efface myself. In fact, being only able to offer you a refusal, it seemed to me that by staying too tangibly before you through a resumption of our relationship, I would place an obstacle in the way of happiness which you might find elsewhere.

Since then his letters had demonstrated that he neither would nor could dissociate himself from her, and also that God had allowed her in the past to be of some benefit to him. This being so, she now thought it her duty to resume her former relationship with him, 'comptant sur vous pour agir comme si vous ne m'aviez jamais écrit la lettre de Juin dernier'. She then elaborated a little on the reasons Caroline had given for her silence on the question of religion:

You don't know how painful I often used to find the discussions we had in the past and how often, apparently beaten down by your close and unforgiving logic, I had to struggle to defeat that which in your reasoning might have shaken my faith and sort out what was true from what was false, and how I reproached myself for not being more courageous and intelligent in answering you face to face. All these memories were present when I wrote to you in June. You have come closer to Christianity since then—and that you will not fall by the way-side is what I pray for. Finally one more word, and I believe that I shall have said enough to show you the truth. You wrote to me in June: 'Yet I hope to know that you are and have been loved quite simply for what you are, may work good for you, even though . . .'. In fact, it would be neither true nor just to say that your approach caused me *only* pain and perhaps my letter could have given you that impression. It is always beneficent and encouraging to know that one has been, up to a point, understood, appreciated and faithfully loved, especially (as has been my case) when circumstances have made one mistrustful of oneself. The delicate affection which has continuously surrounded me has much helped me to raise myself and find my self-confidence again. Therefore I believe much in the power of affection, but I have never wished and do not now wish to find help and consolation in any other human sentiment than affection.

You may perhaps find my letter lacking in logic. What of it? I haven't a logician's head. I have tried to be true and I think I have been. I have allowed weeks to pass since the reading of your letters and all they stirred up in me. So I have been able to write calmly and it is I, myself, who has written. Now, if you still have something to say to me about all this, please do it soon, and then we shall talk of it no more.

Before answering this letter, Tom had withdrawn altogether from the Paris visit. Yet another year was to pass before he saw Marie again.

❦

CHAPTER NINE

A Friend from the British Museum

My dear Marie,

I cannot help wishing you had never written the letter I received last Thursday. I had hoped you had got further on your way back to health and wholesome thoughts and this letter merely undeceives me ... what you say you will do is indeed what I asked you to do, but the reasons you give and the tone of discouragement brooding over the whole!!! The peak of Tenerife because of its sheer declivity and lonely position appears impossibly high, but really there are mountains far higher than that in the world. So your misfortune, by its abruptness and solitariness in a life otherwise so guarded and happy, seems to have browbeaten and dismayed you out of all proportion. Dr Arnold used to pray every evening in Rugby Chapel that those present might be delivered from the base and degrading fear of one another. And it is indeed true that no one can do us inward injury except ourselves. It seems to me that both this letter and that of last June are prompted by fear of me; in both cases I think that had you waited longer you would never have written so.... You use the phrase 'le désir d'accomplir ma tâche *seule*'. Now this is undoubtedly what you feel, and, in pain and darkness as you are, it is not unnatural to feel so, but this is no kind of answer to my contestation.

> Not for choosers is love, but by fate,
> Fate wiser and surer than *we*.

That you would desire to accept my offer straight away I did not expect. The question is may it not be your duty some day to accept it.... I do not know but what underlying all you say the true ground for a refusal exists. Perhaps you have instinctively weighed and found me wanting years ago, although I think it would be kinder to allow of the possibility of the revision of such a judgement after so many years of separation.... But if it is your present suffering and the recent impression of your misfortune, and these are what you urge, these things, unless you fail, will fade away. It could never be right to meet any man's love with the mere desire of living alone, every case must be judged on its own internal merits. What assurance have I that you are not as utterly deceived by these new desires as you were before? This is no small matter in which either of us can afford to go wrong; it is everything for this life, and who knows how much for any life there may be beyond?

What you say of your having thought I was chiefly influenced by the artistic side of your nature confirms my belief that you are totally mistaken. If I spoke to you chiefly on such matters it was only because I felt I had a better right to do so than others. Though you seem to recall my having argued against your religion, my remembrance is of having been constantly checked from doing so for fear of wronging you. I could not but recognize that your religion had been a chief factor in making you what you were.... You exasperated me not a little by your unwillingness to talk about such things, because I was greedy to learn what it was in what seemed to me absurd that so helped you, and if I spoke against it I must have been hoping that you would defend it and thus solve my difficulties. I tell you this because I think you ought to know in what light I read your letter. For the rest you may depend on my never acting upon your knowledge of what I feel in the least degree, so long as your desire remains what it is.

Undated, unsigned, and with several crossings-out in the original, this cannot have been the final version of Tom's response to Marie's exposition of her attitude in regard to him; the severity of tone may well have been modified.

Whatever her reactions were, Marie made no allusion to them when she wrote again on 31 May. She dwelt first on Caroline's Italian tour: 'All the guide-books you lavished on her are a great help, and she will come back to us with an altogether overwhelming amount of information—historical, geographical, artistical, philological and many other icals.' Then, recalling that Tom was 'un fervent de Berlioz', she reflected on a performance of *La Damnation de Faust* she had recently heard. Finally, she declared her readiness to correct further translations and asked for guidance in her reading of Matthew Arnold. Tom, beginning again in his rusty French, confessed to having no appreciation of music unless he could relate it to literature or art; for the most part he listened without apprehending, 'et d'être ainsi dans le brouillard me fait souffrir un peu. Mais avec Berlioz j'ai presque toujour la joie de comprendre.' As this was also a birthday letter, he enclosed a proof of his woodcut of *Peau d'Ane minding Turkeys*, Wordsworth's 'Ode to Duty', Milton's sonnet 'How soon hath Time, the subtle thief of youth', and sent Ricketts's edition of Mrs. Browning's *Sonnets from the Portuguese*: 'I cannot recommend it as poetry, though it is very popular, but as a book to look at it seems to me perfect, the cover especially. . . . Such work as this ought to count high as Philanthropy as well as Art; who knows, if everybody did one thing as well as this, whether all social problems would not be answered shortly . . .'. These were rapidly followed by certain of Arnold's works and his own 'would-be translation' of Browning's 'An Epistle . . . of Karshish, the Arab Physician', which had been ready and waiting since the spring of 1895. 'The poem is one of B's best. The language is very rich and idiomatic and full of energy, but very digressive and not very elevated. The style is almost a poetical equivalent to that of St. Paul.' The correspondence thus proceeded along the former lines, but with one difference. Marie was to become increasingly active in educational and welfare work for the church, to be made Treasurer of the Seine Branch of the Y.W.C.A., and to make her mark as a speaker and chairman of committees. Behindhand in correcting translations and answering letters as she continued to be, she usually managed to send copies of *Le Journal des Missions* and other evangelical publications to which she was an occasional contributor. This introduced a growing element of discussion on questions of belief.

A preoccupation with religious attitudes is also evident in Tom's letters to Fisher, who was now back in Imber, happily engaged on his studies of rural occupations, climbing haystacks to sketch the thatchers at work, and following the local sheep-shearing team about on his tricycle. In a June letter, Tom began by directing Fisher's attention to the early work of J. F. Millet, in which 'selection the most rigorous' had resulted 'in the survival of only the absolutely fittest'. He then switched to a quite different theme by quoting

> Calm soul of all things! make it mine
> To feel, amid the city's jar,
> That there abides a peace of thine,
> Man did not make, and cannot mar.
>
> The will to neither strive nor cry,
> The power to feel with others give!
> Calm, calm me more; not let me die
> Before I have begun to live.

These are the last 2 verses of Mat. Arnold's 'Lines in Kensington Gardens' and they are used as a hymn in a Chapel, a Baptist Chapel in Liverpool, where the Minister has preached a sermon on the Ballad of Reading Gaol! Perhaps these facts are more significant than the Hispano-American War, at any rate they are extremely strange. . . . Meanwhile Dr Lee in Southwark Church gives out a Prayer to the Virgin Mary and is interrupted by Mr John Kensit, and the German Emperor tells his soldiers that all great soldiers have been good christians and sends the editor of a comic journal to prison for publishing a cartoon representing the Devil listening to the said speech, scratching his head and saying, 'Ah, that explains why I could never find Alexander the Great, Caesar or Napoleon. Of course, if they were good christians, then they would have gone upstairs.'

Early in July Tom cycled down to Imber, where he was found lodgings in the village as the Fishers' cottage was so small and he was anxious not to put them to extra expense. '. . . they are right in the heart of Salisbury Plain,' he wrote to his parents, 'and more difficult of access than Stonehenge itself. The distances on the treeless hills are like mother-of-pearl, the fields being very large and various in their tints; sometimes there is nothing at all in sight but this undulating patchwork surface.' This short visit was a source of much mutual satisfaction, not least to Mrs. Fisher, who felt herself socially isolated in the landscape that so enthralled her husband. For some reason, perhaps because the pastoral life evoked biblical subjects in Tom's mind, it was agreed that he should present Fisher with a Bible. 'I promised to buy you a nine-penny bible,' he wrote shortly after his return home,

and lo and behold I have done otherwise. First I thought that maps would be a great assistance and then little by little I enlarged my notions till I send you the whole outfit of a Sunday School teacher. . . . You must remember to look for a spiritual meaning all along, as it is the pre-eminent spiritual record of the human race, and even the early legends, which are as Renan says 'morne, grandiose et immorale', have a spiritual significance for the most part; although agnostics such as we are apt to ignore it, while good christians as commonly misrepresent it.

A few days after the Wiltshire interlude Marie's elder brother came to stay at 39 Southgrove. Henry was then thirty-eight, and after six years as pastor of the Vaudois Church in Turin had recently become one of the pastors of Calvin's salle de la Réforma-tion in Geneva. His programme on this brief visit shows how he shared his father's questing spirit. He heard Dr. Parker preach at the City Temple and Canon Wilberforce at St. John's Westminster, went to a missionary meeting with Miss Mayo and 'appreciated pretty well' an address given by the theosophist Mrs. Annie Besant. He sampled one of the 'Pleasant Sunday Afternoons' designed to relieve the tedium of the Victorian Sunday. At Mrs. Josephine Butler's instigation he listened to a debate in the House of Commons and from a day spent at Dr. Barnado's Home he returned 'quite enthusiastic'. Tom took him to the British Museum and with all the Moores he saw Sarah Bernhardt play Phèdre, ('he thought she smiled too much'), and listened to a performance of *Fidelio* which delighted this most musical member of a musical family as much as it did Hettie.

The home in Southgrove was now seldom without visitors. George had been elected a Fellow of Trinity College and had also become a member of the Aristotelian Society. He stayed frequently over this period, during which, besides reading papers to the Aristotelian, he gave two courses of lectures on ethics to working men at the Passmore Edwards Settlement. He kept his eldest brother supplied with preparatory reading in Kant and Hegel. Sarah, too, came up periodically to represent her College: 'Presently there was a hearty sound and Sarah came in fresh from a hockey victory at Dartford over the team of Mme Osterberger's Physical Training College.' When these two from Cambridge came up together they took Nana to the pantomime if the opportunity offered. Harry stayed twice during the year while he had medical treatment for some obscure complaint. In June, Ida Kruse, a young American introduced apparently by one of Hettie's rent-collecting friends, stayed for a few days while she looked for lodgings, and ended up almost as another member of the family. After she had graduated at Vassar, her father, who was a merchant and banker in Central City, the 'gold camp' of Colorado, had presented her with two years in Europe to study drama, language, and literature. At this stage she was homesick, troubled with a cough and, though she had an engagement with a touring theatre company, somewhat at sea, it seems, as to how to proceed. Hettie mothered her and Tom gave her direction. 'It has never been my fortune', she wrote to him, 'to meet any one who really *knew* before I met you. But you do know.' Hearing him read his *Mariamne* aloud was to her a revelation: the poetic drama was still *alive*! 'You will surely keep your promise to take me through the part at Christmas time? Perhaps I won't make a good Mariamne— I might be a better Salome.' When on tour she asked if she could borrow the manuscript of his Phaedra play, promising to commit the name part to memory and return the manuscript at once: 'I have thought about it many, many hours—night hours when I should have been sleeping.'

In August, again on his hard-worked bicycle, Tom went down to Cockington to spend a fortnight's holiday with his parents—a traditional summer holiday of bathing before breakfast, walks for all moods, excursions by rowing boat or steamer and the sending of Devonshire cream to city-bound friends. Although it had taken his mother, now nearing sixty, a year to recover from the nervous prostration caused by the move from Woodthorpe, her health had since improved remarkably. She was able to enjoy playing croquet on their lawn and taking quite long walks with Daniel. She had her at-home day and a small circle of congenial acquaintances. With Daniel she attended University Extension Lectures in Torquay, on subjects ranging from Bees to Dante, and special attractions such as a recital by the actress Mrs. Kendal. Together they had visited relatives in Bristol and Plymouth, where Annie was now teaching, and Henrietta had travelled to the Sturges in the Birmingham area on her own. Servant problems, however, still plagued her; the most dramatic event chronicled in her weekly letter to her children is her dismissal of the cook after Daniel had broken a tooth on the pastry of a mince pie. At such times of domestic crisis Hettie was usually borrowed from 39 Southgrove for the duration, an arrangement always welcomed by Daniel. It was, in fact, now he who was often ill and depressed. Periodically he suffered attacks of acute pain, of which, as later became clear, he knew both the cause and the cure, but chose to continue to suffer, knowing into what a desperate state of anxiety and agitation his wife would be thrown at the prospect of his undergoing an operation. When well, he walked four hours a day, worked vigorously in the garden, read a good deal, particularly history, and was a formidable member of the Torquay Chess Club. Encouraged apparently by Bertie, he had taken up sketching, specializing in studies of trees, very bold and fresh in colour—and always he played the piano. Nevertheless, without his children about him he found life humdrum, and looked forward to nothing so much as the vociferous influx of them and their friends at holi-day times. If Harry had apparently not visited at all since the move two years ago, Bertie came every holiday, George very frequently, with Desmond MacCarthy and later A. R. Ainsworth, and Annie, Nellie, and Sarah with a large assortment of friends. Tom, perhaps partly because he had so much family life at home, had been a rarer visitor and was so all the more appreciated.

From Torquay on this occasion he cycled back as far as Win-chester and then travelled by train to the contrasting coast of

Broadstairs, where he and Shannon were to spend a week together. Within a few days Shannon, an apt pupil, had 'learned the machine under my tuition', so that they were able to explore the coast and the marshland villages extensively. Shannon enjoyed this way of experiencing the countryside so much that over the next three years, if the weather was good, he and Tom went on a day or weekend cycling trip at least once a month. Ricketts and he had recently moved from Chelsea to Spring Terrace, Richmond. Although Tom frequently cycled over to 'grub' with them (and they now ate better than in the early days at The Vale) or met them by arrangement in town, they were outside his casual calling range, so these opportunities for talk with Shannon, who was anyway inclined to let Ricketts do the talking when in company, were a great satisfaction.

At about this time, through Ricketts, Tom first met Laurence Binyon—and a more fruitful encounter he could hardly have had. Binyon was a year older than Tom. After reading Greats at Oxford, and winning the Newdigate Prize, he had gone straight to work in the British Museum, first in the Department of Printed Books and then, from 1895 onwards, in the Department of Prints and Drawings, of which he later became Keeper. He had already published several slim volumes of verse and his *London Visions II* had just appeared. Although described as a reserved man, because of his standing as a poet and his scholarly, coterie-free position at the British Museum, Binyon was in touch with many creators and appreciators in the world of art and literature; quietly and disinterestedly, he acted as a bringer-to-light and a cross-fertilizer. 'I like Binyon very much,' Tom wrote to his parents, 'he is very gentle and not I think at all a humbug, which is very rare.' Their acquaintance rapidly developed into a friendship which was for Tom more evenly based and without all reservation than any other, and was for both of them more than a matter of common interests.

By September Binyon had invited Tom to contribute a monograph on Albrecht Altdorfer to a series he was editing called 'The Artist's Library'—a series which, it is interesting to note, was to include Roger Fry on Bellini, C. J. Holmes on Hokusai and Constable, Bernhard Berenson on Giorgione, W. B. Yeats on Edward Calvert, Will Rothenstein on Goya, Selwyn Image on Rowlandson, and Binyon himself on Cozens. In spite of Binyon's warning that the £25 which was all the publisher, the Reverend Oldmeadow of the Unicorn Press, could offer, would probably be swallowed up by travelling expenses, Tom accepted this commission. He had now reached the stage when he wished to publish some at least of the considerable body of verse he had written. Ricketts would have liked to accommodate him in the Vale Press, but all his type was committed to a programme covering the next two years. Daniel had therefore offered to pay for a selection of the poems to be printed privately. On hearing this, Binyon said it would be absurd to pay for the publication of such eminently publishable work, and gave Tom an introduction to Oldmeadow. Oldmeadow, as was apparently his way on scenting new talent, welcomed Tom and his poems with open arms and proposed embracing some unrelated woodcuts in the same volume. This Tom did not wish, and, Ricketts assuring him that it would not be to his advantage financially, it was finally agreed that the poems would be published the following March and the woodcuts at a later date. This news was most welcome to Daniel. Of the Altdorfer commission he had written: 'I am glad you have some definite literary work and hope you may make your mark with it, but the time to do it [a year] seems too long and may lead I should think to frittered energy'; of the poems he wrote: 'I trust this volume will only be the first step, and that your fame will resound in the land, giving pleasure to many and raising the tone of life and thought in all who read you.'

Binyon, like Tom, was experimenting in forms of poetic drama; after hearing *Mariamne* read aloud, he suggested that either Forbes Robertson or George Alexander, who was shortly to produce Stephen Phillips's *Paolo and Francesca*, might be inspired to perform it. Tom was dubious. He felt the whole world of the commercial theatre was inimical to the performance of the poetic drama; the theatres were ill-adapted to it, the actors did not know how to speak it, there was little conception of artistic harmony in presentation. Together they discussed the possibility of in some way promoting the formation of a company of properly trained actors under imaginative direction. Binyon looked about for wealthy patrons, Tom consulted with Harley Granville-Barker on the recruitment of actors, Ida Kruse held herself in readiness, and Ricketts was immediately tempted, though it was some years before he actually threw himself into theatre design. The project remained gently simmering for a time. Meanwhile, Binyon did arrange for Tom to read *Mariamne* to Forbes Robertson, the Shakespearean actor they both most admired. Tom described this occasion to Bob Trevelyan:

he was courteous, very wrinkled in the face, very depressed and disillusioned in tone of remark, talked of Swinburne as a contemporary of his youth, said that only Tennyson's Cup and Browning's Blot on the Scutcheon were really practicable for the stage of all that modern poets had writ. The laurel wreaths and their streaming dowdy ribbons, trophies of his triumphs, were piled up against his bookcase, there were plans for a new Theatre on his sofa and a large photo of Mrs Pat framed on an easel, besides there was a miscellany of old armour, books, photos, inkstands, etc. . . .

Although he rejected *Mariamne* as unsuitable for his public, Forbes Robertson expressed admiration of its poetry and said 'he would always be pleased to hear anything else of mine'. So encouraged, Tom sent him the outline of a tragic theme he had found in Froissart's *Chronicles*. Forbes Robertson replied, 'I do not think your subject a good one. It is very harrowing and there is no love interest. To my mind what is wanted in a play is firstly charm and then sympathy. I feel sure that if you could get hold of a good subject you could write a play that would be a success.'

'So you see Binyon has taken me under his wing.' True though this was in one sense, it was not how Binyon saw their relationship. In an early letter, he wrote of wishing for the sake of his poetry that he had got to know Tom sooner: 'I feel still on the threshold of my art. You have got a good way further and I am afraid I have little to give you in exchange for what I learn from you.' When he asked for Tom's help with two lines in a poem he was about to send to a periodical, though evidently surprised at the resulting thorough-going revision of the whole poem, he wrote in reply, 'You are splendid! I really didn't mean you to spend so much trouble, but thanks immensely. Only now I don't quite know what I ought to do; I don't like to get praise for what is not my own, yet I must take some of your lines.'

Tom's invariably conscientious and often most time-consuming response to all appeals for help or advice is very clearly demonstrated in the correspondence of these months. From Lucien Pissarro came requests for manual help with his printing and for advice on the English works that appeared in the Eragny Press. Harry Mileham would enthusiastically describe a composition on which he had just started, lose his nerve in mid career and beg Tom to come down to his studio in Beckenham and give him 'practical advice and moral support'. While on tour, Ida Kruse, who was not finding her life as 'a strolling player' very congenial or instructive, wrote nearly every week asking for guidance on make-up, the interpretation of the part of Juliet, reading in French literature, or her own emotional problems. Most demanding of all was Fisher. He was then working feverishly on the drawings of rural occupations which were to appear as a series in *The Dome* and on etchings for the exhibition of the Painter Etchers. At one point he sent Tom drawings and proofs of etchings for comment every few days, sometimes asking for the verdict on the latter to be telegraphed. Shortly before Christmas Tom rounded off some merciless general criticism by writing,

Suppose you were to make an out and out imitation of Millet or some such at first, would that not be better than making an out and out imitation of the common art student's idea of what an etching ought to be? Nothing is ever won from the ideal without boldness, temerity almost. Be rash and damn 'la perfection bête' as Puvis called it. There, I hope you will forgive me for being so outspoken, as I hope Mrs

Fisher will for ordering a ham to be sent to you which I am afraid may be the devil to cook. It ought to be boiled ¼ of an hour for every pound and ½ an hour for good luck; if you haven't a pot perhaps a foot bath would do.

In October a visit to a Rembrandt exhibition in the Hague was planned. Bob Trevelyan withdrew from this expedition from 'laziness and fear of sea-sickness', Harry Mileham on grounds of work, and Henry Poole, having through the bankruptcy of his father suddenly become the sole provider for the family, had for the time being to forgo all continental pleasures. So finally, it seems, Tom went with Binyon and Roger Fry, whose lectures on Italian Art he was attending. On his return, along with Ricketts, Shannon, and Legros he was occupied in preparing some of his woodcuts for an exhibition of engravings at van Wisselingh's gallery off Hanover Square. His main preoccupation, however, was the selecting and perfecting of the poems to be included in the coming publication under Oldmeadow's imprint. Once made the selection was submitted to Ricketts for appraisal. His first reaction was to write, 'I like your poems muchly as long as they are not about Jews.' Later he withdrew this wholesale disapproval from the poems on biblical subjects, but still argued for certain improvements. 'It certainly must be a fine thing for you to feel as you do as to the critical value of Ricketts' opinions,' Fisher wrote to Tom. 'I can understand it as it is somewhat of the same kind of feeling *I* have for your own—I certainly shall not find in this world one whose opinion I more highly value.'

By the beginning of December Marie had managed to finish correcting the translation of Browning's 'Karshish' which, in spite of sustained and sincere effort, she had failed to appreciate.

Many things seem to me simply grotesque and I can perceive only vaguely the general intention. . . . What truth did Browning want to illumine? From what point of view is he writing? Send me something shorter and simpler. I'll try to correct it quickly. I should so like you to try some straightforward little themes and we should see whether you did not make marvellous progress!

Tom professed not to understand what Marie meant by 'honnêtes petits thèmes' and, to her considerable annoyance, sent next what appear to have been a string of platitudinous copy-book maxims. Having made his point that only the difficult was worth attempting, he then dispatched his first instalment of Arnold's *The Strayed Reveller*, 'Le Convive Egaré'. At the same time he asked her, as a matter of some urgency, to arbitrate on a passage in his de Guérin translation still in dispute between him and George. In a lucid grammatical analysis of the passage, she conclusively upheld George's interpretation.

The year 1899 opened propitiously for Tom. His work for the Vale Press was well advanced, his first book of poems was about to be published, the woodcuts he had shown had aroused interest, he had been invited to contribute to the *Saturday Review*, and his Altdorfer pilgrimage on the Continent was arranged to start in April. He wrote again to Caroline, asking whether it would be acceptable for him to propose breaking his return journey in Paris. Her reply conveyed a warm invitation from her parents, who hoped that he would stay with them for at least a week; she added that Marie was better in health and spirits than she had been for years.

In the meantime, Marie sent Tom for his twenty-ninth birthday *Il Vit*, 'un livre de mon cousin, Wilfred Monod, qui a une conception et une réalisation de la vie chrétienne grande et vraie'. Tom found cause to criticize in this book the Christian claim to authoritative revelation:

After all why should we prefer to have definite mysteries, clear hidden things to mysterious mysteries, hidden things that are secret? ... Then a man holds himself to be better in a *mysterious* way because he is a christian, and this makes him uncharitable ... he judges Voltaire, Goethe and Renan to be worse men than he is, although they were eminent revelations of the ideal under various aspects; and he himself both humbly confesses [not to be], and obviously is not, the eminent revelation of any ideal. ... Then I cannot agree with M. Monod's main proposition. 'Il Vit', though I was delighted with many of the ideas and instances which he includes within his main meaning and thought some of them both new and true. 'What becomes us, embosomed in beauty and wonder as we are, is courage and the effort to realize our aspirations.' This I recognize him to be doing, as I hope to do it too, and in that sense be his fellow worker. If he has greater aid he is luckier than I am, so let him be kind to me. I will try to be kind, because it is good—is beautiful, not because I can, but even though I cannot.

Since they were soon to be able to discuss these questions together, in her reply Marie raised only what was to her the central one—the essential certainty of faith to a Christian: 'the very basis of his faith is not a belief personal to him, it is a living reality, true in itself, by which he lives—how could he live without seeking to share it with others? There is neither arrogance nor narrowness in this.'

This letter reached Tom in Munich, the centre for the final stage of his Altdorfer researches; even though it also brought news of more illness in the Appia family—Marie herself with bronchitis, her father and sister with 'grippe', and Tante Louise in a condition causing much anxiety—it was very welcome. The original plan for Harry Mileham to join him for the whole tour had fallen through and hopes of meeting Bob Trevelyan in Vienna had also been dashed. Binyon had accompanied him to Berlin and on to Dresden. Here they had stayed with Hans Singer, the Director of the Königliches Kupferstichkabinett (Royal Print Collection), an ardent Anglophile who showed them, among other things, the collection of suppressed anti-imperial caricatures, over which he gloated. He gave Tom valuable introductions for the rest of his journey, on which he had proceeded alone, and with no knowledge of German, to Prague, to see the private collection of the Ritter van Lanna, to Vienna, to the Dominican Convent of St. Florian near Enns and then from Munich to Altdorfer's native city of Regensburg, to Nuremberg, Augsburg, and finally Strasburg. These were journeying weeks of intensive study. In Vienna, Munich, and Regensburg, he had introductions to English-speaking authorities; the Ritter van Lanna spoke French, 'calling me "mon petit" though he only came up to my brace buttons', as did Pater Czerny at St. Florians, but elsewhere he was naturally handicapped and bothered by his lack of German. Besides, he was a man who liked company and did not enjoy digesting his impressions in ill-lit hotel rooms with no one to talk to. The Alte Pinakothek in Munich was shut on days when it was supposed to be open, and other galleries closed hours before the advertised time. After Regensburg it rained incessantly. By the time he reached Strasburg, Tom may well have been thoroughly jaded. He spent two days in Rheims, breathing familiar French air, before going on to 119 bis, rue Notre Dame des Champs, Paris.

During his stay Tom wrote three letters to his mother.

14 May. Here I am at 119 bis. The appartement is very similar to though not so pleasantly situated as the old one and not a very great deal though considerably larger. . . . I climbed the 3 flights of stairs with a young lady who turned out to be Winifred Sturge [a Birmingham cousin]. I also found Hélène Appia, Uncle Louis' eldest daughter, stopping here. Caroline was in bed with neuralgia and still is . . . Marie is about and very much the same as ever. I think both she and Caroline are improved in good looks. Louis shows little change. Uncle is getting older no doubt, but there was less change in him this time than when I had seen him before, and they are all as kind and nice as can be. Aunt Helen seems well . . . I have not yet seen Aunt Louise, but Hélène Appia tells me that she thinks she is bodily much better, but that she suffers from a melancholy that runs in the family and from which Uncle Louis suffered a great deal, and that it is rather this than any bodily trouble which is what now prostrates her.

Hélène Appia is a very nice person indeed . . . I have been to the Louvre several times and to the Salon with Hélène Appia, and this morning I went to hear Louis preach and see his fine new church. It was a first communion service and all the girls looked very pretty in their muslin. Henri stopped here from Friday to Saturday evening and seemed much to have enjoyed his trip to Scotland though he had not been able to deliver his address [to an evangelical conference in Edinburgh] in a satisfactory manner as he was put off until there were very few left to hear him.

23 May. I am still here and expect to stop till nearly the end of next week. Aunt Louise is much better and gets up to sit in an arm chair in Uncle's Study. Yesterday, Whitsunday, we all went out to St Germain, the old Palace of the Valois, and spent the day in the woods, though as Aunt Helen and Caroline were both tired and could not walk we did not get far. The weather cleared up and it was very enjoyable, though all except me, and perhaps uncle, got over tired. . . . Caroline is to go to Versailles today, so as to rest and benefit from an out of door life. . . .

[Undated] I am still here, as Uncle pressed me to stay on a little. . . . There has been great rejoicing in the family here over the return of M. Boegner [President of the Protestant Missionary Society] from Madagascar. He is very bronzed and looked happy and successful. . . . Yesterday evening there were a great many people to dinner, a Russian lady and two Scotchmen and a girl who is half Scotch half Italian. . . . The confusion of tongues made the bustle all the more confounding, but every one seemed to be happy. Marie is quite herself and talks and laughs freely. Caroline returned from Versailles on Saturday evening; I had been there a day or two before to say goodbye to her, so she was rather surprised to find me still here.

Henrietta, who had continued to suffer a sense of parental guilt ever since her last meeting with the Appia parents in Cannes, must have been much comforted by these letters. Considering, however, that none of the Moores had seen the Appias' new home and that, apart from the London visits of Georges and Henry, there had been no direct contact between the two families since the broken engagement three and a half years before, they are not as informative as she might have expected. The emphasis on Hélène Appia in the first letter is understandable, for Tom had already heard of this admired Geneva cousin, then in her early forties. She and Tom had, in fact, found themselves in an immediate and trusting accord, which, though they did not meet often, was to prove sustaining to them both.

Apart from the marked prolongation of the visit, the only indi-

cation of what passed between Tom and Marie after their separation of five years comes in a passage she felt it necessary to include
in a letter written shortly after Tom's departure. Having first
thanked him for loyally observing the conditions of their renewed
intercourse, she proceeded:

I don't know what you may have concluded about my attitude during
your stay, but I would not wish you to think that my feelings towards
you had changed, for they have remained the same. . . . Be persuaded
that in my relations with you, whether written or oral, I will always be
guided by the wish to help you and be helped by you. You asked me to
tell you more openly what I thought. I answered that I always tried to
be sincere. This is what I wish to continue to be in all questions which
we may deal with together, but I do not think you have the right to ask
more of me.

It has cost me much to write these lines, knowing that I should cause
you pain and fearing not to be understood—and fearing also your
reply. In fact I don't think it would be useful or desirable that this
letter should recommence a correspondence on this subject and I hope
you will agree with me. . . . Believe me, I am most thankful to you for
the delicacy of your procedure and that if I appear a little hard I do not
basically lack in gratitude.

❦

CHAPTER TEN

The Vinedresser and Resurrection

To Tom's extreme indignation his poems had still not appeared by the time he returned home. That an undertaking to publish in March would not be carried out by June was something he had not considered possible. 'The publisher', he wrote to Marie, 'has spent his time making unnecessarily grand promises and breaking them in an unconscionably thorough manner; he is one of those feverish creatures that are always doing more than they ought to and are in consequence unjust both to themselves and others.' Baulked of making the book her birthday present he sent Marie instead some work of Matthew Arnold, and a proof of his wood-cut 'The hare is running . . .' with the passage from Wordsworth's 'Resolution and Independence' which it illustrates. Marie received this package in the midst of preparations to take Tante Louise to Switzerland for convalescence. While there she was to stay with her great friend Rebecca Piaget in Neuchâtel and then with cousins in Leyzin at an altitude of 1,450 metres. Once in the mountains Marie, like most of her family whatever their ailments, became possessed with the desire, and furnished with the energy, to scale the heights. In Lausanne she stayed with de Beaumont cousins and in Geneva with the family of her god-daughter Geneviève Appia and with her brother Henry, who now had six children. She visited Cousine Hélène Appia, 'qui a gardé un très bon souvenir des quelques jours passés avec vous'. And at the beginning of August she collected Tante Louise, an old lady of great bulk, and solicitously accompanied her on to the Airals Blancs, where her mother was already installed.

During Tom's absence from home, Nellie had been baptized and confirmed into the Church of England; in writing to advise him of the date of her baptism she made clear that she was not expecting *his* prayers. Harry, who had stood godfather, had himself been ordained priest and was now a curate in Kirkby Lonsdale: 'honourable doubtless,' commented his Nonconformist father, 'but unsatisfactory from our point of view'. Sarah, too, had by now become a member of the Church of England, probably through Harry's influence. Gaily sociable at Cambridge, successful on the hockey field, she had just failed the first part of the Natural Science Tripos, and was from now on to throw her energies into the Temperance Movement and church work in the village of Cockington at home. More to her father's surprise, Nellie had to take part of her medical finals again. Bertie had finished at the Slade and was to set up in a studio of his own. 'A first experience with a studio and models I should think likely to be trying,' wrote Daniel. 'I wish Bert well through and out in a larger experience.' Tom's efforts to find a suitable studio for Bertie led to an agreeable renewal of acquaintance with the former Lambeth student Arthur Rackham, who was about to move out of Chelsea at this time: 'he makes his living by book illustration, can make £500 a year when he likes, but prefers to make about half that and enjoy himself a little. He talked a good deal of the iniquity of publishers, but not bitterly . . .'. Bertie was eventually satisfactorily installed and the models for his current painting of Samson and Delilah engaged. Both for him and for Nellie the 39 Southgrove establishment was still needed.

Binyon, like Tom, was one of a large family, but he was geographically distanced from it, his father being a clergyman in the north of England, and none of its members shared his interest in art and literature. For some time he had been wanting to introduce Tom to William A. Pye, the man whose house at Limpsfield in Surrey had become like home to him. He was a son of John Kellow Pye, the pianist and composer who at the age of forty, while retaining his honorary positions connected with the Royal Academy of Music, the National Training School for Music, and the Bach Choir, had taken the curious step of giving up his professional musical career to become a partner in a firm of wine merchants. This partnership W. A. Pye had taken over on his father's retirement. An acute migraine sufferer, he was at this time not able to taste his wares, but their sale was profitable enough to allow him to indulge other tastes. He collected pictures, sculpture, books, and rare plants. While acquiring, for instance, Dürer and Rembrandt etchings, he kept his eyes open to contemporary work. His eldest son, Burns, who was then in an Oriental shipping company, brought him home treasures from China and Japan. Consequently, his house, Priest Hill, built in the style of Norman Shaw and furnished under the influence of William Morris, was full of beautiful objects. Not that the atmosphere was museum-like, for Pye and his wife were immensely hospitable. He was a generous shelterer of relatives and other people in difficulty, and an unassuming encourager of young writers and artists. On Tom's first visit with Binyon, in late June 1899, of the seven variously gifted Pye children only the two youngest daughters, both still in their teens, were at home: Sybil, very delicate in health, and Ethel, a student at the Slade, who was later to elect for sculpture. Among the rare profusion of flowers in the garden a row of white sweet-peas particularly caught Tom's attention; he quoted,

> . . . on tip-toe for a flight:
> With wings of gentle flush o'er delicate white,
> And taper fingers catching at all things,
> To bind them all about with tiny rings.

Sybil, it turned out, had read no Keats, an omission Tom was to make it his responsibility to rectify. 'They are very nice people indeed,' he informed his parents. Soon he had an invitation from Pye to stay with them as often and as long as he liked.

What he pressingly needed to do, however, was to settle down to Altdorfer while his impressions were fresh, making use of the help offered by Campbell Dodgson with the German references, and by Bob's younger brother, George M. Trevelyan, with the historical background. First, though, he had a long-standing arrangement to spend the beginning of July in Cornwall with Binyon on 'a poetry working holiday'. They had a rather rainy week in Tintagel and then went on to Ruan Minor near the Lizard. In the mornings they worked, in the afternoons walked and talked, scrambled on the rocks, and watched the great Atlantic rollers breaking. Their final weekend was spent at Cockington; on the Sunday, Binyon rowed a boatload of Moores twelve miles up the Dart estuary, against the tide. Tom stayed on for a few days with his parents and then paid another brief visit to the Fishers, who had now moved to a considerably larger cottage in the slightly less remote village of Chitterne. Fisher, though his livelihood was still precarious, was as ecstatic as ever about Salisbury Plain, while his wife still bemoaned the 'lack of anyone with whom to exchange an idea'.

Before Tom was back in London, his book, *The Vinedresser and other Poems*, had at last appeared. The little volume, bound to the author's design in green cloth with simple gold line-decoration, was dedicated to his parents; the title poem, 'Sent from Egypt with a Fair Robe of Tissue to a Sicilian Vinedresser. B.C. 276' to Shannon; 'The Panther' (Circe's panther) to Ricketts; 'At Bethel' to his brother George; 'Two of the Lord's Anointed' (David and Saul) to M.A. No explanation of these last initials being vouchsafed by Tom, his friends assumed that he was acknowledging his debt to Matthew Arnold. Reviews were, on the whole, warmly welcoming, though Tom was slightly piqued that the poem most commented on was 'Les Chercheuses de Poux' after Rimbaud. What particularly pleased him was that the friends amongst whom the poems had not previously circulated all had different favourites. George Trevelyan, who after reading the book through three times wrote, 'Please write me down as one of your warm admirers', preferred those on biblical subjects. On a first reading, Pye picked out several of the shorter lyrics, including 'Summer Lightning', 'Silence', 'The Young Corn in Chorus', 'The Dying Swan', and 'The Chorus of Greek Maidens', of which he wrote, 'you have expressed the charm of girlishness as it has never been done before in the language as far as I know'. Roger Fry wrote:

—although I had seen one or two of your things in the Dial and liked them, this book absolutely astonished me. Hitherto all the poetry that has appeared within my recollection I have disliked or liked with a sense of critical reserve—this I feel inclined to accept simply. Your absolute conviction relieves one of all responsibility. . . . I think the poem that gives me the most *intimate* pleasure though I don't think it's by any means the greatest is Tempio di Veneri . . .

In sending the book to Marie, Tom assured her that no opinion on his poetic efforts would be more valuable and welcome to him than hers. He suggested that she jotted down her thoughts on little bits of paper as she read and sent them to him from time to time. If Marie, then still on her peregrination, did as he suggested, she kept her jottings until their next meeting. Caroline was ill and away from home for several months this year and for part of the time her mother was with her, so that, as Marie wrote later, 'since my return to Paris, I have had to be turn by turn, or rather simultaneously, mistress of the house, parish worker, reader and secretary to Papa, nurse and sometimes unwell myself etc. . . .'. Not, as she was anxious to make clear, that she regarded her absorption in these duties as a deprivation. 'My everyday life, which does not leave me the time indispensable to man to find himself and seek God in contemplation and study, teaches me nevertheless many things. And I assure you that I am learning to find an infinity of poetry, of beauty and of grandeur in the human soul, in apparently prosaic life, in many people and things "without beauty and brilliance".'

While in the Valleys Marie had, however, finished correcting the translation of *The Strayed Reveller* which she returned with congratulations and a request for an explanation of the poem's 'esprit'. Tom's reply left her still mystified. 'I understood you to mean', he then wrote, the didactic purpose of the author and suspected that you had secretly told yourself that he had none. I am not sure that he had an intention such as I described to you, it is very possible that he did not think of his poem in that way at all. But as for me almost everything that happens, everything I read or hear becomes immediately the symbol or image of a moral relation, I invented an explanation of my own; I did, however, add that such an explanation detracted from the effect of the poem and that beauty is more operative when experienced directly than when reduced to a formula by the intelligence. . . .

Of the missionary journals that Marie frequently sent he wrote, 'I read them more than once and though I do not find much to say to you about them I draw my profit. We are not sufficiently in accord to have edifying discussions on these subjects, on which I would often be tempted to become disputatious, a weakness of mine.' However, after one such perusal he was moved to write enviously, 'Happy missionary people, theirs is an idyllic and purely human life, in which courage and good will are the only virtues needed!' When she sent him the report of a Congress of Christian Unions in Paris, in which she had taken part and which had encountered some opposition, he commented:

I have a natural distrust of associations, but the smaller they are the more perfect and the less there is in them to alarm those who wish that reason may prevail. . . . Things are always contested in proportion to the claim they are felt to make to being approaches to the ideal. I am sure it is so in the world of art. Flaubert used to say that 'fleas could not resist the temptation of jumping on white linen, nor could critics the temptation of showing how opposite was their nature to that of good work'. . . . So I congratulate you on having to respond to an opposition, which does seem most irrational, and hope that the unions will prosper and long be a source of vigour and pleasure to you.

Marie also wrote to Tom on behalf of her black lamb of a cousin, Ernest Guy, with whom she always remained on the friendliest of terms. He was desirous of improving his English and wanted to spend September with a family on an *au pair* basis. He stayed first at 39 Southgrove, where he was immediately set to work on improving the translation of *The Strayed Reveller*. Then he went off to Wales to teach French to the children of a family connected with the Moores living in Mold. From here he wrote to Tom and Hettie: 'Today is Sunday and we must all be as sad as possible for being agreeable to God. I, however, hope that God is not so melancholic as many people imagine. Else I would not understand why it is so worthwhile to desire his company after death.' On his return he and Tom stayed with George in Cambridge for a weekend, the occasion on which Tom first met Bertrand Russell. 'I found Russell's manner as attractive as what he said was interesting. E.G. thought the life in Cambridge the most "épatante" he had ever come across and said we were at least two centuries ahead of France in material respects. However, I think he was very pleased to be going back there.'

Meanwhile, Tom had more urgent work on his hands than ever before in his life. He had been commissioned to edit the Vale Shakespeare, the first volume of which was to appear in January 1900. The plays were to be printed separately in Ricketts's specially designed Avon type, and the edition was already fully subscribed. At the same time, Oldmeadow, who had been delighted by the sale of *The Vinedresser*, and also by the handsome Unicorn impress Tom had since designed, had asked him to edit a series entitled 'Little Engravings: Classical and Contemporary', an early number of which was to be of his own work. Besides considering which artists should be included in this series and who should write the introductions, for his own contribution he was working on blocks illustrating the Siegfried legend, a theme which had visited his mind ever since Bob Trevelyan had first introduced him to Wagner. The Altdorfer monograph for the Artist's Library series had still to be completed. Assembling adequate reproductions for the illustrations was proving difficult. Ida Kruse was to do her determined best to help in this; because of her worryingly persistent cough she had given up acting for the time being to study theatre and opera in Germany. Tom was now mistrustful of all Oldmeadow's promises as to quality and date of publication. Nevertheless, when a situation arose which caused Binyon to appeal to him to intercede with Bob Trevelyan on Oldmeadow's behalf, he immediately complied. When Roger Fry's *Bellini* had first appeared it had been found to be faulty and had been withdrawn for correction; while Fry was away in Italy Bob had discovered that copies were still being sold, he believed with Oldmeadow's knowledge. Always intensely loyal to his friends and mindful of their reputations, he was now, according to Binyon, 'buzzing about like a bee' in a manner likely to jeopardize the future of the whole series. By the time he received an admonishing letter from Tom, however, his anger had subsided; admitting that he was apt to get carried away by his feelings and then have to retreat ignominiously, he apologized to Binyon.

Shortly afterwards George Trevelyan, who was going to Paris with his elder brother Charles, asked for an introduction to Uncle Appia. 'We had the pleasure of making the acquaintance of your friend Trevelyan and his brother,' Uncle Appia wrote to Tom later. 'I felt that all Englishmen staying abroad at this time suffer from the severe judgements passed in non-English countries on the policy of "Greater Britain".' Tom was not as concerned by the moral implications of the Boer War as either his uncle or the Liberal Trevelyans, though naturally there are frequent references to its progress in his letters. In a letter to Mrs Pissarro he defended the British action as a necessary check to Kruger's growing military power and desire for aggrandisement. To Fisher he inveighed against 'the extreme publicity following every reverse. . . . The losses have really been exceptionally small instead of unusually great. The cause of them is the lack of foresight in the Government, which has always been the fault of the English in undertakings. They had not even an ordinance map of the colony . . .' He instanced Wellington's record at the beginning of the Peninsular War: '. . . and his losses were infinitely greater, amounting to 50 per cent in some of the biggest engagements. Journalists are the curse of the modern world. They always lie. It is just the same as their calling Dreyfus the greatest martyr of the century or the Armenian massacres more atrocious than those of Nero or Domitian. . . .'

In December came a reverse of a kind which touched him more nearly. There was a fire at Ballantyne's printing works. Many of Ricketts's blocks for initial letters and ornamental borders, all Tom's blocks for illustrations to *The Centaur*, all the type set for *Hamlet* and *Othello* together wtih Tom's textual notes, much other type, and a number of the books printed on vellum were totally destroyed. Mercifully, the founts of the type survived unharmed. The issue of the first volume of the Vale Shakespeare was postponed until March, while, under chaotic conditions, the Avon type was recast and the plays reset. It took strenuous combined effort from the printers, Charles Holmes, and Tom to meet this date. For Tom, life at home was full of rather untimely distractions. Ida Kruse had returned from Germany full of a Goethe Festival in Bremen, performances by Eleonara Duse in Berlin, and experiences of Wagner. Her cough was still troubling her and she was going to the Gironde for a cure; in the meantime she visited constantly. Ernest Guy, who had now decided 'to learn the wool trade', had also reappeared. Later he was to travel about the country in the utmost luxury acting as interpreter to a wealthy French wool merchant, but first he lodged in London. Horrified by the fogs, chilled by his boarding-house (where his bedroom window would not shut), he took refuge at every opportunity in the Moore 'oasis' at the top of Highgate Hill. The frequent presence of Ida was an added attraction to him; they monopolized Hettie's piano and sang together. Fisher had by now reluctantly decided that he must return to London to be in closer touch with outlets for his work. For several weeks, singly or together, he and his wife stayed at 39 Southgrove until with Hettie's help they were finally settled in lodgings in Cheyne Row, Chelsea. In March Tom had to write to Bob Trevelyan, who had recently informed him in a matter-of-fact way of his engagement to a musical Miss van der Hoven from the Hague, that he 'would be welcome to lunch but not for the night owing to shortage of sheets'.

For Christmas 1899 Tom had sent Marie Wordsworth's 'Dion', a photograph of Shannon's self-portrait, *Man in a Black Shirt*, and Binyon's poem, 'Statues'. At the same time he had mentioned that he hoped to see her again soon as he and Shannon were planning a trip to Madrid via Paris. This was postponed because of the disaster at Ballantyne's, but on 10 May they arrived in Paris to stay in the Hotel Britannique for four packed days. At the Beaux Arts Shannon was gratified to find that whereas paintings by Watts and Leighton were skied his own work was well hung on the line. Of a neighbouring portrait by Sargent he wrote to Ricketts, 'tissue paper and modern millinery, *but exceedingly able*', and after reviewing Manet's work in general: '*beastly* and *very good*'. Besides visits to the Louvre and Panthéon, they spent much time at the Paris Exhibition, where there was a magnificent collection of early French decorative art, for which 'All the churches, galleries and private collections of France have been ransacked'. Shannon did not speak French and so relied on Tom both as guide and interpreter, especially when they combed the art photographers for good photographs of drawings. However, Tom found time to call on the Appias. Marie was lying on a couch, recovering from a fall. Caroline had a bad eye. Ernest Guy's mother was there, playing Wagner and making fun of Uncle Appia and Tante Louise for not liking it. It was arranged that Tom should stay for a night or two on his return from Madrid.

'Spain is a bleak and melancholy country with old towns exactly the colour of the cliffs on the mountains. It is not beautiful but romantic. The Spaniards are a very grave people with exceedingly sweet manners, which seem more dignified and genuine than those of the French.' This postcard to his parents is the only record of Tom's impression of the country. The five days in Madrid were spent almost entirely in the Prado, to which they managed 'to force an entrance' even on a saint's day. While Shannon sent Ricketts detailed notes of his reactions to the pictures there, Tom left no such account in any of his correspondence. His 'Lines on Titian's Bacchanal in the Prado', published some years later, are, however, a celebration of one intense, contemplative experience. On 20 May they were back in Paris, Ricketts had come over to join Shannon, and Tom was with the Appias.

25 May. I am still here and shall probably stay almost a week more. Every time I come here I feel fascinated by the life in this house and am very loth to leave it again. I am too English, and they make me feel like a serpent that wants to change his skin, only it won't crack wide enough to let him through. . . . You ought to come over here and see the Exhibition and enjoy the Appias.

[Undated] Louis and I went with him [Uncle] and Aunt Helen to St Cloud on Whitmonday. It was a lovely day and we sat and read under the trees. Uncle was very interested in a phonograph which a man brought and set up near our camp. Aunt Helen made coffee and tea with a spirit lamp in a place that was not more private than the Crystal Palace grounds on a Bank Holiday, and there we read missionary journals, etc. In the evening we strolled on to Sèvres, making one halt on the way. We took the steam boat back. It was very crowded, but a place was found for Aunt Helen right in the prow, a gentleman gave up his to Uncle, Louis and I stood. Aunt Helen was rather troubled lest they should let on too many passengers and sink the boat, so we had to count how many went off and how many came on at each pier. We passed through the Exhibition just as it was lighting up; Uncle was extremely pleased to see it from the river, but the motion of the boat gave Aunt Helen a little headache. We got back very late, not before nine, and found Marie and Caroline had been back ¾ of an hour. They had been to the 'bois de Chaville' with their Y.W.C.A. girls and spent the whole day within 10 minutes of the railway but quite hidden in the woods. Which would certainly have been more suited to Aunt Helen, but it is impossible to get Uncle to pass time in that way.

Marie lent Tom the first part of Tolstoy's *Resurrection* to take home with him. This book, which had just been published in France, had so far impressed and moved her deeply and she promised to forward the other two parts as she finished reading them. Tante Louise wrote to Henrietta in English, 'We have all got the more and more attached to dear Tom, I enjoyed much his visit.'

On 7 June, immediately after his return to England, Tom sent Marie a very long letter for her twenty-eighth birthday. He could no longer repress the intensity of feeling aroused during his visit. Writing first in French, he told her that Ernest would be bringing her the first two volumes of the Vale Shakespeare. He enclosed photographs of Titian's *St. Margaret conquering the Dragon* (Madrid), and his *Crowning with Thorns* (Munich), and his own poem 'Of the beauty of kindness I speak', probably composed under the Appia roof. Then, referring to some comment of Marie's on *The Vine-dresser*, he argued that Christian ideas might well be best expressed in pagan form. Though not yet Christian, he was not himself very pagan.

You have formed me too radically for me ever to escape from the Christian way of life. I feel this keenly and painfully. I have suffered much from this force which has taken possession of me, urging my artistic, optimistic, placid disposition to undergo long disciplines and difficult reformations. Your Latin nature, *ensoleillé*, animated and ardent has penetrated to the depth of my being and has forbidden me many things while dictating many others—and all this so gradually, with such an insistent continuity that I feel you are almost more to my work than I am myself. Your father said some good and true things to me last Sunday; he seemed to understand that any violent change of direction ... would be a great mistake for me. I deeply desire that my life and work may be useful and a source of good, but I feel I would be quite wrong to relinquish truths and skills acquired to snatch at others which are not yet mine.

Continuing in English, he spoke of his dream of a reformed theatre and the spirit in which he intended to approach it. Hitherto his life had been all failure apart from what he had achieved as an artist; he would now strive for 'a new spirit, not repudiating my past but transforming it'. If only he had done this sooner,

not my life only but yours too might have been happier, fuller and more perfect. All last year I was tortured because I could not leave off accusing you, though I knew I had not the least right to do so. . . . One more thing I want to tell you about myself: that is that though I have sinned, nobody but myself was concerned or harmed in any way. . . . It was reading *Resurrection* which made me want to tell you that. I have never made any feint or pretence of love to any other woman, nor have I wronged any other.

There follows a passage in which he questions Tolstoy's assumption that the prisoners were merely the victims of unjust circumstance, that social reform and civil justice could cure the evil in mankind.

For me there is only one sin, not to have preferred at any one moment the more perfect to the less perfect, not to have loved God. . . . Love kindles love, that is why charity fulfills the law and gives strength not only to itself but to others to resist and cease from sin. You were so kind to me when I was in Paris and took so much interest in my work that I feel bound to tell you how beautiful I feel that the spirit of charity in you is, and how sincerely I mean never to cease from striving till it has entered my heart too, whatever the future may or may not bring of that which I have most constantly desired. You must not think that because I look on things abstractly I do not feel them; my heart beats and aches as constantly as others. I have been led to 'hide my life', partly from shame, partly I hope from better motives. . . .

Pray forgive me for troubling you with so much about myself. I would like to have written you a different letter, to amuse and please you, but the feeling that there was so much unexplained and misunderstood between us made it impossible to write as I will soon, when I send my play. . . . Now I must get back to *Romeo and Juliet* which is the play I am at work on. . . .

A few days later came *Aphrodite against Artemis*, some requested reviews of *The Vinedresser*, and a letter expressing remorse for the egoism of the last. Also enclosed was his poem, 'A Spanish Picture' (a picture, seen in the Prado, of the dead Don Juan and the squalid circumstances of his laying out); it ends with the verse,

Thou wast an envied man, Don Juan,
Long shalt be envied still.

Thou hadst thy beauty as the proud pard hath
And instinct trained to skill.

Friends had urged him to publish this in the *Saturday Review*, but
he wanted her opinion before doing so. He promised to translate
into English her favourite passages in Mistral's *Calendau*. He asked
her to suggest subjects on which he might write poems; he had in
this way written an ode to Leda for Ricketts. Finally, he offered
her a solution to the problem she had in writing letters when on
the move: 'The Châtelaine Swan Fountain Pen is an arrangement
with little chains which are fastened to the case of the pen; . . . I
think it is just what you want, and it looks rather well hanging
from the belt.' To be sure of getting the right nib she would have
to send him her pen in exchange. 'I should be more likely not to
lose a pen that you had used.' Marie, again in the midst of preparations for a round of visits, sent a postcard referring only to the
Don Juan poem. She had found it rather hard to understand and
felt quite unqualified to make any comment except that the subject
did not much appeal to her. Ricketts, who himself more than once
painted Don Juan triumphantly alive and regarded him as a heroic
figure, did not like the poem either; though published later, it was
not sent to the *Saturday Review*.

Although in a brief note assuring him that his self-reproaches in
the first letter were unjustified, Marie had explained that she would
not be able to write fully until she reached the Valleys in August,
during the remainder of June and July Tom continued to send to
her: the Vale *Antony and Cleopatra*, a pamphlet by Josephine
Butler recommended by his mother, and the *Saturday Review* containing his substitute for 'A Spanish Picture'. When he had finished
reading *Resurrection*, he devoted the greater part of another long
letter to a criticism of the book. The ending, much admired by
Marie, had filled him with a personal sense of outrage. This Prince
Nekludov had been shocked out of his empty, self-indulgent way
of life by the discovery that his earlier seduction of the peasant girl
Maslova had driven her into prostitution, and so indirectly led to

her being sentenced to penal servitude for a crime she had not committed. His efforts to obtain a pardon for her and other innocent prisoners had been frustrated by official indifference all the way up the established hierarchy. He had offered marriage to Maslova, had come to love her, had followed her on the long trek to Siberia. Then, in Tom's eyes, he betrayed and abandoned her for the second time by weakly accepting her decision to marry one of the political prisoners, Simonson, knowing perfectly well that this was a sacrifice on his behalf. After that, having read some passages in the New Testament already familiar to him, and reflected on them quite superficially, Nekludov's heart was flooded with happiness and Tolstoy expected the reader to believe that some wonderful new life had dawned for him. How could Marie find such a conclusion admirable? This letter, Tom knew, would reach Marie when she was again staying with the family of her restless god-daughter Geneviève, and would be going on to her brother's family; he enclosed the lullaby written in the secret notebook six years earlier and explained how it had come to be composed:

I would have published it in my book, for I find it successful enough, but I had not the courage to ask the advice of my friends on a thing which, though altogether objective, has such a close personal association for me. . . . I do not know if it is possible to send a French child to sleep with an English lullaby but if the occasion arises you might perhaps make use of my song which till now has remained unvoiced.

During a peaceful interlude at the Airals Blancs in the middle of August, Marie was able to acknowledge all the enclosures, most of which she had had no opportunity of reading, and give a considered answer to the letters, whose tender urgency had been disquieting to her. She vehemently rejected any justification for celebrating Don Juan's 'instinct trained to skill', warmly approved his poem 'Kindness', promised to suggest subjects should they occur to 'ma veine poëtique bien capricieuse'; she left the Tolstoy debate to a later letter and gratefully accepted the offer of the

Châtelaine Pen, asking only that it should be sent to Paris, 'car en Italie ils sont tellement voleurs à la poste'. She enclosed the programme of a congress she had attended on the Work of Women in the Church, and mentioned an invitation to speak at a conference of l'Etoile Blanche which she had felt obliged to refuse, not being sufficiently clear in her mind on 'le rôle de la jeune fille dans la lutte contre la démoralisation'. The greater part of the ten pages of folded notepaper was, however, concerned with Tom's birthday letter of 7 June. On this she first expressed her astonishment that she could have meant so much to him; being so aware of her weaknesses of character, she thought she was the one to have benefitted most in their relationship. 'Ah well, I know you don't want to pay me compliments and I leave you to your illusions, only grateful if it has been given to me to be of some little use.' Then, for the first time, she entered fully into her reasons for regarding a marriage between them as impossible. In the first place, there was the gulf caused by the difference in their religious views; he did not believe in a personal God, a Father to whom one could pray, nor did he believe in the immortality of the soul. She did not in the least blame him for not sharing beliefs of vital importance to her, for 'chacun croit ce qu'il peut et comme il peut'.

What I mean to say is that complete intimacy can never exist between me and a soul which cannot associate itself with me in prayer, and in the contemplation of a future life. I have very dear friends, and you are of their number, with whom I have precious exchanges and who do not share the same convictions as I have. But the intimacy which you wish with me could not suffer compromise and light and shade. We neither of us would wish for intimacy at a discount. We could not bear it—it would be our misfortune. We could not have less than a complete union and that is impossible.

Hardly less of a barrier was the dissimilarity of their chosen tasks in life. While she approved, and followed with all the sympathy and understanding of which she was capable, his literary and artistic work and aspirations, he must not think that these interests were more than peripheral in her own life. Her vocation lay in her work for the church, and to this her life was dedicated.

How then associate two types of activity, two preoccupations, so entirely different from each other as yours and mine? There could but be parallel lives—that is the negation of happiness or the sacrifice of one or other of us, which neither of us could desire. Don't you agree? Perhaps you'll find it difficult to accept this, because without wishing to pose as greatly experienced, I think I know life better than you do and that you can dream more easily that things are possible whereas I see them as incompatible with reality. I feel so strongly that you would need a companion who could entirely share *your* interests, who could *whole*-heartedly serve the cause which you serve, who could follow through the vicissitudes of your career, which will no doubt be agitated, without reservation, with confidence and enthusiasm. I could not be all that to you. And I know so well how much you need this that I wish you had never known me so that you might have found it elsewhere.

Then there was her commitment to her family. Her most ardent wish was that Caroline should marry, and her parents needed at least one daughter at home.

Our dearest prayer is that they should be preserved to us for long, for very long. Our father is the centre of our life more than can be said. And when they will no longer need me I shall no longer be a young girl, which I scarcely am at present.

If I were a child, if I were 18 years old, if my heart could be easily given and my life take a new direction, then there might perhaps be some possibility that a life in common might melt all this together and harmonize everything. But at my age, and perhaps more so for me than for others, because of all I've been through, and especially because of the lack of flexibility in my character, one cannot take oneself to bits and re-form oneself. You well know that a woman cannot be insensible to a love as faithful and as living as yours, especially when it comes from a being she esteems so profoundly and in whom she has a confidence as great as that I have in you. . . . But I would be tempted to reproach myself for finding some sweetness in it, feeling as I do that I cannot return it. The heart cannot be commanded; I feel mine ungrateful and hard towards you. I feel I do not merit what you give me and I suffer from having to receive without returning.

She knew how earnestly he had endeavoured to grow nearer to her in Christian faith, and was confident this endeavour would continue, even though she was not to fill the place he desired in his future, 'because it is towards the good *in itself* that you wish to aim, do you not? and not at a *means* of coming together?' Finally, she hoped that his protestation of wanting 'to help' rather than 'to conquer' her was still true:

I am persuaded that our relationship can be a source of richness and benediction for each of us, and you can count on me to give it willingly the time and seriousness possible to me. But I *must* feel that we wish to help each other and *not* anything else. I must feel both in our correspondence and when we meet that you're not trying to conquer me; you must be confident that I am giving what I can and not ask for more. It has cost me much, my dear Tom, and it costs me now to ask so much of you. But if you knew how all this has tormented me lately. Now I shall feel relieved. Can you understand me and not be irritated and discouraged?

In future let us go forward like two faithful friends whose paths cross, separate, and meet again in an energetic and sometimes joyous course towards the highest summits.

Always believe in my faithful and very real affection,
Your cousin and friend, Marie Appia.

CHAPTER ELEVEN

꿿꿿

An Irish Bard and a Death in the Valleys

MARIE waited a fortnight for a reply to her letter, an unprece-
dented delay on Tom's part. Then, recalling that letter of Caroline's
that had gone astray, she sent a postcard of inquiry. This crossed
with Tom's weighty answer. He first expressed his gratitude to her
for explaining the reasons for her rejection and his sense of relief
on finding these were what he had originally supposed:

I think you are quite right in what you say about being bound to
Caroline and your family. And you know that seven years ago, right
from the first, the religious difficulty seemed to me almost insuperable. . . . Of course, underlying all the other causes the real reason
why you cannot and have not loved me is that I am not lovable. I felt
it then, I feel it now. You cannot help condemning me. I condemn
myself, and probably God condemned me. But ought I to accept any
of these condemnations as final? . . . Will you not hear me when I ask
you to hold over the judgment that experience forces on you, to fight
against it, not to acquiesce in it, not to write to me, not to think to
yourself that without posing for 'une vieille expérimentée' you can
say 'je crois que je connais mieux la vie et vous pouvez rêver plus
facilement que les choses sont réalisables quand je les vois incom-
patibles avec la réalité.' Did not those high officials use just this line of
argument to Nekludov? . . . Are not they who dreamed in great
number among those who succeeded as we see success when we look
back into the past? I can wait, Marie, my dream will hold out; you say
you will no longer be young but I shall always be older than you; you
say it will be more difficult to realize then, but ought we to expect to
be weaker and more ignorant, or ought we not to hope to bring to
these difficulties more experience, firmer wills, larger hearts? . . .
Even today, even now may we not be more truly married in the sight
of God than thousands who are happy in supposing themselves so? I

can see no necessary connexion between 'parallélisme' and 'la négation du bonheur'. The unity of marriage is not one of function, hardly ever is it one of thought, but then it is hearts that love, not heads. . . . Is it ever right to say, 'I am divided from you by an abyss. I will call across to you. I will help you as much as I conveniently can, but it is useless to think that we can meet.'? Oh, such ideas . . . must wall in the mind that resorts to them, this is the artist and the bourgeois, the aristocrat and the serf, the pharisee and the publican over again! . . . But no, you did not mean *that*; you only wanted not to encourage my hopes in what you feel to be a desperate case. Oh, but Marie, don't think it so! You wrong me, you wrong yourself the moment you do! Hope, hope that I shall grow so worthy of your love that you cannot help loving me as I love you! If you ask that I should be silent and not importune you, may I not ask this of you, that you will hope to love me? At least, that if I am loyal to my promise, you will not let me feel that you are yielding to thoughts that slowly and surely are building impassable barriers between us. How can you expect me to succeed if you do? Oh, it is not *too likely* that I shall succeed!

I marvel at your astonishment at finding you have meant so much to my work. I should have supposed you would have expected it. You opened the gates of a new world of beauty to me, and though I did not abandon that which I already knew, I have ever since been trying to bring them together and to harmonize them. I do not see how it could have been otherwise; if you had meant nothing to me I should not have loved; it was because you seemed given to me in one very real sense that I was led to hope you might become mine also in the fullest and most complete sense. . . . You lay down all the qualities I shall need in a wife and you say, 'I cannot give you these' but if I have found in you what I most need, why should you prefer your guesses to my experience? . . . And I know that this [her assertion that their vocations were incompatible] is conformed to received notions, but is it true? No, a thousand times rather would I see in the divergence of our tastes and interests not only an obstacle but the invitation to a success . . . 'Impossible.' Impossible, impossible! and look! what has happened of any importance in the past that was not called impossible. . .? That you cannot feel it now is reason enough for now, but why should you fight against a relationship growing up between us that (when you are set free, as in all probability you must be at however distant a period) shall naturally result in our marriage? Do not think you deceive me in your kind efforts to meet me in the art world, I know and feel that your heart is and must remain in the world of your present activities, but am I necessarily excluded from all participation in them, or are you from mine? . . . It is not wholly in the air this dream of mine, there are foundations laid. The design is neither yours nor mine; let us build and not quarrel as to whether the building is designed for a temple, as I believe, or a club, as you think more probable. When the walls are raised, when the rooftree is in place, we shall at least recognize what the architect intended.

On their differences in religious belief, she had attributed to him more certitude than he possessed. Man's understanding of time was so limited that he could surely have no rational conception of immortality; in a Tolstoyan context, he later added, 'I do not think any future can make up for injustice now. . . . "The kingdom of heaven is within you" seem to me the most hopeful words that men have ever heard; to believe in them, not as an intellectual proposition, but as a veritable experience always ready to be tried, seems to me infinitely more alluring than any kingdom in the skies.' Nor could he understand what was meant by a 'personal God', though he could, in a figurative sense, follow Jesus in ascribing good, received and desired, to 'our Father'. Nevertheless, he was firmly convinced that, though arrived at and held differently, the faith that inspired them both was essentially the same; it was his poverty of attainment that most divided them. This conviction was restated in a second letter, virtually a postscript, in which he repudiated Marie's hitherto unchallenged assumption: 'Vous ne pouvez pas prier.' 'I believe that it is a difference of words that separates us, and that has in the past left me with a spiritual hunger to which you must have been blind.'

Why, he next asked, did Marie reproach herself for finding 'quelque douceur' in his love, knowing she could not return it?

You should seize on every opportunity of finding 'quelque douceur' as the very means given to you of rendering me a return, there is no return but this, and this you guard yourself against. Why? More especially if you suffer not to be able to render it. There is no debt and no account in love, only as Shakespeare says 'acceptance bounteous'; if you cannot accept all, accept as much as ever you can ...

After a further defence of Don Juan, he returned to another treatise by Wilfred Monod Marie had sent, *L'immoralité de la moralité*. While in agreement with this in the main, there were certain points that 'make me feel very warlike and ruffle all my feathers':

And really his pictures are not complete pictures, they are rhetorical and one-sided. Nor should a delicate nature, I think, have talked as he talked about La Fontaine; surely he knows better than that? His condemnation seems to me stupid in the same sense as the man's state-ment that he liked the gospels and the fables because they were both moral. What is beautiful about Fontaine is his temper, not his thought, and there is a real resemblance to the parables in their temper, which enables him to attain that naïve simplicité and sunniness which is the great charm of the fables, nor is it true of all of them that the point is merely worldly. ...

O Marie, you must not think that because I argue against some of your words that I am insensible in the least to the great proof of affection that your letter is in itself. I welcome it, I thank you for it, I rejoice in it and am more and more determined to be worthy of it.

I am all expectation for my lesson on Tolstoy's book and hope to be an apt pupil.

I hope and believe that we shall meet on our journey towards the high summits far sooner than you are as yet able to hope or suppose, but whether it will be side by side or divided by real or imaginary abysses, we will press on, will we not? That is agreed!

And now with love to all yours and very much for yourself,

I am your affectionate cousin and friend,

Tom.

Much pain must have been suffered in the course of converting what could only have been a cruel disappointment into so confi-dently steadfast a manifesto; and much intellectual travail in the effort to harmonize, to the satisfaction of his own conscience, the two worlds of beauty revealed by the two rooted objects of Tom's devotion, Marie, the dedicated church worker, and Ricketts, the creative, agnostic aesthete. The strain of this solitary struggle may well have been responsible for the discord in his working relationships particularly evident at this time. He wrote an angry note to Holmes, complaining that he was interfering with the Shakespeare texts. Shannon then accused him of suffering from 'high stummick', reminded him that he had been particularly asked not 'to rag or worry Holmes' while he was seeing the books through the press and told him, 'Your letters are apt to be emphatic and pompous and irritating.' Holmes himself referred to this episode more moderately: 'Over the Shakespeare proofs I got into hot water once or twice with the patient editor, Sturge Moore.' Relations with Oldmeadow, however, reached such a pitch of acrimony that Binyon was driven to intervene and wrote offering to conduct Tom's future business with the Unicorn Press himself. While admitting Oldmeadow's shortcomings, he expressed himself equally strongly about Tom's:

I will spare no trouble. But you must understand that I am not going to be guarantee for any printer, engraver or binder; if you expect them to produce things up to promised dates, I don't and I'm not going to worry myself to death if they delay, though I shall do my best to prevent them. What do you say? . . . Whenever any question has had to be decided you have (it seems to me) demanded just what you wanted, without the slightest reference to expense or the cost of the book or the time required and when things have not been at once just what you wished, you have immediately flown to unmeasured expressions. Perhaps you think it wrong to be polite to publishers, but you know you are, even in ordinary discussion, given to saying things which in most people would sound absurdly rude. Shannon and Ricketts have noticed it too. Of course, your friends don't wish you otherwise, I'm sure I don't, but business is different and I think your method of showing dissatisfaction is the most ineffective possible. . . .

Characteristically, Binyon rapidly followed up these home truths with a note: 'Since writing all that jaw I have been dreadfully afraid I may have offended you. I dare say I said far more than I

ought to have or meant to, but I meant well, I'm sure you know.
... Do pitch into me, I shall feel happier if you do, and then
forgive me.' Tom accepted Binyon's offer gratefully and then
carried on pitching into Oldmeadow at one remove.

When in September *Altdorfer* finally appeared, it was widely
welcomed as setting the work of a little-known artist honourably
in the German tradition. Among Tom's friends, Ricketts and
Shannon were for once united with Roger Fry in enthusiasm. Fry
had, indeed, become increasingly desirous of discussion with Tom
—on his forthcoming series of lectures on Italian Art, on an
article he was writing questioning Berenson's theory of Tactile
Values, on his own current preoccupation with 'surface quality'.
Tom liked him personally, admired his lively intelligence and
erudition, but attacked him for his intellectual approach, for
treating the appreciation of art as though it were a matter of
applying general scientific principles, instead of a particular
personal response matured through experience. He was later to
accuse him 'of never having been in love with a picture'. So
vigorously did Tom espouse his own favourable responses, that
Fry, disabled by an accident, laboured on crutches to Shannon's
show at the New English Gallery. He sent Tom his draft review of
the exhibition. The reservations it contained offended Tom's
loyalties and he responded, in Fry's words, 'by heaping insults on
my head. . . . It is a little hard that this superhuman effort of toler-
ance on my part, this attempt to find my way out of my fortified
position, should lead me to fall a prey to the one who perhaps
more than any other has helped to entice me out.' Ricketts later
noted in his journal, 'We were astonished by a two column article
on CHS in the Athenaeum . . . the bulk of it the most intelligent
praise. It turned out to be by R. Fry, certainly the last man I would
have suspected.'

At Fry's lectures Tom usually forgathered with Binyon and
other friends from the British Museum. At about this time, however, Binyon (who seldom dated his letters before he became engaged to be married), sent him a note explaining in confidence

why he would not be attending the lectures any more. It was to avoid meeting there the young artist, Miss Monsell; he had been 'deep in love with her for some time' and she had finally refused him. 'I have been very wretched but am tired of grieving and lamenting and am not crushed at all. I know you will be sorry but you need not be troubled about me.' Strangely, perhaps inhibited by his own secret situation, Tom gave his closest friend little sympathy or support in this disappointment. When, nearly three years later, circumstances moved him to express remorse for such callous behaviour, Binyon replied, 'I fancied at the time from things you had said that you thought artists ought not to marry and that you were glad for my career that my chance had not come off, though didn't want to hurt me by saying so. But I was sure you were sorry for my pain and had no reproach against you in my mind; so don't trouble about it.'

Tom's suggestion to his mother that she should see the Paris Exhibition and enjoy the Appias had been followed by a pressing invitation from her sister. After much consideration and correspondence Henrietta decided to go with Sarah at the beginning of November, just before the Exhibition closed. Sarah was only exercised by the problem of finding a suitable person to carry on her numerous charitable activities during her absence; Hettie, who would be at Cheriton looking after their father, was not eligible, 'she must have a church woman and a total abstainer'. Henrietta, apart from some anxiety as to how her health would stand up to the undertaking, had apprehensions about the family reunion. Originally, Tom had intended to stay in Paris at the same time. Then Binyon mentioned an October exhibition of Japanese prints he was particularly anxious to see and Bob Trevelyan, who managed to combine a bachelor freedom of movement with his happy married state, was eager to come too. Tom therefore wrote asking Marie if he might pay a brief visit in mid-October.

Marie, just returned from the Valleys, much preoccupied with opening up the house after its 'sommeil de l'été' and with a reorganization of parish work, wrote a hurried note welcoming this suggestion. She thanked him for his two recent letters, the second of which, in particular, 'm'a vivement touchée et même impressionée'. She still, however, believed that it was more than a difference of words that separated them on religious questions and regretted his continuing prejudice against Christians:

You don't know Christians—you know my father, Louis and Henri —but in England you have not seen Christians at work. You've created in your mind a narrow, dogmatic, hard-on-non-Christians Christian, and then you accuse him of the ills of humanity. Matthew Arnold, with his high-flown despisal of 'popular theology' and his logic, often seems to me very illogical. But enough—I run the risk of getting cross. Goodbye. We'll take this up again by word of mouth in a few days.

From the letter Tom wrote on his return it appears that their attempts to continue this debate were constantly interrupted. Just before being summoned to her father's assistance, Marie had asked Tom how he thought the divine spirit acted upon mankind. In his considered reply, Tom borrowed Arnold's analogy between human and divine love:

And as a lover can pass whole days in the presence of his mistress even though he is far from her, we can live with Jesus Christ and in the presence of our Heavenly Father. . . . he thinks of her, he often recalls her beauty and he has the desire continually to be near her—to see her in imagination, to talk audibly with her, though in silence. From this practice comes the constancy, the firmness and the intensity of his passion; so it is with the heavenly beauty of the idea of God and Jesus Christ; although we do not see it, we behave as though we did in recalling every gift born of this idea, every word inspired by it and in attributing to it every perfection of which a conception has entered our hearts. It is also by this method that every work of art is created . . . for 'Faith is the substance of things hoped for, the evidence of things not seen.' . . . Just as the lover always knows that he may perhaps be mistaken and that he attributes to his mistress a character she does not possess, so the intellect can admit, though the heart denies, the possibility that his revelations of a divine beauty have no relation to the reality. And all the more readily when this same intellect affirms that reality, such as we know it, may be an illusion of our senses. Our hearts are then freer than that of a lover to stake all on the conception of perfection that possesses us. The true reality may not be real, and to call the things that we believe truly real 'facts' is to degrade them, for they are more real than the material creation or we are lost.

On his return Tom had also immediately written a reassuring letter to his mother:

Hettie tells me that you were advising Sarah not to take things for paying calls and visits in, as you expected they would not like to take you about to see their friends. I don't believe for a moment that they will feel in the least like that, but, on the contrary, be very happy to introduce and take you about as much as you are inclined to go and the occasions allow. They are quite the same as ever they were and will not feel the least inclined to hide you because of the Harry affair. . . . I am sure you will enjoy Paris immensely; it is always most refreshing to go there and the Appias are as good as it is possible to be. . . .

Trevy and Binyon lunched at 119 on Wednesday and were both very pleased. Trevy talked a great deal and made everybody laugh several times; there were Ernest, his brother and Raymond Penel besides.

Henrietta did enjoy her visit immensely. While not able to undertake the energetic programme arranged for Sarah with one or other of her cousins, she managed to spend two hours at the Exhibition on most days. This she found 'most interesting', and was only disappointed that the panorama of the Trans-Siberian Railway (in which she had shares) was already closed. She renewed friendships of her girlhood with the Monods and Soeur Waller, the revered Dutch diaconesse, who in 1871 had slipped Georges's letters to England into the Dutch diplomatic bag. She accompanied Marie to a meeting of the Y.W.C.A. and attended a Réunion at the Maison des Missions, presided over by Pasteur Jean Meyer, whom she remembered 'as a tiny child in petticoats who could only just toddle by help of his Father's hand'. Tante Louise invited her to her Refuge. Here there was a moment of embarrassment when the old lady unexpectedly delivered herself of a tirade against a sermon she had read by Dr. Tipple, the Baptist Minister at Upper Norwood, whom the Moores so much admired. Henrietta thought it best to make no comment. Otherwise all was harmony. She appreciated the warmth and animation of the Appia household, and noted with a certain envy the industry and devotion of the servants. Though these are not recorded, the quiet, intimate talks with her sister probably gave her the greatest satisfaction of all. The sisters were not to see one another again.

For Christmas 1900 Tom apparently sent Marie some sketches for a series of woodcuts of the Parables from the Bible on which he was then working. She returned corrected his translation of passages from Emerson, an author who had pleased her greatly, and enclosed another sermon by Wilfred Monod. At the same time a book by Henry Appia, presented to Henrietta, was circulating among members of the Moore family. Already, in Turin, Henry had preached 'le christianisme social', a doctrine for which he had become more widely known in Geneva, particularly since his appointment the previous year as Professeur at l'Ecole de Théologie of the University. His father enthusiastically identified himself with Henry's views, which, as he explained in a letter to Tom, he saw as a response to the call of the new century; the churches had become too much like mutual welfare societies with benefits realized in eternity; they were fortresses of spiritual well-being, ignoring the sea of injustice and human suffering beating on their walls. Young men like Henry and Wilfred Monod were urging Christianity to grapple with the social problems of the time 'et ne se confine pas dans les discussions surannées du passé'. 'I do not recognise any defined *theory* in Henri Appia's book,' commented Daniel, 'but approved his ideas in so far as they showed a broadening of his mind and an appreciable departure from dogma. The terms Xtianity and Socialism are far too indefinite to found theory on.' Having digested both Monod's sermon and Henry's book, Tom sent Marie his comments in what she justly described as 'une philippique'. One of his general criticisms was that her brother and cousin are trying to galvanize christianity, not to regenerate it, though that is obviously what they are intending to do. If you preach that men have a right to justice, property, comfort or what not, you preach what will inevitably make them first discontented, then angry that their rights are withheld from them and ultimately accusers and enemies of those who enjoy the things they imagine they have a right to. If you make the kingdom of heaven a material future state, you make them not only worldly for the present but 'otherworldly', as George Eliot said, for the future.

From this letter, evidently written early in 1901, until May 1902 all Tom's side of the correspondence with Marie is inexplicably missing. As he was normally the most active party, on a ratio of about three letters to one, much of the content and feeling of the interchange over this period remains hidden.

Shortly before this baffling blank intervenes, Tom had mentioned in a postcard to Marie his recent 'acquaintance with a believer in spirits who is quite intelligent; it is very interesting to hear him talk, but he fails to convince me that there is any better ground for his beliefs than for the miracles of the past. He is Irish and his beliefs are quite common property in the west of Ireland. He is not a Christian though some who think like him are.' This was W. B. Yeats, then thirty-five years old and living in rooms off Woburn Square when he was not in Ireland. Of their early association Tom later wrote, 'His derision of the puritanical and scientific bases of my bringing up roused me to contend as much as his witty, dream-soaked talk delighted me.' Talking and contending were imperatives for them both, and if Tom had not Yeats's eloquence, his fabled gift for sustained monologue, he was well able to hold his own in logical argument and philosophic discourse. He continued to consider Yeats's appetite for any hearsay about spirits as indiscriminate, and to regard his involvement with spiritualism, clairvoyance, and the magic of MacGregor Mathers's Order of the Golden Dawn with a sceptical, though far from incurious, eye. In spite of the difference in the range of their experience and achievement, there was common ground on which to meet. Both had been art students who turned to poetry, carrying a Pre-Raphaelite allegiance with them. Both were 'fanatics for mythology'. And what brought them immediately close was their critical appreciation of each other's verse. 'Yeats', Tom wrote to Bob Trevelyan in December, 'is the most obstreperously enthusiastic auditor I have yet had. He even ventured to interrupt me with an exclamation of approval. An audacity which I forgave, though it made me read a good many lines very badly and kept me in anguish for fear of its repetition until the end.'

The more or less dormant project of forming a company of actors able to speak verse was now reanimated by Yeats's interest, an interest based on stormy experience. In 1898 he had become co-founder, with Edward Martyn and George Moore, of the Irish Literary Theatre. On his own and in collaboration, he had already written a number of plays in prose and verse. And these, in spite of the rows connected with patriotic susceptibility, religious orthodoxy, political schism, and personal vendetta endemic in the Irish theatre, had been performed. Though there had been rich acting talent to hand, few of the productions had satisfied him. Gordon Craig's theories on staging appealed to him strongly and he had bardic ideas on the speaking of verse, which only the actress Florence Farr could as yet demonstrate. A company in London would enlarge the possibilities of production and be a stimulus to the 'literary theatre' movement in both countries. Yeats invited Binyon and Tom to dinner to meet Lady Gregory, Florence Farr, and the doctor turned poet John Todhunter. There was much subsequent discussion on the practical problems. The not entirely converted Tom was persuaded to take lessons in elocution from Florence Farr and so better equip himself for training young players. 'You must write some short sweet songs for me to shout when I become a master bard,' he wrote to Bob Trevelyan.

Before this, Tom had offered his hitherto only privately circulated *Aphrodite against Artemis* to Macmillan (later the publisher of the four volumes of his collected verse) and met with the response,

'Our experience does not make us sanguine about the success of a short verse play and fearing that the publication would only end in a loss we are obliged to decline to undertake it.' Binyon then advised him to return to the Unicorn Press, and on this occasion Oldmeadow acted with dispatch. 'Now that I have your play in print', wrote Yeats,

I think even better of it than I did when you read it. I am much more satisfied with your verse and your theories of verse than I was. You certainly get vivid effects out of your use of modern words and I do not now find any of the verse too intricate in its thought, though I sometimes regret an inverted phrase. The play should act admirably and one regrets, vivid as they are, the few little things that do not come within the limits of the stage. If they were not there you would have an admirable chance of being pirated in America at once. [This, he explained, was what had happened to his *The Land of Heart's Desire*, much to the pirates' profit.] All seems to show me that if one writes actable little plays now, without too many characters, they will find their way to some stage. I think you have done the best play of the kind there is. I hope you will soon publish your *Herod* [*Mariamne*] too. . . . Theseus himself is I think the finest, but all the characterization in your play is good—perhaps 'the maidens' do not come of very 'good family', but they are all the more vivid.

Ricketts and Shannon were at this time shocked by the publication of a disparaging book on Joshua Reynolds by the art critic Sir William Armstrong. 'You are the right and only person to answer him,' Shannon wrote to Tom, urging that it would also be a chance 'to show up this preposterous notion of *un*originality. . . . if you would only write it in your best Altdorfer manner you will make a great success and I believe it might well prove a turning point in the matter of art criticism'. Tom's *A Defence of Reynolds* appeared in the April number of the *Monthly Review*. Its initiators were delighted, and so were the author's parents. Henrietta read the article aloud to Nana, then a guest at Cheriton, 'who was very much interested and said she was proud to have been your nurse'. Roger Fry's verdict was guarded: 'I think you have great polemic powers, you see your own point of view very clearly and you have plenty of picturesque expletives'; on the whole, though, he considered the article to be stronger in feeling than in exposition. This was Tom's first venture into journalistic art controversy, waters whose undercurrents of feud and influence were later to bewilder and exasperate him. He was back on firm ground in considering Binyon's suggestion that he should write a book on Dürer, and also in allowing C. R. Ashbee to use one of his completed woodcuts for the Essex House Press, while refusing on principle to do work for him on commission, a principle that the possession of a modest independent income made it easier to maintain.

By now, Tom had evidently written to Marie to the effect that he was too busy to pay his usual spring visit to Paris. This announcement was received 'avec protestations', and hopes that he would manage to tear himself away from his 'austères travaux' to spare them a few days in the early summer. In her letter Marie mentioned the family's concern for Henry's health; it appeared that he was suffering mental strain from overworking in his double capacity as pastor and professor. Later in April Marie took part in a conference of the Italian Christian Association held in Genoa. Afterwards she stayed a few days at the Airals Blancs. She had never before been in the Valleys in the spring, but failed to enjoy the tranquillity she hoped for there, 'car une Appia en cette saison est une si grande rareté que tout le monde voulait me voir. . . . And what has become of your French? I hope the hoar frost has not paralysed it. It seems to me that you're not very zealous in doing translations, and you know that I would be most willing to make some visits to Emerson with you.'

Busy as Tom was on editing the Vale Shakespeare, apart from his other activities, his life was certainly not austere. The round of gallery and theatre-going with various companions continued, as did the cycling excursions with Shannon, which included a trip to Wells in May. Occasional weekends were spent at Priest Hill, where Tom did not neglect opportunities of enlarging Sybil Pye's knowledge of poetry. She asked his advice on lessons she was giving two or three mornings a week to a small group of young children from the neighbourhood. He suggested 'the Socratic method', but her parents thought she was too young for Plato. He then had the idea of writing verses for her to read with the children and this led to a correspondence between them.

During the early months of this year Tom's circle of acquaintances widened appreciably. Through Yeats he got to know John Masefield, at whose home 'we had strawberries, cream and honey and talked about lyrics'. At the Pissarros he met the Belgian poet Verhaeren and the educationalist Cloudsley Brereton. He dined with the master etcher William Strang, 'a very Scotch man', and with Will Rothenstein. He became friendly with George's fellow Apostle, the barrister Charlie Sanger and his wife Dora, and through them met Desmond MacCarthy again and Goldsworthy Lowes Dickinson. At a meeting of the Art Workers' Guild, 'Emery Walker wanted me to say I would become a member but I don't think I shall ... I stunk of stale tobacco the day after, besides there is nothing to be gained but hobnobbing'. Tom was soon to change his mind about joining the Guild, and also his opinion of its Master for that year, Selwyn Image, whom he then described as 'quite a miniature Dr. Johnson, which is just what he would like to be'.

There was a considerable mingling of old friends with new: Bob Trevelyan was introduced to Yeats; Binyon was taken to see Mileham in his studio and John Tweed working on his statue of Cecil Rhodes; Poole was taken to dine at Roche's, the French restaurant in Soho, which provided an excellent meal for eighteen pence and had become a sort of informal club with a nucleus of men from the British Museum. Fisher, though another to benefit from Binyon's interest, was then in no position to enjoy any social life. 'Very stupidly', according to Hettie, he had more or less imposed on his wife an experimental separation of a year, during which he hoped she might develop her own artistic interests and skills and thus cease to be so negatively preoccupied with the uncertainties of his own career. The need to make her an allowance increased his financial difficulties. Although he had various long-term commissions, immediate demands forced him to work day and night on illustrations for a special edition of the *Illustrated London News* commemorating the reign of the late Queen. Pleased with his work, this magazine then asked him to produce an illustrated article on Carcassonne. 'If you overwork too much,' Tom admonished him, 'you won't be able to go. It would show real elasticity to determine in future to take things gently, leaving time for digestion. You are too apt to be merely a boa-constrictor in regard to experience.' And Ida Kruse was now back in America. The cure in the Gironde not proving very effective, she had given up thoughts of joining Frank Benson's company. During her brief stay in London before sailing home, it was probably Tom who introduced her to Yeats and arranged for her meeting with Gordon Craig. In May she wrote from Black Hawk, Colorado, where the high, dry native air had almost effected a complete cure. She was riding three hours a day, going alone into some rocky canyon and reciting the *Chorus of Grecian Maidens* at the top of her voice. She had ideas about 'dance plays', and had heard that the steel millionaire, Carnegie, wanted to endow a theatre—and needed guidance!

What Tom gave Marie for her twenty-ninth birthday this year cannot be gathered from the postcard she wrote him on 14 June. She was too anxiously preoccupied with the news of her brother Henry to do more than include a general acknowledgement. Henry, with his wife Thérèse and the children, had been for some-time at the Airals Blanc, where he had seemed to be progressing satisfactorily. But now he was critically ill with what was thought to be sunstroke. His mother and Caroline had immediately gone to the Airals Blancs and were telegraphing daily to Paris. Henrietta wrote offering to have the children at Cheriton. Marie, by this time also at the Airals Blancs, replied, 'It is actually impossible to send the children away, and he is now so weak and unconscious that the noises can not disturb him.' On 28 June Henrietta received the telegram, 'Allé paisiblement à Dieu.' It was probably of a tumour on the brain that Henry died, aged forty, in the middle of a career that had been an ever-growing source of satisfaction to his parents. His widow was left with six young children to care for.

During this time of anxiety and grief at the Airals Blancs, Cousine Hélène Appia from Geneva was on a visit to England with a friend. By every account, Hélène Appia was an exceptional person. It was not just that she was a woman of culture, widely read in the literature of several languages, a lover of art, a gifted pianist, numbering among her close friends the mothers of Albert Schweitzer and Karl Barth. What seems most to have impressed all who knew her was the serenity she radiated. She had looked after her widowed father, whose closing years were, as she had already told Tom, often troubled by black moods. Since his death she had lived alone, but always responsive and available to the needs of family and friends. In her letters to Tom, which had so far been mainly about their literary preferences, she had mentioned how much she would like her younger brother, Adolphe, to meet him. Ever since hearing from Ernest Guy that after meeting Adolphe Marie had ejaculated, 'Quelle splendeur d'un homme!' Tom had been curious about this cousin. He was a stage designer of genius, whose influence was as penetrating as that of Gordon Craig.

Hélène stayed briefly at 39 Southgrove in May, long enough to be taken to the Guildhall by Bertie, to the Wallace collection by Tom, and shown over the British Museum by Binyon. But it was a talk she had with Tom during her second visit to London a month later that was most important to her and made her write to him, 'Vous êtes mon meilleur souvenir d'Angleterre.' She had never before confided in anyone the causes of her constant concern for her brother Adolphe; he was a homosexual, addicted to drugs and subject to frenzies of suicidal despair. These were matters which, for Adolphe's sake, she did not feel able to mention in her own circle, so she had been left to care alone. She did not interfere or attempt to reform her brother, but waited until he turned to her, as eventually, it seems, he always did. Her situation in relation to Adolphe is a recurrent theme in her letters to Tom over the following months. 'I feel quite *at home* with your letter. You say in good words what I have felt for years—this loneliness, the result of not belonging to a milieu, not quite to the one and not quite to the other.'

You tell me you envy 'the great number of Adolphe's personal attractions', but you don't know *what* you envy and you have no idea how happier you are just *as you are....* I should like you to be his friend; I told him just yesterday that I seldom had a friend who inspired in me more 'sécurité' than you do and that is a blessing.... We are happy together Adolphe and I—it can never be a very bright happiness, but instants of quiet intensity and mutual comprehension, through much sadness to some glimpses of joy.

And after Tom and Adolphe had met:

This meeting will have made you better understand the profound and obscure anxiety of my life.... To see marvellous faculties and a fine nature like his going daily towards shipwreck without being able to do anything. Nevertheless I still have some confidence and faith, which I stick to, for it's the only way in which I can help him, the only act of love which I can at present make. And perhaps also you now understand that it did me good to speak to you one day of this heavy secret. I have such great need for truth and I am obliged to remain silent always. Never shall I forget that hour in your room when your good and frank look met mine. I believed that in those eyes I could be completely true.

In the knowledge of subsequent history, Hélène's mention in one of these letters of Adolphe staying happily with his friend Chamberlain at Berchtesgarden strikes an incongruous and sinister note. Berchtesgarden was then the home of the Hungarian Countess Zichy. She had a small theatre in which she encouraged Adolphe to realize his settings for Wagner's musical dramas. Houston Chamberlain, an expatriate Englishman, had written two books on Wagner and was later to marry his daughter, Eva. He was also possessed by a pan-Germanic dream, based on pseudo-scientific racial theories, which he propounded in the two volumes of *Die Grundlagen des xix. Jahrhunderts*, published in 1899 and 1901. This book had considerable and long-lasting appeal in Germany and Austria. Since it naturally appealed to Adolf Hitler, Chamberlain was to play a significant part in the rise of the Nazi movement, and of Wagner's posthumous association with it. Their common interest in the arts, however, not politics, brought Adolphe Appia and Chamberlain together. Both men read Tom's *Altdorfer* with approval while at Berchtesgarden. When Hélène later sent Tom Chamberlain's book he passed it straight on to G. M. Trevelyan, whose comments have not survived.

It was also in the month of June that Tom 'house-dogged' at Spring Terrace while Ricketts and Shannon were in Paris and was for the first time invited to the home of their particular friends, the Michael Fields. Michael Field was the nom de plume of the poetess Katherine Bradley and her niece Edith Cooper, then aged fifty-four and thirty-nine respectively. Katherine was 'Michael' and Edith 'Field' (or Henry) and they used the masculine pronoun in referring to each other. Believing, like the Brontë sisters, that the work of unknown women would not be read with proper seriousness, they had adopted the name for the publication of their first book in 1883. These early lyrics and the verse-dramas, which they composed jointly, aroused admiration, and there was speculation as to the author. For some time the true identity of Michael Field was known only to Robert Browning, who was deeply moved by their work and became tenderly attached to them personally. When the authorship first became common knowledge, the two ladies were considerably sought after and acclaimed. Thereafter, the interest in them and their works gradually waned. Partly, no doubt, for this reason, but also because Edith had become increasingly subject to rheumatic illness, they had then withdrawn into their own partial self-sufficiency and a small circle of the congenially discerning. To this circle Ricketts and Shannon had become progressively more central ever since Will Rothenstein had introduced them a few years previously. In 1898 'the Painters' had found for 'the Poets' The Paragon, a little eighteenth-century house only ten minutes' walk from their own, looking down the river to Richmond Bridge and across to meadows with tall elms and cedars. It was then decorated, furnished, and hung with pictures, largely under Ricketts's direction. The Poets moved in from Edith's family home in Reigate, bringing with them doves, whose cage was hung in the drawing-room, and the adored dog, Whym Chow, who had a large wired run in the otherwise aesthetically satisfying garden. Ricketts designed bindings for their works and jewels for their persons, and both he and Shannon kept a watchful eye on their wardrobes. From their garden the Poets brought flowers, of which Ricketts was extravagantly fond, to Spring Terrace, and they entertained the Painters to exquisite, yet sustaining, dinners. And there was constant exchange and discussion of work completed and in progress.

From 1888 onwards the Michael Fields had kept a journal, a full and fascinating record of their 'Works and Days'. From this it appears that at the time Tom came on the scene, Ricketts was the paramount male figure in Katherine's life; he played capriciously along with her, but, as he was later to acknowledge, felt more admiration and affection for Edith than for any other woman; Edith's thoughts were then much occupied with Bernhard Berenson, whom she had just seen again after a five-year separation. As an artist, Shannon fully sustained his part in the quartet, while as a man, courteous and often silent, he remained aloof from any sentimental cross-involvement.

Tom did not feel immediately at ease with the ladies. 'Their manners, though a second nature,' he wrote later, 'were more elaborate than any I had encountered and intimidated me. . . . They insisted on evening dress, and clothes I wore so rarely were a barrier in themselves.' However, Katherine reacted with characteristic impetuosity to his first visit: 'Moore, the Poet, comes to dine with us. Good at last to have intercourse with a poet, not a critic. Long, he says, he has been promised to meet

Michael Field; but after all Ricketts could not bring us together, he could only bring us round him! . . . We spoke of secrets poets alone can speak to poets about, of things Ricketts mustn't meddle with. . . . I think he impressed me more than any one I have ever met, having a soul of his own—not a will or a temper—a soul.' A few days later he was invited again and talked of the poets he most admired. 'He is thoughtful,' wrote Edith,' and waters his own thoughts from his own fountain—they are home-grown and very fresh.' He soon became 'Tommy' or, sometimes, 'the albatross'. When the poets went for their summer stay in the New Forest, letters were exchanged and Tom sent them the first draft of his verse-play *Omphale and Herakles*. Edith wrote,

Your verse is as fresh as cabbages in a dewy garden. There is scarcely any poet's work that positively creaks with sappiness as yours. . . . Your imagination is full of eyes, it sees almost more than it should, things that are quite *behind* the range of most vision. And you steal up to the gods with the still feet of a savage. . . . Frankly, I don't think you are quite the born dramatist. You are too inquisitive at moments of passion, your dramatic scene is too pictorial for strife, you are too delighted with ideas to forge characters . . . like some of Rodin's work, it [the last Act] seems to me too full of idea, too vague in genesis to be pleasurable and therefore poetically objectified.

In the journal Edith wonderingly noted some errors in spelling committed by 'the dear albatross': 'one's respect and affection grows with every wrong letter'.

Now that *Aphrodite against Artemis* had appeared in print, it was necessary to secure the acting rights by the curious procedure then in force. The play had to be read on the stage of a licensed theatre before a token audience. Two of the performers had to know their parts, a certain sum of money, which could afterwards be returned, had to be collected at the door, and a poster advertising the play displayed outside. Ricketts, who with Shannon formed part of the audience at the Dalston Theatre on 30 July 1901, evidently took a mischievous pleasure in recording his impression of the proceedings:

An Irish Bard and a Death in the Valleys

We all met at the Austrian [Restaurant] like conspirators, chaperoned by Binyon and Streatfield, who had written some occasional music for the play in a beautiful manner. We found the party consisted of a batch of mere boys in their teens, Miss Morris, rather patronizing, and a good-natured, middle-aged actress, Miss Florence Farr, who has figured in countless Stage efforts—Ibsen, etc, etc, etc. T. S. Moore wore a cheap straw hat with a beautiful wavy brim and handed us each a twopenny ticket at the tube as if we were at a school treat. At Dalston the theatre seemed to be closed, and Oldmeadow, the publisher, who was supposed to have been there to manage things was nowhere to be found. I had entered into conversation with Miss Farr about her part in the Countess Cathleen ... Had she found her clothes trying? Yes, she had. 'You see, Mr Yeats had insisted upon my wearing mauve, a most trying colour, a mauve tunic just below the knee, you know, and over that a great common purple cloak ...' Inside the theatre there was a pandemonium of charwomen cleaning the place, clouds of dust on the stage, and a rural scene 'Cottage in the corn' as background. When the curtain was raised, the young chaps who were to read the chorus of Greek girls became so nervous that their part was cut out. Enter Miss Morris from the left, 'Am I to come on now?' There follows a speech inaudible from the back of the stage [front of the auditorium?] answered by Binyon, inaudibly, and during about an hour nervous people walked on and off reading long speeches in inaudible voices, interrupted by noise from the charwomen, ''Arris, are you there?', and by noises from the street, an occasional child's head peering through the scenery. When the play was over and the stage properly strewn with corpses, the curtain man was nowhere to be found, though corpse after corpse sat up and called, 'Curtain!' When Phaedra in a tart voice said, 'Curtain, please!', the man turned round and said, 'Woo says so?' and when told by Aphrodite, the only professional, we wanted the curtain brought down, please, he said, 'You mean the Act Drop, Miss?' I was enchanted by Moore as he listened with a wrapt face all the time; Pissarro and his wife turned up to our surprize, and a pressman, pledged to secrecy, listened from a box. Each reader thought he had been most audible and effective and came forward afterwards to be complimented.

In accepting her part, Miss May Morris had written, 'Reading a

Greek play in cold London daylight, and in modern clothes, is not an easy thing, though in this case the beauty of the language should make it easy. I hope somebody will tell me how to take it; whether rhythmically or "mit Gefühl"; whether the readers recite straight at the audience or whether there is any turn of head or action of hand?' And afterwards, shocked by the actual experience: 'Instead of receiving a copy of your play, I think that all the criminals of that Dalston afternoon ought to be severely punished and reprimanded for so murdering the poetry of it. You would have been much to be pitied if you had heard, but I gather very little of our speech got over the footlights. The Phaedra is immense and I should have loved a chance of doing her something like justice.'

Tom had now to turn his attention to urgent domestic matters, for the home at 39 Southgrove was to be broken up. Nellie had qualified and was to gain experience at Newcastle Infirmary where Dr. Morison, the Head Surgeon, had formerly been assistant to her paternal Uncle George. Bertie was to spend a year in Florence. His parents would hardly have afforded him this opportunity unless he had shown achievement as well as application, yet there is little indication in the letters of where his talents lay. It is recorded that he made for Binyon so faithful a copy of a Raphael drawing that it was taken for an original; and in a letter written the previous December his father remarked, 'Bert makes each of us sit for him daily and there is some prospect of his producing recognizable portraits.' Whatever his technical competence as an artist, it was not felt that he could cope with a studio and life in Florence on his own, so Hettie was to accompany him. She had been taking Italian lessons at the Berlitz School in preparation for their departure early in October. Meanwhile, 39 Southgrove had to be cleared of a seven-year accumulation of possessions and Tom had to find somewhere else to live. More than he perhaps realized at the time, he was to miss the cheerful, dependable family base to which he had grown accustomed, and, in particular, the congenial, tonic companionship of his sister Hettie.

❦

CHAPTER TWELVE

Hobby Horse House and Priest Hill

DURING this unsettling period Tom was working on two articles setting out the aims of the theatre scheme and appealing for support, both financial and histrionic. 'A Plea for an Endowed Stage' and 'The Renovation of the Theatre' were to appear in the January and April 1902 numbers of the *Monthly Review*. He had now completed his elocution course with Florence Farr and, though still doubtful about her method, had gained some understanding of the voice as an instrument, which he was always ready to put into practice. On 6 September, Edith Cooper wrote:

Sturge Moore comes to dinner to read some of his lyrics. His reading is like a Gregorian Chant sung by saints in ecstasy; it is severely modulated and vibrant. It has the peculiar virtue of conveying speed without changing time. He read his 'O swift, O proud' with a passion of intonation, a vocal clang which swept through his hearers, his 'Loki' and then the lovely blank verse lines on the Bacchante of Titian, written before the picture a year ago. . . . We like to think that our white walls have given back the voice of a poet.

Katherine added,

Chow however did not understand. He was disturbed by the sudden fall of unwanted sound on the air, as when I cough or make unearthly cries. He went straight up to Moore and laid his nose affectionately between his knees, with the expression, 'Can I do anything for you, Sir?' I shall never forget it.

Two days later Tom came again to read poems by Browning and Shelley, and was interrupted by the arrival of Logan Pearsall Smith, anxious to discuss his project for a new edition of Palgrave's *Golden Treasury*. 'It is curious how the humble, awkward poet without scholarship dominates the Oxonian gentleman amateur,' Edith noted; and after Tom has left: 'LPS remarks that Moore's simplicity is self-conscious and indulged in, as certain people wear sandals.'

Before long Tom had persuaded Edith to read her poetry to him. This is further evidence of the sense of 'sécurité' that his clear blue eyes inspired, for she shrank from reading her own work aloud. Although she had earlier expressed amusement at the 'sprawling and non-conformist' effect that Tommy made initially, she had now reached the conclusion that he was 'the only suitable person' before whom to risk this self-exposure: 'Tommy hangs with an intentness on the scene that makes me think of the Eagle's above a man who will soon be a corpse—I feel the claws of his interest fasten.' A less happy occasion was that on which Tom came to read the first draft of a one-act play on the Cid, *Roderigo of Bivar*. The Michael Fields listened appreciatively to the first scene, but were then disconcertingly moved to laughter by the heroine's reaction on discovering that her lover had killed her father. 'Tommy is enraged; but seizes the rein of his rage and holds it with self-control.' Such behaviour from auditors apt to be hyper-sensitive to the reception of their own work was indeed affronting and the session was somewhat abruptly terminated. They wrote a letter of explanation rather than apology. Ricketts and Shannon agreed to mediate, but urged the Michael Fields not to give ground, their laughter was after all justified. It was three weeks before Tom came again, at his own request, 'to read a little play on Paris and Oenone'.

We smiled praise on the poet, became good. . . . Of course, after what had occurred and after his own lesson [in a letter] 'that on a first hearing of a poem or play it is fair only to mention what has given pleasure or what if blamed can be easily remedied', we find the play 'very interesting, with a splendid end, etc—but it needs more rapidity.' 'I am glad you like it so much; it is not mine, it is Binyon's.' Now I understand the goatlike malice about Tommy's lips while reading. . . . But this is a hateful revenge, that attacks us with comedy and gives the laugh against us to Binyon and Fay [Ricketts] and those Pan-like lips of the author of Roderigo.

There was a special edge to this prank in that, at this stage, the Michael Fields classed Binyon as one of 'the little Museum people' with whom Tommy insisted on being friendly.

'Tommy' was often the subject of conversation between the Poets and the Artists at this time, and the latter's proprietary attitude emerges strongly. On one occasion, when Ricketts had been speaking of the difficulty they had had in getting their achievements recognized, Edith noted, 'they hope to train up Tommy to be a sort of Ruskin to them. He has elements of the preacher, and therefore of success in England.' On another occasion they had been in reminiscent mood: 'Tommy was found at Croydon and transferred by Rox [Shannon] to Lambeth, 'I made him with my own hands,' boasts his master. 'Tommy is handmade,' we cry together. . . . He [Ricketts] tells me whenever I am in doubt about myself to think of a Tuscan portrait. I suppose he thinks he has handmade me into an Isolta Simonetta.'

To Ricketts's disappointment, Tom in his search for accommodation, 'missed by a few hours the old rooms in Red Lion Square occupied by Rossetti and later by B.-J. and Morris. It would have been great fun if he had taken them.' However, he was well pleased by the rooms Tom finally took in 20 Fitzroy Street, which also had creative, if less famous, associations. The house belonged to the architect and designer A. H. Mackmurdo, who had originally lived there with that man of many talents Herbert P. Horne, the poet Lionel Johnson, and the Selwyn Images. Mackmurdo had founded the Century Guild Workshops, and from 1886 to 1892 Horne and Image had together produced the Century Guild's magazine, *The Hobby Horse*, a handsome folio precursor of *The Dial*. Although the community had been broken up by Horne's remove to Florence and Lionel Johnson's death, the house was still known as Hobby Horse House and the Selwyn Images were still there. A young doctor called Hulbert was now a lodger and Tom was to take Horne's former rooms; as the resident landlord, Mackmurdo was responsible for providing their meals and domestic service. The melancholy move from 39 Southgrove took place at the end of September, with the usual complications; the removal men arrived hours late; Tom's desk jammed so firmly in the stairway that Nana's husband, Mr. White, had to cut a slice out of the bannisters. In a state of exhaustion, Tom went down to Limpsfield for a long weekend with the Pyes.

Hettie and Bertie recovered at Cheriton before setting out on their progress to Florence, of which Hettie, a ready correspondent, kept Tom informed. First Rouen and then Paris, where the Appias were able to give them many useful introductions and had already arranged hospitality for them on arrival in Florence. Marie took Hettie to see the 'charmante, petite' new headquarters of the Seine Branch of the Y.W.C.A. After experiencing the crowded steamy room there, which could provide meals for a hundred members, Hettie felt that 'it would be rather more "charmante" if it were rather less "petite".' Altogether, Hettie seems to have found herself more at home when they reached Cousine Hélène's apartment in Geneva. There were two swallows' nests over the front door, and it was 'old, roomy and peaceful. It faces on to a quiet by-street and the other side looks on to a pretty court with a chestnut tree in the middle. It is on a little hill so you look right over the houses to the lake and the mountains beyond.' While there they called on other Appia relations, and dined with Hélène's brother Paul, 'very neatly dressed and extremely vivacious'. He was the father of Marie's god-daughter Geneviève, 'a thin, lively, intelligent-looking little being'. On their subsequent journey, with stays in Milan and Bologna, Hettie described Bertie as being 'torn between desire to economise and fear lest I should suffer discomfort'.

By the end of October they were in Florence, lodging with worthy friends of the Appias, of whom Hettie drew portraits not untinged with irony for Tom's benefit. Unlike Bertie, she was not prepared to be accepted as a member of the religious sect to which they belonged, for we are inclined to think small beer of their service and their ideas which are like those of a dissenting community in England. ... I would willingly go to their church, for I want to get to know them and be allowed to help in their dispensary clothing club and such like, but if they cannot have me without I subscribe to their creed (and perhaps it is mean of me to try to get the advantages without the disadvantages), I must try to find some other way of being philanthropical, for I think *all ladies* (at least all ordinary ones) ought to try to be so.

She was allowed to help in the dispensary, and so joined a group of philanthropic ladies of mixed provenance—Dutch, American, a Russian princess, a Scotswoman of royal descent. No less than her experience as a rent collector, Hettie's humane appreciation of the comic will have made her a valuable member. When Bertie had found a studio to his liking with Herbert Horne's help, they moved into lodgings with a non-English-speaking family.

A letter that Marie had begun in the Valleys and finished in Paris after Hettie and Bertie's visit must have reached Tom in the middle of October.

I have often thought of you this summer. But you have not been aware of it. Alas! you will have guessed that we have spent this summer very differently from any other, and letter-writing has more than ever been difficult for me, because of so much to do and above all from lack of courage. I knew from my cousin Hélène, whom I had the pleasure of seeing for a few hours in Geneva in July, that you had been thinking of us. But may I say this? Amongst the flood of telegrams and letters, the numerous expressions of sympathy, your brief lines, your long silence seemed to us a coldness on your part, in you who know our family life, who had known and appreciated our Henry. No doubt there are wounds that most need silence, that the least touch re-opens and makes bleed. But believe, O son of cold Albion, that true sympathy, which comes from the heart, which weeps with the heart that weeps, very rarely comes amiss.

Marie then explained that she, her mother, and Caroline had felt the need of a few days in the healing atmosphere of the Maison des Diaconesses before taking up life at home again. After thanking

Tom for sending her *Mariamne*, his Reynolds article, and more translations of Emerson, she turned to their debate on responsibility for the gulf between Christians and non-Christians. This letter evidently moved Tom to propose an early visit to Paris, for there are two communications from Marie about the difficulties in fixing a date. Their spare room was occupied until Tante Louise made up her mind when she was going to Cannes, as she usually did during the winter months, and though Caroline was temporarily in Belgium, collecting material for a memoir of Henry, she might return at any time. It must eventually have been decided that it would be better to wait until the spring. From Marie's second letter it is clear that Tom had expressed dissatisfaction with himself and a want of inspiration in his work. He had also mentioned his recent acquaintance with the young French art critic, Bréal, who had known Marie as a child and was now married and a neighbour of the Pyes. Marie remembered the vivacity of this 'ancien compagnon': 'Mais pourquoi au monde ont ils été se fixer en Angleterre quand ils ont le bonheur d'avoir la France pour patrie?' She added a fierce postscript, referring to what Tom had written about her mother's mourning state. 'How can you think that she could ever "wholly recover" from such a thing? I trust that none of us will ever recover from a wound of this kind. The place of our brother will always remain the same in our hearts; we guard ourselves jealously against forgetfulness and consolation.'

Tom was not happy in his new accommodation, relegated to bachelor quarters, having meals in common with Hulbert who, though 'a very nice fellow', was not a chosen companion. The household was, moreover, badly managed. The Michael Fields had known Hobby Horse House in its heyday, when Selwyn Image had designed the binding for their *Tragic Mary*, and Herbert Horne had invited them to the first Arnold Dolmetsch concerts, held in his rooms. They were shocked at the change when Tom invited them to tea: 'There is something ill about the place—it looks dirty and has an isolated air.' They procured some striped chintz from Liberty's to cover Tom's sofa, and urged him to have the main room redecorated 'with one *light* wall'. But Tom then thought he would move elsewhere in the spring, perhaps find a cottage near the Pyes in Limpsfield, and meanwhile there was one great compensation in the shape of Selwyn Image. 'He is quite wonderful, almost a saint in some ways—always serene and comfort-creating; his wife is very nice too.' Image had gone up to Oxford in 1863 destined, in the tradition of his family, for the church. While there he had attended Ruskin's Slade lectures and felt drawn towards a different vocation. After eight years as a curate in London he relinquished holy orders for art, and became mainly a designer—of stained-glass windows, of endpapers and title-pages and other applied decoration. Besides being a loving observer of birds and flowers, he was a master lepidopterist, breeding beautiful Japanese moths in his rooms. At the time of Tom's arrival he was lecturing on the 'Desecration of Bloomsbury'. There are many testimonies to the sweetness of his nature, his courtesy, and consideration; 'the sort of person', Michael Field observed, 'who sees that people put their toes in mustard baths when they are ill'.

Afternoon tea appears to have been the only meal at Hobby Horse House that could be given a distinctive flavour. After his first visit Ricketts commented, 'the dear chap was very nice, having got us some extra special cake', and there is record of Tom serving delicacies such as Hymettus honey and rose-petal jam. He dined out more than ever, took Nana to the pantomime, and spent many evenings with Yeats after his return from Ireland in November, 'full of the success of *Grania* in Dublin'. At weekends he seems seldom to have remained in London. Bob Trevelyan, who had recently dedicated a book of poems to Tom, welcomed him at the Mill House, Dorking, where Roger Fry was a near neighbour. In December G. M. Trevelyan asked him down to Cambridge to discuss the forthcoming theatre articles; of all George's interested Cambridge friends he was the most actively enthusiastic about the theatre scheme. He was collecting names of likely supporters and was prepared to finance the circulation of the articles in pamphlet form to them, to Lord Rosebery in particular. Much of their discussion took place on a long walk, interrupted only 'by bread and chicken under a haystack', in that north-east wind that blows straight across the Cambridgeshire flats from Siberia. They breakfasted with Lytton Strachey: 'he and George Trevy agreed together that I had no imagination because I was not so enthusiastic about Shelley as they considered it necessary to be'. Later the Moore brothers played ping-pong together, and Tom was pleased to talk about Adolphe Appia's work with John Pollock, a history student, who had become deeply interested in stagecraft and was just off to study the workings of the theatre in Vienna.

Most frequently, however, weekends were spent at Priest Hill, often with Binyon and occasionally Yeats as well. W. A. Pye, who from the first had been involved in the theatre scheme, had devised a little collapsible stage which could be erected in an alcove in the north room. The pattern on Sundays therefore became rehearsing scenes in the morning, walks in the afternoon, and in the evening either reading aloud or playing ping-pong, a game which seems suddenly to have penetrated every spacious household in the country. Sybil later remembered Tom as having 'a particularly fierce and effective service, but too kind to win when playing against us girls'. Bréal often formed one of the party and some-times brought with him the French painter Simon Bussy, the appearance of whose name in Tom's letters perplexed Henrietta; she knew, of course, who 'Trevy' and 'Binny' were, but who was 'Bussy'?

None of these activities or associates, not even Yeats, explains how it was that Tom then fell under suspicion of being 'a Polish conspirator'. Unknown to himself, he was for a time under police surveillance, which was only lifted after members of the staff of the British Museum had been narrowly questioned about this tall, bearded figure, who, like so many others, came and went with papers under his arm. Such misdirected zeal naturally diverted all Tom's friends greatly.

Tom spent Christmas at Cheriton. There was now quite a Moore colony at Cockington, for Daniel's sister Selina had moved there after her husband's death, and his elder brother had then come from Jersey to join them. The family circle was, of course, not complete; Harry, though now again pleased to visit his parents, was kept away by his duties as curate in Kirkby Lonsdale, and the absence of Hettie and Bertie was keenly felt.

Back in London, after the first theatre article had appeared, Tom wrote to Bob Trevelyan.

Though millionnaires and supporters with influential names have made no response to my appeal for a renaissance of English Drama, young ladies desirous of performing, or at least of attaining eloquence, have responded and I have regular weekly engagements with them, and think so far I am not wasting my time. One of my friend Pye's girls has proved very encouraging; she is very sensible and extremely delicate—if there were more substance I think she would go far. Miss Wilson, 'the lady with the terrible eyes', is also much improved.

Mona Wilson, daughter of Canon Wilson of Clifton College, was, in fact, a Rossetti-like beauty, and also the first woman to achieve seniority in the Civil Service. Other pupils included Roger Fry's sister Isabel, Miss Calhoun, an American, and two with considerable amateur experience, Miss Flora Mayor and Mrs. Gwendoline Bishop, who later married Clifford Bax. The last Tom considered 'the best naturally endowed of any I have tried. Her voice is very good and her manner without any obvious fault. Though I may have some trouble with her when it comes to gesture . . .'. The rather older Miss Fanny Johnson, whose father was a Cambridge philosopher, had written short plays herself, and Tom valued her suggestions of suitable plays to read: Maeterlinck's *The Blind*, Ibsen's *Love's Comedy*, Verhaeren's *The Dawn*, and Webster's *The Duchess of Malfi*. After some personal tuition the students progressed to rehearsing plays for informal performance. Among those performed were Goldsmith's *The Good-natur'd Man* and *Twelfth Night*, of which Fisher could unfortunately later only remember 'the rich deep voice of Selwyn Image and Yeats' droll mismanagement of a soda-water syphon'.

Both Sybil and Ethel Pye attended Tom's classes; it was Sybil who proved so promising. After her father had expressed some concern lest she should overtire herself, Tom wrote to her:

... if I have yielded to the temptation which your success and kind alacrity created, I hope you will forgive me. In all arts respect for the materials with which the artist deals is an absolute law. And in elocution and acting that material is part of the artist and still better reason has he to be extremely careful not to overstrain it. . . . 'Use all gently' as Hamlet says, and I have no doubt you will achieve splendid results as well as establishing your own health.

As Keats complained it is terribly hard when our minds become filled with the idea of excellence 'to have to stop short and be nothing', but though it is hard it is well worth while. I was for many years almost incapacitated by weakness and am still far from strong, but I do not count the quiet and still times the least useful or least successful, quite the other way.

He suggested that sometimes she should just watch the rehearsals; such observation would be helpful to her, the performers, and to him: 'I feel a great confidence in your good sense and the centrality of your disposition.' In thanking him for these 'kind and encouraging words', Sybil wrote,

I do not think rehearsing really tires me except after I have been teaching; in the morning I have to be so much on the alert all the time, and then the keeping up of one's enthusiasm in all subjects so that one can transmit it to the children is rather a strain sometimes. So that I occasionally feel as if I had not much brain left for other things.

The verses Tom was now writing for Sybil's pupils evidently played a considerable part in their learning. His aim was to express in simple form the joy and edification that children could derive from everyday experiences and actions, such as eating, washing, sleeping, walking barefoot. The original form was often changed in the light of the children's reactions. The verse on hands, for

Charles Ricketts, from a pastel by
William Rothenstein

Self-portrait by Charles Shannon, from a lithograph

Robert Trevelyan

'Our Brother Tom'

Marie, aged twenty-two

instance, underwent considerable alteration. 'I am inclined to think,' wrote Sybil, 'it is rather a mistake to introduce the question of blood into the Hand poem, especially if written for children as young as mine. They were very pleased with the idea of a poem on the hand and seemed distinctly interested at first, but the latter part passed very much over their heads. They were all very delighted with the "little woodmouse" and the "geese", too.' Although Tom argued that blood was something children knew, and ought to know about, the final version was bloodless. '. . . little Nicholas was very enthusiastic and wanted to learn it at once! The children were especially pleased I think with the idea of the "hands of soldiers and of kings" having once been helpless baby hands; it was difficult enough for them to realize that their own hands had ever been so weak (not even able to pick up the pencil box, as Harold put it) without thinking of strong grown up hands.' Somewhat later Sybil wrote,

I sometimes find it difficult to get at their opinions of the poems; they are not naturally critical at this age, or rather not given to *pronouncing* judgement on everything they hear, and I think it is better that they should not be; so I am loth to say 'What do you think of this?' too pointedly. But when they know the poems they ask to hear the ones they particularly like; the other day someone remarked that we had not heard the sleeping one for sometime, and as soon as I had read it Harold said, 'Oh, Miss Pye, if I'd remembered it was like that, I would have asked for it *long* ago!' It was such genuine and spontaneous admiration that I thought I must pass it on to you. [The 'sleeping poem' was the lullaby written for Marie's god-daughter eight years previously.]

After expressing his pleasure at this tribute, Tom continued,

I wish you would always tell me what you think about the poems, I have a deep respect for your opinion, far more than my contentious disposition has, I fear, allowed to appear. Indeed, I am always defeating my desire to learn and always very vexed at doing it. . . . Your instructions have not been thrown away on me, for yesterday I won Image's sincere commendation for the salad dressing [made to her recipe], though it was a little too salt, and in view of this I hope you will consent to impress your thoughts about the poems on me and not merely content yourself with reporting how the children take them.

Sybil had been chosen to play the role of Oenone in Binyon's play *Paris and Oenone*:

You must begin to think out the action, always remembering that the fewer the gestures the better. Large, slow, rhythmic movements are I believe the secret of dignity on the stage. I wish you had seen Frau Klafsky [the Hungarian soprano famous for her Wagnerian roles], then you would know how they could be combined with passion and vehemence. But I very much expect you will know in spite of having missed her. Miss Johnson told me that it was her experience that no one could teach well who had not a gift for acting.

In writing to Tom for his thirty-second birthday, Marie sent special good wishes for the success of the theatre project. She also asked if he could be of assistance to her cousin, Julien Monod, who wanted to work for a year in a good London bank. Through what channels Tom fulfilled this request is not recorded, but fulfil it he did and in due course became firm friends with this young man, 'who works too hard, like most Frenchmen'. He was equally successful in providing for the needs of a theological student cousin spending a fortnight in London, as Marie gratefully acknowledged: 'You are a guardian angel to all our young cousins staying in London, and I cannot thank you enough for your great kindness to Jean Vallette who has returned full of the memory of your goodness.' That other cousin, Ernest Guy, was not now in need of advice or hospitality, for he had for some months been in Australia, on a secret mission connected with the wool trade. He maintained a provocative correspondence with Tom, who continued to guide his reading of English literature. He was considering whether to return home by way of America, with a pursuit of Ida Kruse in mind, or to have a look at the French in Quebec, or to take the opportunity of exploring Japan.

Hettie and Bertie, meanwhile, had endured an unexpectedly cold winter in Florence. Neither of them was given to complaining, and Hettie continued to describe occurrences and characters with much of her usual relish, but at the end of February she remarked in a letter to Tom,

I am sorry you do not make jokes any more and hope you won't forget how. I miss them terribly. I have to make all the conversation now so you may judge how gay it is. Poor Bertie is so beset with fear of wasting time that he seems to me to get slower and slower. Naturally being alone in the studio all day is not enlivening and his careful calculations do not allow for any sociabilities or 'sillyings about'. I am out a great deal as I have always hitherto accepted all invitations for walks, picnics, afternoon calls etc, so I detail my experiences and have occasionally tried jokes, but these have been met with such ponderous literalness as does not encourage.

After having been persuaded to accept an evening invitation to the Berensons, 'poor Bertie' himself had written, 'When all these people treat me so kindly and respectfully I sometimes feel that they might be treating me so because they expect from me a capacity like yours or George's, and that they might be rather disgusted when they find I have not got it, but am decidedly dull. However, I must do what I can'.

Tom decided to spend the money earned by the two theatre articles on a fortnight in Florence, before the week now fixed for his visit to Paris early in May. Binyon was persuaded to accompany him. He had hoped that he would also meet Cousine Hélène there, for she was making an Italian tour at the time, but to their mutual regret she arrived the day after he left. She stayed a month and was a great consolation to Hettie. Of Tom's first experience of the riches of Florence there is no record, only a postcard to his parents saying that they had spent a night in Pisa on the way and arrived to 'find Hettie and Bertie well, but subdued'. When he had left, Hettie sent a note after him to explain that she had not said goodbye properly, 'because I did not like the people to see me crying'. She was worried, too, because Tom did not seem as well as when he had left 39 Southgrove.

'I'm afraid Hettie alarmed you unnecessarily about my health.

Anyway Paris did me a great deal of good,' Tom wrote to his parents. He had found the Appias 'all pretty well, though Aunt Helen is often absent in expression'. He had visited John Tweed at Rodin's home in Meudon, and while he was there Rodin had returned unexpectedly from Switzerland:

He has an enormous establishment like a factory and he works constantly. Mme Rodin told Tweed he used to work even while he was taking his meals. Now, he is, of course, quite rich, but he must spend a great sum on the work he is doing as his processes are very elaborate and he keeps several casters constantly employed and a great number of sculptors, perhaps 30, and several men of all work. . . . He was very nice to me and talked a good deal, yet thought it necessary to send me apologies by Tweed because he was tired after the journey. . . . Adolphe Appia arrived [the following morning] and I had some talk with him before going to lunch with Tweed and two French friends, and about 4 o'clock I met him again and had more talk in a restaurant. In the evening I went to a Bach concert with Marie and Caroline. Ernest has been to dinner; he is full of his travels, specially in Japan. I am to lunch with him Vendredi. Today I am going to church and then to the Louvre or Salon with Marie, and possibly Uncle and Caroline. Monday last I called on Pissarro's father; he was very charming. Pissarro was there too and Tuesday morning I went with him to see the Wood Engravings at the Beaux Arts. The catalogue and hanging are about as faulty as they could be; however, my things haven't suffered, though Image's name does not even appear . . .

A small engagement diary of Tom's for 1902 has survived. The only entries in it are for the five days beginning on 13 May. The first reads, 'Returned from Paris. Bussy's show—met Bob and wife. Tea with Bin. Made resolutions concerning discipline and M. and S.' On the 15th he wrote to Marie, first enlarging on something he had said to her about Adolphe.

A nature so rich as his in many ways where I am of exceptional poverty must always be attractive to me, but at the same time his apparent despair made me feel a little afraid of him, made me ask myself if in ten years time I might not also have given up the struggle against evil. He told me that a certain drink he was taking was a very fatal mental poison, and that it was gaining a hold on him. I said, 'Then why do you continue to take it?' He said, 'Why do you ask that? Look at me!' And he took my hand and squeezed it and smiled so sadly. . . . I think the position he takes up on certain questions amounts to anarchy, just as I think the position held by Ernest and Raymond [Penel] in regard to women amounts to anarchy. . . . Though I can see things from more or less a large and unprejudiced point of view, I cannot bring myself to feel them so; my temper is narrow and sectarian, which makes it very difficult for me to create and retain relations with people whom my judgement condemns, and my consciousness of this difficulty and desire to minimize it often puts me into the false position of seeming to acquiesce in things and judgements which really are in direct contradiction to my convictions. I am always more or less in this difficulty when talking to Ernest and felt the same thing with Adolphe; often the best I can do is to say nothing.

It did me a great deal of good to talk with you and I only wished we could have talked more, as naturally it is the disagreements which get discussed first and are the least profitable. You have no idea how lonely I am in regard to the things which occupy the first place in my thoughts; I have no friends who are willing to treat such matters as open questions or, if they will allow them to be open, want to treat them seriously or regard them as important. Yet it seems to me that if the business of poetry is to find a spiritual interpretation of the world, as Matthew Arnold believed, there are no questions of greater importance or that more concern a poet. But all my aesthetic friends want to sever art from morals entirely, while I am always working at uniting them. At the bottom we are all so horribly afraid of the darkness that we try to keep as much in one mental locality as possible, yet the only chance of finding something really solid would seem to lie in groping about and feeling after what we cannot see but desire to find. It was a very great pleasure to me to find your outlook so much nearer to mine than it used to be, and I think my aims have grown much nearer to yours, though of them we did not speak.

Several of Tom's friends had before this decided that as 'ambassador of the Renascent Theatre' he ought to possess a dress suit. Ricketts and Shannon had supervised the purchase of this. He wore it for the first time the day this letter was written, at a dinner in honour of Rodin, largely organized by Tweed:

MacColl's and Wyndham's speeches were very good. Rodin looked very pleased. After dinner the Slade and South Kensington students were admitted to hear the speeches and at the end of the evening they took the horse out of Rodin's cab and dragged it from the Café Royal to the Arts Club, where the servant had to be called up from bed to prepare them a supper, which was not over till 3 in the morning. Shannon and I left shortly after 12. We were all photographed by Flash light. Shannon was visible in the print, but I was behind a pillar. I enjoyed the evening very well.

The Michael Fields now asked Tom to bring Yeats to dinner with them. Besides the usual exquisite repast, with which three choice wines were served, they prepared wreaths of green smilax for this occasion, which Edith recorded on 6 June:

Yeats and Tommy come.... His shyness makes Tommy more familiar. The stranger manifests that we are somewhat intimate after a year's friendship. It is an easeful truth. At dinner Yeats is fearfully shy at first, doctrinaire and 'causy', but he gradually becomes warm and vivid in his monologuising. He is dark with a Dantesque face—only not cut in Italian marble. His hair dribbles in a Prottlethwaite manner over his brow.... His eyes are abstract and fervid; when he speaks of spiritual things and shakes back his forelock, there is a smile like an atmosphere on his eyes and brow. The mouth is for speech—speech—the hands flap like flames. At first the gesture spells one; then it irritates, because it is a gesture and is not varied. We put on our smilax wreaths. Tommy looks like a primaeval forest god, terrible and the source of panic and of the cruel laughter of simplicity. Yeats feels he is wearing spectacles and the twine looks conventionally poetic on his hair. Then we cast the wreaths on to Whym Chow's neck.

Yeats is not of us—as Tommy and the Artists and Bernhard [Berenson] are; he is a preacher. He preaches some excellent things and some foolish things. He knows our plays well and seems to care for them with insight.... His wit is rhetorical not the instinctive mischief and drollery, the moment's wild happiness in some contrast, that is so engaging in Tommy.

Yeats reads a little prayer to the psaltery—a most charming poem—all the archangels appear with shoes of the 17 metals. Also he entoned as if to the psaltery Keats' Bacchic Ode. . . . We have been saying that we envy men their conversations with each other. 'Men don't talk well with each other, they talk well to women. There must be sex in good talk,' says Yeats. Tommy, lying Panlike on the sofa, echoes this with fervour. 'A man has no ideas among men—but he goes home to a cook or a countess and he is all right,' sings Yeats. Therefore he is a believer in many flirtations and believes that Goethe's wisdom was born to him of women.

Some days later Katherine attended a lecture recital by Yeats and Florence Farr in the Hall of Cliffords Inn and afterwards commented,

In speaking to the psaltery there is nothing of further accomplishing in speech. Music trifles a little, that is all. I did not like hearing Florence Farr taking Shelley's Pan on her lips. Her voice has been trained, but there is no ancestry in it. . . . But what an audience, and Yeats doomed to lecture and strive artificially to recall the figure of the poet with the lyre. . . . It was ghostly as waxworks are ghostly, too solid for a real ghost.

At the back of the Hall crowded with notable literary figures and drama critics Tom was standing with Binyon 'in a frightful draught. Yeats was not as good as I had been led to expect. However the evening was a success on the whole, though Mrs. Emery [Florence Farr] was simply awful in Atalanta in Calydon, tearing rhythm, sense and everything else to rags.'

The psaltery played by Florence Farr had been made for her by Arnold Dolmetsch, 'the only man in the world now', as Yeats wrote to him, 'who knows anything about the old music which was half speech.' Dolmetsch had discovered that Yeats could not recognize the inflexions of his own voice, and so could only accompany himself rhythmically. Florence Farr, on the other hand, could accompany her 'golden voice' tonally, and reciting in a small room achieved an entrancing melodious effect. In the projecting of her voice in a larger auditorium, however, the harmony was often lost. Eventually Yeats, rather brutally describing Florence Farr as 'a chalk egg on which I have been sitting for years', abandoned the attempt to get verse spoken as he wished on the conventional stage. At this time, however, he was in crusading mood, and in the training of the young ladies was concentrating, with Dolmetsch's help, on chanting to the psaltery. Tom, whose ear was probably neither more nor less musically sensitive than Yeats's, had so far been concerned only with unaccompanied speaking.

On Friday 20 June Tom received an urgent card from Marie. Her father would be arriving in London early on Monday morning as the French delegate at the reception to be held for King Lewanika, the Christian chieftain of the Barotse on the Zambesi. Would Tom be so kind as to arrange accommodation for her father? A note of commissions and instructions from Caroline followed by hand, stressing the need to direct and watch over her increasingly absent-minded father, who must be reminded to take his spectacles 'and if he goes out in the evening must have his shawl or paletot'. So fearful was Tom of oversleeping that he got up and arrived at the station an hour early, and the train arrived an hour late. He brought his uncle back to breakfast,

and we spent some time, I copying out his speech for the afternoon and he writing letters. Then we went to the British Museum. I got Streatfield to show him the Medal Department, where he was much interested in some medals of John Huss, and afterwards in seeing the tile records of the deluge and the Coronation Exhibition, where he made me copy out the prayer said while the crown is placed on the head. . . . After that we had lunch at the Express Dairy Company and I took him to the tube station as he had to go to the city and I had to get back as two of my ladies were coming. I met him again at the Bible Society's after the Reception of King Lewanika and took him on a bus to Nellie's, where we had dinner and Annie came in to coffee afterwards. Either he caught a cold on the bus, or in my bed (I slept on the sofa downstairs), not being accustomed to sleeping with open windows. On Tuesday I took him to Wilton Crescent near Hyde Park, where he was invited to a private audience with King Lewanika. That afternoon I went to the Constitutional Club to meet Herbert Swears, a man in the Bank of England connected with 5 or 6 dramatic Clubs, who has undertaken to find men for our experimental performances. . . . We [Tom and his uncle] dined at an ABC, off eggs, not by my will but by his, and then went to Exeter Hall where we found a French prayer meeting in progress, in which Uncle joined and gave the news from Paris. . . .

He seemed much impressed by the King's [Edward VII's] illness and looked upon it as providential, as designed to fit the king for the responsibilities which he had appeared to be undertaking in rather too light a spirit. He was as much absorbed in his interests as ever and, apart from the cold he took which was already better by the time he left, appeared in very good health. He said poor Aunt Helen was feeling the anniversary of her 3 weeks watching and waiting . . .

This long chronicle letter to his parents, written a fortnight after Uncle Appia's visit, recounts two other episodes. Binyon, who had been commissioned to write a play for Mrs. Patrick Campbell, had invited Tom to meet her in his rooms.

She was very much the actress in private life and her manners were not such as one would desire to have considered as a model. She is finer to look at close than on the stage, but constantly talked about other actresses in a most petty and spiteful spirit—all except Sarah Bernhardt for whom she expressed a monstrous adoration. Mr. and Mrs. [S. Arthur] Strong came in to tea too. . . . They want Mrs. Pat to put on Agamemnon and play Cassandra. He was a great friend of Renan's and is reckoned a first rate scholar, is Librarian to the Duke of Devonshire and the House of Lords and is supposed to be very influential and a terrible enemy if you offend him.

This formidable person, who was also an art connoisseur and Professor of Arabic at London University, took an immediate liking to Tom and his works and was to prove the reverse of an enemy.

The other occurrence was included at Nellie's special request. She, like Annie, was now again working in London; she felt she had learned a great deal as an anaesthetist at Newcastle Infirmary, through watching Dr. Morison at work, for 'the operations were so neatly and quickly performed, and he was so simple about it and made no fuss'. When Yeats left for Ireland at the end of June, Nellie and her friend Miss Roberts moved into his rooms in Woburn Buildings. And there Miss Roberts was at once bitten by a bed bug. Mrs. Old, the servant Yeats inherited from Arthur Symons, was most indignant and insisted that Miss Roberts must have brought the bug with her, 'but she thoroughly searched the room and parafinned the bed and used Keatings with a lavish hand and Miss Roberts had a quiet night, though Nellie was not sure whether she had been bitten'. Mrs. Old was hardly candid, for Yeats had already told Tom of a similar occasion, in which he had finally caught a bug and kept it under a wine glass for her to see before she could be persuaded to take action. Henrietta was not able to respond with Nellie's buoyancy to a domestic drama of this kind. Indeed, it only heightened her regret that these children had left the healthy air of Highgate for the dark heart of London, where, according to newspaper reports, 'diseases raged'. She checked, very rightly, on their vaccinations against smallpox, and urged them both at least to take as much exercise as possible.

During Yeats's absence, Tom was left in charge of the ladies who spoke to the psaltery as well as his own protégées. He was already extremely occupied. His *Danaë* was shortly to be set up at Ballantyne's, and he was helping the Pissarros with the printing of *Peau d'Ane*. Oldmeadow was most anxious to publish his verse-play on Absalom, and this he had been reluctantly convinced needed revision after Katherine Bradley had written, 'Trevy and Binyon are right to say things are too long, and not say why. It is the hand of a friend laid on a shoulder; "You bore me, stop!"' Another play, on Judith, was going the rounds in its first draft; three evocations of Greek myth in dialogue form were not quite ready for publication; D. S. MacColl had written an article on Rodin which demanded an answer; the Vale Shakespeare was still not completed. Moreover, he was now house-hunting again.

Though Bertie was to stay on in Florence until the spring, he was now sufficiently well established there to manage on his own. In August, he and Hettie were to visit Sienna, Perugia, and Assisi on their bicycles, and then Hettie would be returning to England. She needed considerable reassurance that Tom really wanted her to set up house with him again. As matters then stood, there was no more welcome home-maker he could hope for.

CHAPTER THIRTEEN

✤

Two Proposals

RICKETTS and Shannon had recently moved from Richmond to Holland Park. They had been offered the spacious studio-flat on the top floor of Lansdowne House, a tall building erected at the bottom of Lansdowne Road by their most munificent patrons, Sir Edmund and Lady Davis. This was an upward step in more than one way, reflecting as it did the now established reputation of the two men as creative artists in their different fields. The fruits of their remarkably wide-ranging connoisseurship could here be displayed with fastidious abandon and were appreciated by a growing circle. Even this aesthetic establishment found room for a ping-pong table, on which Shannon and Tom were fairly equal contestants. The Michael Fields, at first greatly afflicted by what they could only regard as a desertion, bitterly referred to the new home as 'The Palace', though Ricketts assured Katherine that the lift would be strewn with roses when she visited, and the Artists continued to dine at The Paragon every Thursday evening. Ricketts confided to his diary that the years at Richmond had been the happiest of his life—'leaving meant the end of youth'.

In mid September Tom jubilantly informed Bob Trevelyan that he had rented 20 St. James's Square, Holland Park, 'only 7 minutes from Shannon, with a garden, hot and cold bathroom, 4 bedrooms, 3 sitting rooms, kitchen, scullery, pantry, cellars, cupboards, etc. for £55'. Pending Hettie's return, however, he remained at Hobby Horse House, now renamed 'The Chantry' by Roger Fry. There were weekly chanting sessions with Dolmetsch and Florence Farr and now also Miss Owen, a friend of Yeats's benefactress Miss Horniman, who accompanied herself on a small harp and, in Tom's view, chanted more successfully than Florence Farr. He had become infected by Yeats's enthusiasm, and was convinced that Bob could learn to chant with his wife Bessie's help; he tried to convert the young art student, Wyndham Lewis, who read his own sonnets with such powerful effect, but he expressed a dislike of 'operatic reading'. Among his lady students Tom had become much in demand, socially and vocally. At Mona Wilson's, her cousin, Henry Sidgwick, professed a desire to take lessons in elocution; Miss Calhoun wept for Mariamne at an evening reading; Isabel Fry invited Tom and Bertrand Russell to dinner together and the renewal of this acquaintance revealed an 'extraordinary similarity' in literary taste, leading to further meetings. Entries in the Michael Field journal, such as 'Tommy comes and stays for 6 hours', show that these friends were not as a result neglected. They had now asked him to become their literary executor.

Arthur Strong had also several times invited Tom, both to read to him and his archaeologist wife Eugenie and for discussions on the book he wanted written for the Library of Art series he was editing. On one of these occasions Holman Hunt was present; he was so impressed by Tom's appearance that he first declared he had the face of a saint and then that he would look splendid in Cesare Borgia's clothes. 'Of course,' said Ricketts, 'he would like to do him in magenta and ultramarine as a Believer.' A forewarning of further work ahead came from G. M. Trevelyan, who with Lowes Dickinson and others was planning a new review 'with really good literary, artistic and dramatic sections. My own admiration of your prose and poems is shared by all members of the committee, who earnestly hope for your help.' An invitation to discuss this matter further at Wallington, the family home in Northumberland, had to be refused as it coincided with a trip to Bruges already arranged with Binyon. Meanwhile, the reply to MacColl's article on Rodin had appeared in the *Monthly Review*. Tom was astonished at the mixed reception. While his brother George, one of his severest critics, approved, as did Desmond MacCarthy, John Tweed pronounced it incomprehensible and Will Rothenstein was so enraged that he sprang to MacColl's defence in the *Saturday Review*. Roger Fry, too, appeared to find the article over-contentious, but at the time of writing he was overridingly concerned with an encounter of his own with Ricketts. He maintained that because he admired Ricketts's and Shannon's work he had persistently endeavoured to remain on good terms with them; on this occasion, however, a remark he had made about Bréal had been met with such dismissive scorn of himself and Bréal and their pretentions as art critics that he vowed he would never go there again, 'but let us have a wrangle before long. I enjoy that because you are a person with whom one not only *must* but *can* differ, which is a great thing.'

On her way back to England Hettie stayed a few days at the Airals Blancs. Marie had always been on spontaneously affectionate terms with Sarah, but hitherto, as she later confessed, she had found Hettie somewhat intimidating; she now learnt to know and appreciate her better. At this time, one or more of Henry's children usually spent their summer holidays in the Valleys and Marie was so occupied with her two eldest nephews, Théodore and William, that it was not until Hettie had gone on to Cousine Hélène's that she found time to answer Tom's letter of 15 May. She paid particular attention to the suggestion in the first paragraph that he might some time lose 'the desire to struggle against evil': 'But Tom, how can you think this? I re-read this phrase a number of times, asking myself if I had misread it. When one has tried, as you have until now, to fight against what is evil and ugly, one has faith in oneself and should not even suppose that one might stop on so good a path.' On the difficulty of maintaining a candid relationship with people of whose conduct one could not approve she greatly sympathized, but urged openness and, above all, perseverance in the effort to understand: 'Comment aider ton prochain si on ne le connaît pas?' She then argued at some length against Tom's contention that faith and hope were the same thing. To illustrate some points, she quoted for the first time from the sermons of F. W. Robertson, that 'broad churchman' who from Trinity Chapel in Brighton had radiated spiritual comfort so widely in the mid-nineteenth century. Tom sent her next his Rodin article, evidently with no letter, for in acknowledging it by postcard on 17 October, Marie inquired whether her letter had been received: 'Nous vous savons très occupés, mais un petit mot de vous nous fera toujours plaisir.'

By this time Tom and Hettie were comfortably settled into 20 St. James's Square, with the help of Marianne, a French servant highly recommended by the Appias, and a 'moving-in present' of £50 from their parents. They were happy to be together, in a home of their own which could be shared with their friends. None came more gratefully than Fisher, now legally separated from his wife, living penuriously alone, kept financially afloat largely by the *Illustrated London News*, for which he had 'covered' the Coronation. Among friends new to Hettie were Pollock, just back from Vienna, and Wyndham Lewis, persuaded to read 'his tales' in his own way in private. The elocution and chanting sessions were resumed in this friendlier setting. But within a month, Hettie was abruptly recalled to Florence; Bertie was in hospital suffering from some form of gastric fever. He proved to be so seriously ill that Hettie summoned her father, who remained until the crisis was past. Bob and Bessie Trevelyan, passing through Florence early in December, were allowed to see Bertie for a quarter of an hour in hospital. It was not until January that he was well enough to travel back to England and spend his convalescence in Torquay, freeing Hettie to return to Tom.

For Christmas, Tom sent Marie further volumes of the Vale Shakespeare, *Peau d' Ane*, his poem 'Though she was a great king's daughter' and a letter beginning, 'I have left your last letter written on 20th September almost as long without an answer as you are accustomed to leave mine. I felt I could not answer it in a hurry or when I was tired after a day's work.' He then proceeded to a further rebuttal of her claims for the authority of religious revelation, and concluded: 'The heretic of one age becomes the authority of another, but the great tradition of religious thought is continued from heretic to heretic and the orthodox have little or no share in it.' Before embarking on a spirited defence of her 'orthodoxy', Marie expressed the warmest appreciation of his presents, particularly 'la poësie si belle, si élevée, si vraiment poëtique, melodieuse et bienfaisante ... toujours elle évoque à mon esprit ma douce et forte Cousine Hélène.' It was, indeed, Hélène who had inspired it.

To Sybil Pye, Tom sent a volume of Matthew Arnold, in the confident hope that she would develop 'a thorough-going taste' for his prose.

I don't know one person who really cares for Mat. A's prose and reads it constantly, and can't understand the indifference and even dislike it begets in most people. He always subdues me at once and makes me entirely receptive, like a child or a sponge. I feel his mind encloses mine on nearly every side. . . . Do you know his Comments on Christmas? It is most beautiful, I read it every year and I think you would like it too; it is bound up with St Paul and Protestanism in the Popular Edition. But perhaps you know it already; you have a way which makes me always surprised that you don't know all the very best things. I remember how surprised I was that you should not have known M.A.'s poetry—you looked as if you knew it.

Just after Christmas Tom went to see Gordon Craig's production of Laurence Housman's *Bethlehem* with an amateur cast. He wrote with his customary candour to Mrs. Gwendoline Bishop who had played Mary:

I was very much impressed by Bethlehem in all respects except the speaking and words. Craig's part appeared to me perfectly successful; if there were any faults they seem to have been imposed on him by the conditions, and one could not blame him for that. I thought you did your part admirably, and should imagine that you carried out Craig's idea to perfection. My friend Mr C. S. Ricketts was even more struck with your performance than I was. . . . Masefield tells me that you were first rate in Ashbee's play at Camden, which he very much enjoyed. I wish I could have gone down with him, but I have been and am very busy, so that I fear if the Countess Cathleen is done at once, as was our intention, I shall be able to have very little to do with it; but I think perhaps Yeats will do his Hour Glass now and wait to do Cathleen until the Autumn, when I hope you will be back and willing to do the title rôle; ... Thank you for sending me the lilt; Miss Owen either would not or could not make anything that more than faintly resembled the way you did it, and I am afraid that we shall have to wait for your return to hear that again too.

Tom was, in fact, forced to hand over to Yeats and Binyon for about two and a half months all his responsibilities for lessons and rehearsals. Editing Shakespeare had to take priority for Ricketts had decided to close down the Vale Press in June. He had printed most of the books he most wanted to print; it would have involved immense labour to replace the losses of the Ballantyne fire for a new programme; under Holmes's capable management the capital outlay had already been returned eightfold. When the last volume was printed, like William Morris before him and Lucien Pissarro and others after him, Ricketts was to throw the founts of his type into the Thames.

That last volume was Tom's *Danaë* with illustrations by Ricketts. In the first half of 1902, three other of his works in verse were published: the three-act play *Absalom*, dedicated to W. A. Pye, by the Unicorn Press, and *The Rout of the Amazons* and *The Centaur's Booty* by Duckworth. The two last, bound in nut-brown paper with the wood-engraving of a burly, crouching Pan intently playing his pipes on the front cover, were sold for a shilling and were widely enjoyed. His experiences in art journalism over the same period were disillusioning. In January he became, almost unawares, art critic to the *Manchester Guardian*. He was not pleased by the way one of his first two articles, on the Burlington House Exhibition, was cut and mauled about without any by-your-leave. Although such flagrant mutilation did not recur, it was hard for a man who not only wrote slowly and amended often, but also reverenced printing as an art, to feel comfortable in the employ of even the most reputable of daily newspapers. After a few months he relinquished this post, suggesting that the young art critic A. J. Finberg, whom he was anxious to befriend, might take his place. Meanwhile, Strong had entrusted Tom with his finely produced book on the Chatsworth Drawings to review for the recently established *Burlington Magazine*. And here Tom found himself in what he described to Bob Trevelyan as 'a wasps' nest'. His article had, apparently, first been accepted by Fry, who, along with Berenson and Horne, was then adviser on Italian art. Berenson then questioned the attribution of some of the drawings, whereupon Fry told Tom that the *Burlington* must be authoritative, the misattributions must be mentioned, and anyhow the drawings were 'a poor lot'. Strong was very ill and could not be consulted. The editor, Dell, suggested a shift of emphasis to 'general aesthetic principles' rather than particular instances, and Tom indignantly withdrew the article altogether. Rightly or wrongly, he considered that Fry, who admitted to a grudge against Strong, had yielded so readily to editorial pressure from discreditable motives. Ricketts, whom Tom is more than likely to have consulted, would probably have backed Strong on the attributions; there is a later story of Berenson remarking blandly at a luncheon party, 'Ricketts and I always disagree about attributions' and Ricketts retorting, 'Oh, don't underrate yourself, Berenson, you are occasionally right.' Bob refused to discuss the matter; Berenson and Fry both being his friends it would only upset him.

Tom rarely referred to his health in his letters, but at this time it was clearly a source of some anxiety to his family. In February his Aunt Helen wrote inviting him to come and have a little rest with them before Easter, while Tante Louise was still in Cannes. Marie added a note: 'Inviter quelqu'un de fatigue à venir *se reposer chez nous* parâit vraiment grotesque', but it would be a change and she hoped he would come. She was perhaps not surprised when he regretted that he was far too busy. She was herself then in great distress at the loss of one of her oldest and closest friends, Emma Jalla, who had died shortly after the birth of her second daughter; the first daughter, Graziella, was another of Marie's godchildren. Somewhat later she sent Tom the account of the life of this missionary's wife that she had written for the magazine of the Y.W.C.A. When she next wrote, sending slightly belated birthday wishes, she was in Geneva, looking after her nephews and nieces so that their mother could have a holiday. It was her first visit since her brother's death. Théodore, now fifteen, was at boarding-school, but needed as much mothering when he appeared at weekends as the other five children, three of whom were unwell. She was happy to be with them but extremely occupied.

During March, with Yeats again in Ireland and Tom still not free of Shakespeare, there seems to have been a lull in chanting, elocution, and experimental performances. Yeats, however, did not hesitate to enlist Tom's help in his Irish theatrical activities. He first sent him 'a bundle of plays' to be forwarded with all possible speed to the censor and then 'gabbled through on a properly licensed stage' for copyright. Tom was, of course, familiar with the procedure, which in this case entailed recruiting nineteen gabblers at short notice. Then, Yeats asked him to design the stage setting for his *The Hour-Glass* which was shortly to be produced in Dublin with the Fay brothers. Tom's design was used, though the correspondence on this and another design for *The Shadowy Waters* indicates the difficulties of fulfilling the author's vision within the limits of an unknown stage across the Irish Sea, especially as Tom's experience in stage design had apparently so far been confined to Masefield's miniature theatre. Later this month, at a meeting chaired by Walter Crane, Tom, along with Yeats, Arthur Symons, Gilbert Murray, and Edith Craig, was nominated a member of the committee of The Masquers, a society founded there and then with the aim of performing 'plays, masques, ballets and ceremonies'. Though somewhat dubious of the society's potential for realizing its aim, Tom recruited a number of members, including Henry Poole, who having just won an open competition for his design of sculpture for Cardiff Town Hall, was well able to subscribe.

The need to concentrate on Shakespeare had not much interrupted Tom's intercourse with the Pye family, and not at all his correspondence with Sybil. Besides sending her further poems for the children, he was now anxious to hear her judgement on the 'grown-up' poems, hitherto sent primarily to her father. As Easter approached there was a frequent exchange on the choice of pictures from the Art for Schools series to be given by Tom and Binyon to all the children in her little school as end-of-term prizes. Tom was now in a position to return some of the hospitality he, and recently Hettie too, had received; both Pye daughters had stayed the night on certain occasions, such as the one on which Sybil was invited to dine with Miss Horniman, Miss Owen, Dolmetsch, Masefield, and Binyon. On 11 March Tom wrote to Marie, thanking her for the moving memoir of Mme Jalla and telling her of his current enthusiasm for Goethe's *Sprüche in Prosa*, with the comment, 'His was a great and beautiful character.' He continued:

The most delightful part of my life lately has been making friends with Sybil Pye; she is a very frail and tiny person, exquisitely delicate, who teaches a little school of four boys and one girl who come to her father's house every day. You would like her very much; she is very quiet and very wise and seems always to do exactly what she means to. . . . She also has a very rare distinction and great claim on my regard in that she likes Matthew Arnold, both prose and poetry, quite as much as I do and I know nobody else who does that.

Marie answered this letter on 20 April, first declaring that Goethe's character, as far as his relations with other people were concerned, 'has always seemed to me hateful—the word is perhaps a little strong—but anyway undesirable and *ugly*, in some respects at any rate. Unless one raises supreme egotism to the rank of supreme virtue, as Nietzsche does. Perhaps Goethe was a "superman" ahead of his time.' But Goethe was not the cause of her writing:

What you say about Miss Sybil Pye particularly interested me. I have often thought of her during the past months and especially these last weeks since your note to Hélène of which she read me part in Geneva. And now your letter seemed to be a direct answer to my preoccupations and to show me clearly my line of conduct. This young girl who shares so completely in your tastes, who knows so well how to correct you and to inspire you, is she not exactly the woman whom I have always wished for you? Capable of understanding you entirely, and of associating wholly and without sacrifice with your preoccupations, your work and your hopes? Don't contradict me. Perhaps I reveal to you sentiments which you did not wish to avow and which are nevertheless real and legitimate. Don't fight against them any longer. Don't accuse yourself of unfaithfulness—you are entirely free. You have taken no engagement for the future. . . .

A certain coldness, shall I say it? a certain roughness on your part during these last months made me feel that a certain distance was taking place between us. And I was truly relieved to find its cause. . . . It seems to me that we are entirely disengaged one towards the other. I asked you to keep silent, you remained silent. You asked me to leave the door wide open between us. I tried, I believe in all loyalty, to do so without any reticence. In spite of this, my sentiments did not answer yours as you had hoped. Naturally yours were disturbed and left room for others. The situation could not be prolonged indefinitely so; the most desirable solution was that you should be able to find . . . a being capable of giving you the happiness which you need.

If she had in any way in the past helped him in his search for a religious faith, she was grateful; she was now, however, convinced that their interpretations of Christianity were, and would remain, essentially different. She hoped that the friendship between them would continue and prove in the future to be 'cette "true relation between us" que nous cherchions et n'avions pas encore trouvé'.

And since it's no doubt the last time that I shall speak to you about all this, allow me to add this: if I was allowed to be of some use to you in the first part of your life, it is to *you* that I owe, at the time when I doubted of myself and of life, having regained confidence in myself and in life. It is a debt of gratitude which I can only pay by wishing for you the most complete happiness.

And now goodbye my dear Tom, perhaps we shall see each other in the Spring in Paris and perhaps you will then have good news to tell us. No-one will rejoice more than your friends at No. 119 bis.

Twelve days before this letter was written, Tom had proposed to Sybil Pye. To judge from a surviving draft of his letter to her, it was not a confident proposal. The difference in their ages (some eleven years) and material circumstances, the fact that neither of them possessed assured health, his uncertain prospects and weaknesses of character were all mentioned. 'Indeed,' he wrote, 'I feel it must be almost a miracle if you can care for me enough even to desire to know me better.' Nevertheless, he felt that there was a deep affinity in their tastes, inclinations, and aspirations, and that if she could trust him he might in many ways add to the happiness and effectiveness of her life. In any case, he owed it to her to explain clearly his hopes and hesitations in regard to her so that he could be guided by her decision on the future course of their relationship. Sybil's answer came the next day:

Dear Mr. Moore,

I need not tell you how hard it is for me to write what I feel to be the only possible answer to your letter, offering me so kindly and considerately what I cannot but feel to be far more than I have ever deserved. I have never felt for you anything more than common friendship and gratitude for the kind interest you have taken in me and my work; and I feel that I would be wronging both you and myself if I allowed myself to think that this feeling could change. The knowledge that it cannot grieves me more than I can say when I think of the pain I shall most unwillingly cause you.

I will not write more for I feel that nothing I can say will make my rejection of your love seem less cruel and ungrateful. I can only ask you to believe that if I had felt it within my power to accept and return it, I should have been most truly glad, and that I am always as far as it is possible for me to be,

Your sincere friend
Sybil Pye.

Tom wrote again at once:

Your letter hardly surprised me and I cannot say how deeply I admire you for being able to write it, but that is all of apiece with the rest. What I gave to you I gave freely, nor is it in my power to take it back, nor could I wish to do so. But I accept your rejection as wholly.

... Perhaps you would rather not, just at present, that I sent you any of my work to read, but later on I hope you will have neither reluctance or fear in renewing our intercourse on the old terms.

'Things are what they are', and have to be accepted and turned to good if we can. I beg of you not to grieve for what you cannot help; that you have caused me to suffer is nothing in comparison with the fact that you make me desire and help me to bear that suffering bravely to a good end. In that you may rejoice and, I believe, you shall hear and see nothing of me to cast a doubt on that joy which is only your due.

Two letters from Sybil followed:

11 April. If anything could make me feel less the weight of the sorrow I have laid upon you it is the knowledge that you are too good and strong to let it come in the way of the work you have set yourself to do. ... As you say, I feel I would rather wait a little while before reading any more of your poems. Of all that your friendship has done for me, the new paths it has opened and the new beauties and pleasures it has pointed out, I cannot speak, for I know the one thing you ask in return I cannot give, I can only thank you many times. ... I do hope that after some time has elapsed we may renew our intercourse on the old terms.

15 April. Since writing to you last I have discovered that my Father and Mother would rather we did not correspond. As I feel absolutely that they are the best judges in this matter, I desire to abide by their decision, and I ask you to do the same, knowing that I may trust you to abide by my wish.

If Tom had been half prepared for Sybil's refusal, this ban on all communication between them imposed by her father 'for a considerable period' was an undreamed of and brutal blow. Though Pye had written assurances of his own unimpaired admiration and friendship, to Tom his intervention implied a lack of confidence wholly unjustified. Doubly wounded, he turned in his misery to their mutual friend Binyon, who did not fail him:

I can't say how much I am troubled by your news. I feel it almost as something that has happened to myself . . . I will certainly find occasion to ask Pye what his thought is. I shall not see him till we meet in

France; I wish it were sooner for your sake. I don't doubt his wish to spare you both pain, but I think with you his fear is exaggerated; I believe it would be wiser to let Sybil judge for herself. This is what I shall tell him. At the same time, I would distrust myself a little just at first, till things become calmer and clearer in your mind; if you do not press, Pye will relax too, I'm sure. . . .

If I have unconsciously said or done anything lately that jarred or pained you, please forgive me, nothing could have been further from my wish. Thank you for what you say of me; I would like to think my friendship has helped you in any way, or in any degree corresponding to what yours has done for me. Do not imagine deficiencies and wrongnesses in yourself that are not there. I know at such times one has a savage insight into one's own weaknesses; but what you write of does not exist in other people's thoughts of you. If I repeated all that many very different sorts of person have said about you, I would make you blush; you might think it of little worth at this present moment, compared with what you want; yet don't forget it.

I have perfect faith in your coming through this bad time whole and strong. But you will need distraction. Can't you get away—abroad? Do tell me if I can do anything. I could go away with you, I think, a little later, if you wished it.

Binyon, the busiest as well as the most generous of men, was relieved to hear that Tom was thinking of going to Paris. He had by now written to Marie, regretting any harshness of tone in his recent letters. This he attributed partly to hurried writing, partly to a sense of the futility of continuing their religious argument, and partly to the feelings she had divined. He had been aware of

perhaps in some degree deceiving you, for though I had the most ardent wish not to break or diminish in the least the friendship between us, I was conscious that it had in my heart a different foundation from what it once had. I hope that foundation is both truer and more lasting. It is a very great gratitude for all that you have meant to me, and that is almost everything. . . .

Now I must tell you that I have no longer any hopes that Sybil Pye will return my love. She is my friend, but has no inclination to be anything more to me. I value and prize her friendship too much to try to force her inclination, especially when I think on all the past. I need not say any more and of course, if I come as I hope to Paris, I shall not want to talk about these subjects. And I hope you will not speak of it to anyone.

Two pages in defence of Goethe followed.

Marie replied on 25 April, assuring him of her discretion, sympathizing with him in his disappointment, but unable to refrain from a reproach:

You have accustomed me to so much regard and loyalty that I allow myself to tell you that I would have found it more loyal on your part if *you* had gone ahead and warned me of your change of sentiments, instead of leading me to guess it and obliging me, so to speak, to go back over it all.

You may find me severe, exigent and susceptible ... but one does not try a woman's heart as you have done, one does not ask of her what you have asked of me, without freeing her as soon as one becomes conscious that one is free as far as she is concerned. . . . You know I can never hold something against someone without telling them. So, as we are to meet, I wanted to look you straight in the face without reservation. Excuse my frankness, which is perhaps unjust. Now all this is finished, forgiven and forgotten.

Vulnerable then to any reproach, Tom admitted to having been wrong in not telling her earlier of his change of heart:

The change came about so gradually and I fought against it so long, clinging to what was leaving me for many reasons that I cannot yet explain to you and perhaps you could scarcely understand. Even now, looking back, I cannot determine when I ought to have told you. Last time I was in Paris I returned having renewed my loyalty and determined to resist the attraction I felt toward Sybil, because I felt her parents had wished to warn me from her, in many ways I could not make her such a husband as she deserved, and also my affection for you had such deep roots, was so much a habit of my mind, that I felt it to be impious to abandon it. No doubt I should have seen that the mere existence of such a struggle was sufficient ground for releasing you from the supposition I allowed you to continue in. I cannot explain, I can only confess and accept the pardon you so generously give with a full heart.

Besides providing distraction, the week in Paris in May had a soothing effect. Tom was thankful for Marie's companionship, now, it seemed to him, without constraint on either side. Cousine Hélène was there too, radiating calm as always, though inwardly troubled. 'Il y avait dans vos yeux', she wrote to Tom afterwards, 'une lumière qui fait du bien, et vous m'avez aidé sans le savoir.' He met Adolphe Appia again, this time with Fortuny, who was helping him in his revolutionary use of stage lighting; he urged them both to come to England. As usual he went to the Salons, and made notes for a *Manchester Guardian* article. While still in Paris he wrote to Pye, who since Binyon's mediation had at least demonstrated how much he wanted the close friendship between them to continue. 'It would be impossible to give you any idea of how much it has meant to me to be able to come every year to this house, and now that all friction caused by religious differences has melted away it is a greater boon than ever. . . . My old uncle grows more and more beautiful every year and now adds to all the energetic virtues a sweetness and simplicity which make him a true saint.' He was later to tell Pye that he looked on his home, 'as representative of the English ideal as I have always looked on my Uncle's as representative of the French. . . . There is the same mutual confidence, the same joy in common and sympathy and everything shared openly.'

In his thank-you letter to Marie, Tom apologized for having burdened her with his discontents:

I think you hardly realize how difficult an artist's life is. He must live as it were two lives and is in constant danger of sacrificing the one to the other. . . . 'Quand notre mérite baisse, notre goût baisse aussi,' as La Rochefoucauld puts it. Morality is, as Flaubert said, the 'base non plus le but de l'art,' and so works of art rarely help directly towards self-conquest but presuppose it, and in a young man they often presuppose what doesn't exist and so betray him.

A few days later he wrote again, much shaken by a visit to Arthur Strong, who appeared to be on his deathbed. They were not exactly intimate, but this eminent scholar, who enjoyed power, had offered him friendship rather than patronage. Death had not so far come the way of any of Tom's near relatives or friends, and he was now moved to reflect, with some remorse, on how he would have been affected by such losses as Marie had recently suffered. 'Even such a short separation as I now endure from Sybil Pye . . . makes me want to be like a wild beast and hide away until my wound is healed, so that at times even the presence of other people in the room irritates me. So you must forgive me if I have failed you in your sorrow, and believe that I felt you would prefer silence.'

There was about this time what Henrietta described as 'an epidemic of engagements' in Tom's circle: Pollock to Gladys Holman Hunt, Simon Bussy to Lytton Strachey's sister Dorothy, C. J. Holmes to a cousin, Miss Calhoun to a Balkan statesman, G. M. Trevelyan to Mrs. Humphrey Ward's daughter Janet, Julien Monod to Mlle Narville. And on 21 May Binyon wrote, announcing in the strictest confidence his unofficial engagement to Miss Cicely Powell. 'Forgive me if my news seems to accentuate your grief. I could not help writing to tell you. . . . It was last Sunday that it happened, in Surrey, under Leith Hill.'

Tom tried to settle down to his work on Dürer. He took Pye to see the Michael Fields, where they were warmly received, for Pye came bearing rare flowers from the garden at Priest Hill. Then, at the end of May, Uncle Appia came to London and stayed part of the time at 20 St. James's Square. With the help of Bertie, who was now taking a course at the South Kensington Institute, Tom managed to see that he was never unaccompanied. He even contrived to fit into his uncle's impulsive programme a meeting with Pye, who was as much impressed by him as he had been by Hélène Appia two years previously. 'I enjoy going about with him,' Tom wrote to Marie. 'It was very beautiful to see his joy after the two meetings, which he thought both successful; his enthusiasm is wonderful and puts me to shame. All things work

together for the good of those who believe in good as he does.'
Uncle Appia took back with him to Paris two presents from Tom
—Matthew Arnold's *Last Essays on Church and Religion* for Marie
and his *The Study of Celtic Literature* for Cousine Hélène.

Cousine Hélène sent her thanks on 2 June. She was returning
home that week, leaving Caroline and Marie, whose life was really
'trop fatigante', with regret; Marie had become so exhausted that
she had been ordered complete rest and sea air: 'You should make
some move towards her, it seems to me that at this moment she has
need of you.'

This communication set off a rapid exchange of letters, bearing
witness to the excellence of the mail services of the day. Tom
immediately passed the news on to Henrietta and wrote to Marie,
urging her to come to Torquay, where his mother and Sarah
would be delighted to have her and if he could be there too they
would do each other good:

We will teach you to be paresseuse there—how to profit by time
without being over-anxious to employ it—how to find without seeking.
You need indulgence and even though you think it a nasty medicine it
will do you good. There is no place in the world where it is more easy
and natural to be lazy than at Torquay. . . . Do, do, do come! Won't
you? Say, 'Yes'!

Marie, writing in a large, scrawly hand because she had scalded
her right elbow, surprised and touched by his letter, nevertheless
doubted whether, if Cheriton were like Woodthorpe, she might
not feel a stranger there, though Tom's presence would naturally
make her feel more at home; what she thought she really needed
was two or three weeks on her own, perhaps in Brighton or
Worthing or the Isle of Wight or somewhere nearer, but not too
close, to Torquay. Caroline, writing simultaneously in great haste
and agitation, stressed first the doctor's prescription of bracing sea
air, sea bathing, and no physical exertion, and then Marie's 'need
for solitude and silence, both for physical and spiritual refresh-
ment, and for the time she wishes to devote to our biographical

work on Henry'; Marie's embarrassingly ambivalent attitude to Torquay *might* be resolved if he were there too; the whole situation was extremely delicate, any 'pénible rencontre' must be avoided, but she relied implicitly on Tom to understand and advise. Tom, who had now, in dismounting from his bicycle, very severely sprained his right ankle, wrote again to Marie. After giving due consideration to other south-coast resorts, he suggested that she should accept the invitation to Torquay for the first few days, during which she could decide whether to remain there or to move on elsewhere. He added that Cheriton was not in the least like Woodthorpe, that his family, being far less sociable than hers, would find nothing at all odd in her wanting to be alone, that she would only have to tell him just how she wished to spend her days, he would then tell sensible Sarah, and his mother would be guided by whatever Sarah said. On 5 June, Marie, overwhelmed by the understanding and consideration shown her, accepted unreservedly the invitation she had received from her Aunt Henrietta.

Meanwhile, Louis had been summoned by telegraph from a stay in Geneva to take his sister to the seaside resort of Dieppe until further plans were clear. To and from Dieppe, where it rained continuously, postcards regarding times, routes, and accommodation sped across the Channel. In their course, Marie insisted that she was not 'malade' only 'un peu fatiguée' and was told that there were 'les saines imaginaires' as well as 'les malades imaginaires' and that she would not be called an invalid provided she consented to be treated as one. Finally, Marie and Louis arrived at Victoria Station on the evening of 12 June. Bertie met them, took decisions about their luggage, and conducted them to 20 St. James's Square. The following day Louis returned to Paris and Marie and Tom travelled down to Torquay.

Early during their stay Tom wrote to several of his friends explaining that he was out of London, taking the opportunity of this holiday after having been confined to the house with a sprained ankle. He told Bob Trevelyan that he was still only able to walk a short distance, and that George, 'fat and saucy', was with them for a few days. In answering a letter from Pye about his *Danaë*, he introduced his Appia cousin, there for a rest.

I expect to be very happy these next two weeks as Marie is more of a companion to me than any one else I know, we understand one another's ways of thinking so well. . . . She is more like my uncle than any other of his children, though very, very different in some respects. I should so have liked to bring her to Limpsfield. She is all that Emerson describes in his Social Aims. She is too brilliant and lively for me when other people are there, but when we are alone she slows down to my pace.

On Friday 26 June Cousine Hélène replied to a letter Tom had written about Marie: 'I don't think it right when you say it is impossible for you to become ever for her as much as she is for you. I think *you could*—and I think it depends on you now much more than before. Sometimes happiness is near when it looks far. Je puis me tromper, mon cher ami, mais quelque chose dans mon cœur me dit que vous avez tort de renoncer.' The probability is that this letter did not reach Cheriton until the Monday. On the Sunday afternoon Marie and Tom went for a gentle walk along the shore. It was not Tom who raised the subject of marriage again while they rested under Corbin Head, yet the Moore parents, strolling along the cliff top, saw the couple emerge from its shadow in a manner which left no doubt in their minds that the subject had been both raised and agreed upon. They waved congratulations.

The fullest account of how this came about comes in a letter written to Pye shortly afterwards. 'Something had happened' which must at once be told and explained to the friend to whose daughter Tom had so recently proposed. The long history of his attachment to Marie was indicated up to the point where she had guessed his intentions towards Sybil:

She wrote wishing me every happiness and apparently accepting my action with a free heart, and she says that she really believed that she did so until after her letter was posted; then she felt—well, you can imagine from what has now happened what she felt. And when I wrote and told her that Sybil had rejected me, she was thrown into the torment in which she has lived ever since, and which has so broken down her health. I was quite blind to what was passing within her, and when I found her even kinder to me than she had ever been I attributed it to her feeling more secure from knowing that I loved someone else, and also to her compassion for me. . . . It was Hélène Appia who understood us both much better than we understood ourselves and wrote and told me what I was to do, and insisted in Paris that Marie was to come to England for her sea-change.

I cannot tell you how overwhelmed I was when I discovered that the cause of Marie's depression was not, as I had imagined, the unsettling of her religious views, but that she feared she would never win back my love. It was impossible for me to do other than I have done, though at first I longed for time, and to be anywhere but where I was, in order to feel and think clearly. But soon I felt that everything was best so, and could only rejoice since she gave me not only herself, but all my past life and all my hopes, both of which I had lost and knew not where I should find them again.

꧁꧂

CHAPTER FOURTEEN

Preludes to an Epic Wedding

THAT Georges Appia gave an unreserved blessing to the engagement between his daughter and his nephew is clear from the letter Tom wrote to his 'Dear, dear Uncle' on 8 July:

Your letter has given us both a joy and peace supreme. I feel I shall never be able to thank you enough for the confidence you repose in me and for the priceless treasure that you give to me and of which I hope not to rob you in the least degree. . . . You will understand that I am very anxious lest, in the emotion of the present times, I should be led to go further in religious sympathy with you than I have as yet obtained the right to go, and then later on be forced to disappoint you by withdrawing. . . . As I tell Marie, she is my elder in these things and therefore she must lead and guide and teach me. . . . And I hope to make myself your spiritual son as well as your son in law, and feel myself already to be your son by affection and respect.

The religious differences, which had once seemed so divisive to Marie, appear, in fact, to have been resolved more by the gradual broadening of outlook on her part and an access of humility on Tom's than by any radical change in beliefs. Somewhat later, his uncle expressed the wish that Tom should be baptized before the marriage, and to this at the time he agreed. On reading the baptismal service 'for such as are of riper years', he was horrified to find that this involved affirming a steadfast belief in the Apostles' Creed. As he immediately wrote to Marie, he had been prepared for a symbolical purification, a dedication to a life in the spirit of Christ, but he had 'no desire or idea of ever asserting a belief in Christian Mythology'. He asked Marie to explain his position to her father, with the aid of part of the chapter on 'The Proof by Miracles' from Matthew Arnold's *Literature and Dogma*. When

Laurence Binyon, from
an etching by William Strang

Sybil Pye (*right*) and her sister Ethel on the terrace at Priest Hill, *c.* 1925

Tom and Marie Sturge Moore, 1904

Marie eventually found an opportunity to do this, Georges listened attentively and then said, 'Ce cher enfant, naturellement je ne lui imposerai aucune liturgie que le trouble.' His conviction that God had given his daughter 'un homme du bien, qui cherche la lumière' was firmly rooted.

On their return to 20 St. James's Square, Hettie embraced Marie and said she had long wished 'it would happen'. Alice, the good cockney servant who had replaced Marianne, was delighted and diverted by the thought, 'Mr. Tom will be much 'appier when he marries Miss Appia', and even more so when Hettie pointed the analogy with Alice's own intended, a Mr. Jolly. It had, however, been decided before Marie left for home that the engagement should remain secret until her health was sufficiently restored for her to ride the flood of felicitations and emotional farewells that would inundate her once it was known in Paris. Tom had therefore to suppress his urge to tell almost everyone he knew immediately, though he was free to tell his close friends in confidence. Binyon had been told at the same time as Pye, and had sent Tom a poem written since his own engagement; Tom copied out the last stanza for Marie, with his own underlinings:

> Oh Love, my Love, the dear light of whose eyes
> Shines on the world to show me all things new;
> Falsehood the falser and the true more true,
> And tenfold more precious all my soul must prize.
> O let us cleave fast to the heavenly powers
> That gave us this, whose unseen spirit flows
> Pure as the wind and sensitive as flowers,
> Nor ever can be chained. Let stormy night
> Cover the bleak earth with these whirling snows,
> Our hands are joined, our hearts are brimmed with light.

Bob Trevelyan, the next to be told, made a special journey up to London to shake Tom by the hand. But to Ricketts, the friend who lived just round the corner, the news had to be broken rather than told, and this was done by letter on 12 July.

When I spoke to you last night about jewelry, I was wanting you to either make or find rings for me and my cousin Marie Appia as we have quite recently become engaged against all expectation. But I was afraid you were not in the right mood to hear such a shocking confession.

It is a very long story, and when I spoke to you and Shannon before going away I imagined its happy termination more than ever impossible. But it turned out otherwise. . . . I feel sure you will like her as she is very lively, clever and talkative and quite French and not at all like me.

I hope we may well be married before Christmas; my father has promised to help and though we will not have much, what we will have will be quite certain, so perhaps the risks are not so great as with people much better off. As we have been the very greatest of friends for ten years and known each other for 18, if we have made a mistake in the choice of one another we shall deserve all the misery we shall get. But I have not the slightest doubt that if circumstances are only moderately favourable we shall be extremely happy. There has been enough of ups and downs to make a good novel, only as other people besides ourselves have been very intimately mixed up in them, I cannot talk about them, at any rate not yet.

She is very anxious that her happiness shall not estrange me from you at all as she has as great an admiration for you as I have myself, and quite recognizes that I owe everything to you that I do not owe to her. I hope you will forgive me for acting so very much against your advice and believe that it was from no lack of respect and admiration for you. I really think she will make intercourse between us easier; I always feel I am too chill and slow-witted to keep pace with you, and I have long felt the same in regard to her. She is an extremely popular person and most people of both sexes more or less fall in love with her when they make her acquaintance. We are not making our engagement known just yet, so please tell nobody except Shannon, above all not the Michael Fields. But nobody at all if you please.

In the margin of this letter, by the words 'against your advice', is written, 'I never advised. C. R.' In Ricketts's journal is the entry, 'News of TSM's intended marriage—feel quite dazed, wrote felicitations.'

My dear old Chap,

Shannon and I join in wishing you every human happiness; my old affection for you is so sound that your marriage can make no difference, at least to me, and I am looking forward to seeing your bride and falling in love with her myself.

I shall have the greatest pleasure in seeing to the ring if you wish it, but in such a case one chosen by yourselves might be more charming. At any rate I shall turn jeweller on my own account and make for your wedding the pendant of pendants, which will tear all lace and scratch babies.

I am so glad that you are both old friends and that your bride has the same admiration for your work that I have myself, that she is an intelligent French woman and not a slack English girl. I am also glad there will be no wolf at the door, as he is a real live person.

Like Shannon I am looking forward to any further news at its proper time.

Yours affectionately,
C. Ricketts.

This letter, which Ricketts immediately followed up with a visit, Tom forwarded to Marie, pointing out, incidentally, that he had not said she admired his own work. 'He approves of you and means to make the best of you. I am so glad! Though you must not fall in love with him, even though he does with you.'

Marie's home-coming had been an emotional occasion. If her father greeted her with joy, her mother could not disguise her distress at the thought of the coming separation. Caroline, concealing no less anguished thoughts, had composed a poem 'To Tom and Marie' which was placed in her sister's room on a little table she had made and ornamented in pokerwork with Wordsworth's stock dove, who 'cooed and cooed and never ceased'. Louis quietly and affectionately conveyed an admixture of shared happiness and personal regret. Impressed though they all were by Marie's radiant spirit, she was still very thin and easily tired. Appointments for exhaustive medical examinations had already been fixed. The resulting advice was that for three months she should spend the mornings in bed, follow a special diet, have injections for anaemia, treatment for pains in the back, and a thorough overhaul of her teeth. Thereafter, in the opinion of Dr. Charles Monod, marriage should effect a permanent cure. Almost immediately Marie, with her mother and Tante Louise, set off for the Valleys. At Culoz two nephews, fourteen-year-old William and his younger brother Georges, joined them. A helpful young cousin, Mina Vallette, was to arrive at the Airals Blancs independently.

Throughout this period of separation Marie and Tom wrote to each other daily. At first Marie's letters were coloured by remorse —for the suffering she had caused him in the past, for having been so neglectful of her health—but this was soon washed away by the trust and ardency of Tom's. All his long-unexpressed love and tenderness poured out in endearments, diminutives, extravagant nonsense, and poetic flights. 'I desire', he told her, 'to drown you in an ocean of love, from which you will never again escape but become a mermaid in love's sea.' And when she feared she had spoken indiscreetly about their past relationship, 'You are free, dear, free as a bird in my love. Fly where you like, sing as you desire, my love is the air in which you live, for which you are made, your wings are meant to buoy you up in my love and your song to fill my love's volume as a skylark's fills the sky.' He looked out those secret poems, written before he had 'the right to say sweet things' to her, and sent her several of those based on memories of his childhood stay in the Valleys—among them,

> To braid a crown of daisies
> Meet for your dusky hair—
> To lead you through mountain places
> Suiting your solemn air—
> Hear your laughter, buoyant thunder,
> Like the torrent's tunnelling under
> Coloured rocks to issue glancing
> In a thousand small jets dancing
> Down a stair of rinsèd stones—
> To heap your lap with scented cones,
> Fir cones, would make a giant of joy
> Out of a timid and awkward boy.

'I have never had a confidant, even Binyon I never tell about most of the things I think oftenest of, but with you I shall talk about everything. All that will not be so new to you as it is to me, and so if I am too greedy and do not understand the limits of such confidences, you must have patience with me and teach me better.' Marie declared she, too, wished confidence to be limitless, to hide nothing and know nothing was hidden, to enjoy a sharing such as she had never experienced even with Caroline. Tom was the initiator of most of their exchanges, and his letters, in particular, have a kaleidoscopic quality, switching from one language to the other, as they range in fluctuating mood over memories of the past, aspirations for the future, inner preoccupations of the present, Ecclesiastes, or whatever part of the Bible Marie had selected for simultaneous reading, daily events, practical problems. Conquently, reading Marie's letters and writing his own absorbed so much of Tom's working morning that at one point he determined on every other day to send only a postcard. His postcards were closely written and the perimeters packed with assorted endearments. To this Marie put a stop 'because they are so dreadfully indiscreet and chatterbox at the post office'. An attempt at least not to write between receiving letters was equally unsuccessful as long as Marie remained in the distant Valleys, for the pain of not receiving a letter had to be expressed. 'It is really ill-done to love one another like this when we have to be apart and have not even the time to write,' Marie lamented. 'But in spite of all my efforts I do not know how to love you less and do without you.'

The most pressing practical matter to be discussed was the programme considered by the Appias to be a condition of an early marriage. In the first place, Tom must come out to the Valleys late in August so that various matters could be talked over *en famille* and their daughter's fiancé presented, as a matter of customary courtesy, to their numerous Vaudois friends. Then, if Marie were well enough, the marriage could take place towards the end of the year. As, however, she would still be in delicate health, she must on no account be exposed to the notorious ills of a winter in London. They therefore proposed a three-month honeymoon in Italy, a month in Paris, and a return to England 'avec les hirondelles et les beaux jours' in April. The Moore parents were totally opposed to this plan. Daniel could see no point in Tom suffering the expense and interruption to his work of a visit to the Valleys in August unless it were to be married there, and implied that the sooner Marie were married and removed from the Appia *ménage* the better it would be for her health. Hettie half-jokingly remarked that this strong objection to a second *fiançailles* arose from fear of another broken engagement; Marie was not amused when this observation was passed on to her. Tom, though naturally longing to be with Marie again, was now acutely aware of the need to earn regularly; he wanted to finish his book on Dürer as soon as possible to be free for other work. As for the three-month Italian honeymoon, this appeared both to him and his parents an absurdly extravagant notion for a couple of modest means. Only if he were commissioned to write on some aspect of Italian art would the expense be justified, and anyhow, if the English climate were somewhat cloudier, the houses were better made and the drains decidedly superior. There was also the likelihood of Marie's becoming pregnant during the honeymoon to be considered. Tom had already written to his father on the question of child-bearing being more dangerous for women over thirty—an anxiety that had been scouted: 'You must remember that your mother was 31 when you were born; I should judge that morbid fuss is at the bottom of most cases in which fear of child-bearing over 30 is a prominent feature.' When Tom raised this further point it was his mother who replied. 'Papa seems to feel he has already said all he has to say, but perhaps in some respects I am nearly as well qualified to speak'; the discomforts of the early stages of her own first pregnancy had been so aggravated by being on holiday in Scotland instead of at home, 'that I have never been able to bring my mind to wish to see that country, with all its beautiful scenery, again. So it is not an imaginary evil that I want dear Marie to be saved from, altho' I know it is quite possible she might not suffer in the same way.'

All these objections were put to the Appias. Marie, although she had thought that three months in Italy would be a happy and fruitful experience for Tom, had all along insisted that she set no store by it personally: 'Pourvu que je sois avec toi le pays m'est *bien* egal.' And writing on 21 July from the Airals Blancs, she faced the possibility that Tom would not be joining them there in August.

> The weather is ravishing, the plain has a light blueness, the rock of Cavour is black as ink and the sun makes the Catholic church in the foreground sparkle like a mosque in the east. Our pretty little oak wood is full of mystery and attraction, and I ask myself in a low tone, so low that I am surprised that my pen should hear it, whether—in a few weeks time I shall be walking there alone—alas! alas! I fear so and I am fully decided not to count on anything else for the moment.

Her mother's views on early pregnancy, drawn from experience in four different countries and often in temporary homes, are not recorded. Her father accepted that Tom's work must be given priority, but seems to have assumed that Providence would favour the Appia plan. As indeed it did, in that Arthur Strong, miraculously rallied from his illness, commissioned a book on Correggio, the first chapter of the Dürer was to appear as an article in the *Monthly Review*, and Duckworth had agreed to publish a selection of lyrics. With Hettie's help, Tom estimated that three months *en pension* in Italy for two, plus fares and incidental expenses would come to £89 (later revised to £120, to be on the safe side) and this, he thought, they could now afford.

Their future financial position and its implications were at the same time gone into carefully. Besides his annuity of £105, Tom would continue to receive the allowance of £50 from his father, and he should be able to earn at least another £100 annually from his writing. Marie was to have a yearly allowance of £120 from her parents, and the Moore parents had already given them a wedding present of £200, so that 20 St. James's Square could be redecorated and more comfortably furnished without cheese-paring or delay. Tom compared notes with his friends. Binyon's future father-in-law had been 'scandalised' by his meagre income, derived from his salary as Assistant Keeper at the British Museum and a considerable output of creative and critical work; Bob Trevelyan was so well off that he didn't have to worry; the Finbergs had so little that Tom obtained Marie's permission to lend them £20 to tide them over a particularly lean period; Roger Fry, with an assured income of £600 and two children, found himself hard up. 'Children are very expensive,' Tom advised Marie. 'Half a dozen would cost a fortune', so they had better think in terms of two to begin with. If they lived in the country things would be cheaper but, after all, inner resources were more important than worldly position or material comforts, and to-gether, 'two fires on one hearth', they should always be able to gen-erate warmth, enough and to spare, for themselves and others.

A constant preoccupation, expressed in Tom's earlier letters in various veins of exhortation, was, of course, Marie's health. His wife 'must be a healthy little Saint, not an emaciated, dyspeptic, consumptive, neurotic Saint like the common run of Saints'. 'Cover your little bones with comely stuff for kissing.' And she must never forget that she was the inspiration for his life and work. Then he was shocked into a different mood by Ernest Guy's announcing on his arrival for a stay at 20 St. James's Square that Marie was very ill and might be suffering from the same disease that killed her brother Henry. Although Tom did not believe this to be true, his anxiety became intensified. He insisted on a daily account of Marie's bodily state, and at the least mention of an ache or sign of fatigue lectured and scolded her for overtaxing her strength, blamed her family for imperceptive negligence, and be-came convinced that he was the only person capable of looking after her properly. When she begged him not to torment himself and her, assured him that she was conscientiously following her regime, and acting with the utmost prudence, he promised not to behave tyrannically, even though her nature drove her to wear herself into an early grave. Then she contracted a headache through shepherding Tante Louise about La Tour in the full heat of the afternoon sun, and the lectures began again. The Airals Blancs at that time was perhaps not the ideal place for a rest cure for one of Marie's temperament. She could not prevent herself feeling responsible for those around her. Her mother still needed emotional support; her aged and ailing aunt had to be patiently listened to and dissuaded from the impracticable undertakings that constantly entered her head; Mina Vallette, devoted and helpful though she was, had anxieties about her future to confide and burst into tears on learning that Marie was to marry an Englishman ('I wear her tears', wrote Tom, 'as a chaplet round my heart'); her fatherless nephews expected her to play with them, and William, though an affectionate and sensitive boy, had to be restrained from upsetting his elders by playing the fool; both boys slept in the room next to hers and had alternately to be treated for bruises and coughs. And everyone, within and without the household, knew that Marie spent the mornings in bed, so that she received a procession of solicitous, or sympathy-seeking, callers.

However, by the end of July she was feeling stronger and had put on three kilos in weight. 'But you must not imagine that I am becoming very fat, I have always been rather thin et très plate, my poor husband.' 'If I had been a man to fall in love with a woman's body,' Tom reassured her, 'I would never have fallen in love with Marie Appia. But, no, never for a moment has a body had superior attractions to a character like yours.' Nevertheless, he wanted her to know that, though a virgin, he was a sensual man; the doctor he had consulted about masturbation before he first proposed to her had told him he was of a type that should marry young. There are frequent references to his physical desire for her, his longing for children, his hope that their sexual relationship would be a sanctified joy, guided by tenderness and mutual respect. He expressed some fear that the ardour of his caresses might already have seemed immoderate to her. 'You have never shocked or distressed or offended me while we were together . . . I think that the body is a holy thing which must be cherished and looked after, which we must enjoy without reproach and not in any way despise or treat as an enemy.' She admitted to almost feeling jealous that he rejoiced as much in thoughts of becoming a father as of becoming a husband.

On 6 August all the Airals Blancs party except Tante Louise, too unwell for the exertion, moved up in stages to the Uverts. At first it was overcast and sultry even there. Then the air freshened, the cloud lifted, Georges and Caroline arrived from Paris, and Marie began to find her mountain legs again. It was agreed the time had come to make the engagement public. Tom had already confided it to a number of his friends, including Fisher (with a warning not to tell Ernest Guy 'or all France will be informed'), John Pollock, Bertrand Russell, with whom he had been discussing his Dürer, and, in spite of the caveat to Ricketts, the Michael Fields. Edith, thinking first of the executorship, wrote in the journal, 'Alas, our bequests can never tread "the Appian way"! It is a shock—and for Ricketts! It breaks up that little celibate company—and we lose a friend, for no man who is married can be a friend. . . . For him marriage was predestined, he is very marriageable. Mercifully, she is a French woman, he will be prisoner in the first division thanks to that.' Katherine hurried to The Palace to commiserate with the Painters: 'They are hiding their displeasure. Fay [Ricketts] regards marriage as a kind of death.' Among the friends who were now informed, Harry Mileham called Tom 'a very clever humbug'; he had looked forward to finding a humble place in a brotherhood 'with a TSM as Superior and Director and the rules of St. Francis of Assisi for the better working out of conscientious convictions in a good cause'. Shortly before telling Ernest Guy, Tom happened to have discussed the pros and cons of marriage with him in a 'superbly impartial manner'; he was therefore a little disappointed that Ernest expressed no surprise on hearing he was engaged and immediately guessed to whom. Perhaps the briefest reaction to the news came from the last member of his own family to be told, his brother Harry: 'I believe I ought to write and congratulate you, but haven't the least idea how to do it. I hope you and Marie will be very happy together. I should think you would understand one another very well.'

Of Tom's friends, Marie had so far only rather fleetingly met Fisher, Binyon, Bob and George Trevelyan, and Henry Poole. She had heard a great deal about Ricketts and Shannon. 'I shall rejoice in getting to know *all* your friends. It will be a circle so different from that to which I have been accustomed up till now. It will be full of unexpectedness and novelty. I hope that they will not freeze me with their northern coolness and that I will not frighten them with my southern demeanour.' 'You must not fear to be frozen by my friends,' replied Tom, 'you will find that I am the most English among them in this respect; you have nothing to fear, nothing worse than me.' More of these friends she would be meeting were naturally introduced in the course of the correspondence. Tom wished she had been there to guide the discourse when he dined with clever Miss Fry: 'I'm sure Miss Fry would be very interesting if she talked about her work or listened to me talking about mine, but for her to talk about my work and me to listen and remonstrate is absurd.' Later that week, his hosts the Sangers 'are very nice and very good people; she works at good works among the poor and he is a barrister who specialises in statistics. They are ultra-modern and were horribly shocked at my consenting to be married in a church; people who respect themselves ought to have nothing to do with even the mildest forms of superstitious ceremonies, etc.' Coming back by train from a visit to the Strongs, he compared them with the poor family who had shared his compartment on the way there.

Those children, who smelt so bad and were so dirty, were so loving in their ways to one another and with their parents and had such happy eyes. The Strongs have not got happy eyes, poor things, quite the reverse. I like him and his wife very much but am sorry they are so political and bitter. . . . One feels always in his presence that he can't afford to rest. This is partly, of course, physical but partly also moral. . . . It is sometimes depressing to feel one's inferiority so much as I do with him and Ricketts, especially when one is thinking of marrying a woman who is worthy of the finest intellect and whom one has perhaps cheated by being very much in love with rather a long time.

A letter of 9 August, the occasion of Tom's first visit to Limpsfield since March, begins on the train with assurances that Marie could never feel jealous of 'la petite Sybil', to whom his love would never have turned had he not despaired of winning hers. Several pages later, he is watching the butterflies in the garden at Priest Hill, while Pye sits beside him, laughing over the Shaw play Tom has brought for him. Sybil and Ethel are, uncustomarily, at church. At lunch Sybil appears slightly confused, and neither sister congratulates him. As the train takes Tom home he can how-ever write: 'Darling, I have had a very happy day and a long talk with Sybil. I don't think she has the least feeling against me, she talked quite openly, and I think her heart has been given to some-one else ... I am, oh, so glad.' While breaking the news of his engagement to Ricketts had gladdened Tom, both because of the way it was received and because the extent of his loyalty was thereby openly defined, this scrupulous re-establishment of rela-tions with Sybil satisfied his tender conscience that his passing infidelity to Marie had in no way been unfairly rewarded.

He now turned to preparations for his departure on 18 August for a three-week stay in the Valleys. Marie wanted him to bring a cabinet photograph of himself, or better still a likeness by Shannon. Shannon, though willing, was not a worker to be hurried, so Fisher was invited to breakfast, and made four rapid sketches. The jeweller had to be pressed to finish Marie's engagement ring— a single pearl in a simple gold setting, with 'Love truth for truth proves love' engraved inside the band. Presents had to be bought for everybody, not forgetting a steam-boat with a winding key and a hunting-horn for the two nephews, reported to be highly excited by the acquisition of a new uncle. Marie, meanwhile, gave thought to the manner of their meeting and their conduct during the visit. In company they must be 'très sobres'. 'Tu sais, mon amour, que je n'aime pas plus les tendresses en publique que certains épanchements sur carte postale.' She hoped that on the first evening they could go out alone together 'et dans le silence de la montagne, tandis que les étoiles de Dieu seulement nous verrons, nous prierons ensemble et nous demanderons à Dieu de bénir *chacun* de nos instants ensemble'. With the last sentence Tom was in full accord, but he protested that he had hidden his affection for so long 'that now your love has proved it to be well founded I have a constant desire to show it to everyone . . . and people like to indulge lovers up to a certain point. But as you feel otherwise, darling, I shall be delighted to repress this tendency.'

After dining in Paris with a very weary Louis, who would not be freed from his parish duties for a further week, Tom set off on the night-and-day train journey last made when he was fifteen years old, and still vividly remembered. A hot bath, bed and breakfast were provided for him at the Airals Blancs, and the next morning the donkey was ready to convey him and his luggage across the Pellice valley, over the ridge to Rora and on up the rough mountain path to the Uverts. All the rooms there were garnished with greenery and a two-part song of welcome, composed by Caroline, was 'sung by William and George, standing one on each side of the fireplace, which was decorated with ferns, and over which was the illuminated inscription "Deux fait mieux qu'un". They looked very beautiful and roguish.' Afterwards they crowned Marie's 'dusky hair' with a wreath of white meadow flowers and presented Tom with a buttonhole of the same. The following evening the stone hearth was transformed into part of a cavern in which two benevolent gnomes, with 'made-up beards and improvised hunches' were hammering on a Vaudois anvil. Their dialogue, entitled *Autrefois et Aujourd'hui*, was devised by Caroline and interspersed with songs by Mina Vallette. It evoked, with ingenuity and humour, the presence in their territory eighteen years before of a dark, vivacious girl, with a pet lamb and a train of other creatures, and a fair, shy boy, who had reappeared there together again. All this Tom described in a letter to his mother, in which he reported that Marie was so much better that it seemed certain the marriage could take place before Christmas, and the Appias were hoping that all, or almost all, the Moore family would then be able to come to Paris.

After the descent to La Tour early in September, the Appias became engrossed in preparations for the annual Vaudois Synod, for which the foreign delegates were already arriving. Only on one evening, when the younger members of the party at the Airals Blancs went on a moonlight picnic by bicycle and donkey cart in the plain of the Po, was there opportunity for Tom and Marie to wander off alone together. Marie responded to all personal and social demands with a self-neglectful grace that Tom both admired and deplored—and knew himself incapable of emulating. He later wrote that during the last part of his stay he had felt himself to be 'in the wrong place', to which Marie retorted that he had perhaps been 'in the wrong frame of mind'. She conceded that her family's constant endeavour to love their neighbours as themselves could lead to an agitated and exhausting way of life, but at least they were able to respond to the needs of others and did not feel resentful of circumstances imposed from without. Whereas he had always been able to organize his life and follow his own inclinations far more than most young people she knew. He had made good use of this privilege, but nevertheless, 'you have got into the habit of making others bend, rather than bending yourself. Isn't that true?'

Tom returned home via Geneva so that he could meet Marie's numerous relatives there and, above all, give thanks to Cousine Hélène to whom they both owed so much. She told him that only by mastering the nuances of the French language could he appreciate how witty Marie often was, and also reinforced a view of his own: 'She is capable of a different and better life than she lives now. She does not possess herself, nor can anybody else possess her, where she now is.' As the train across France passed through Sens, Tom was reminded of his walking-tour with Harry Mileham in 1894. 'How much I thought of you on that walk, you were almost all day long in my mind, and perhaps you hardly thought of me once during the whole time. You must have patience with me now, because I was very patient for you then; though I know it must be hard to find me so slow and stupid in learning to speak French and behave properly.'

During Tom's absence 20 St. James's Square had been shut up. Hettie and Bertie had gone to Cheriton, and Bertie would not be returning, for he had finally persuaded his father that Rome would be the best and cheapest place for him to have a studio. Alice had been on holiday, and, as she was nervous of opening up the empty house on her own, Fisher undertook to do this on the evening of her return. Something in the stillness and suspended life of the house moved him to make a reverential inventory of the contents of the rooms as he entered them. In Tom's bedroom, a black iron bedstead and a kitchen table painted olive-green under the window; on the walls, a huge enlarged photograph of part of Titian's *Bacchanal*, reproductions of Rossetti's portrait of Swinburne as a young man and his *How they met themselves*, of Piero di Cosimo's *Death of Procris*, Velázquez's *Philip of Spain*, Watts's *Ariadne*, Shannon's *A Wounded Amazon*, and facsimiles of Rembrandt etchings, the big one of the presentation of Christ over the mantelpiece; on the mantelpiece two of Moore's own student sketches in wax, one 'a huge female figure with little figures about it, one has climbed up to have its arms about her neck, another is crushed under her right hand. Ah! there is a canvas face to the wall by the bed. It is *very* beautiful, his own portrait of himself. I have not seen it since he was working at it at Highgate.' On the landing, a triumphal procession by Paolo Ucello. Then in the front room, two fine Hokusai prints—a snow-capped Fujiyama and his 'great curving wave in white and blue and grey'—several of Shannon's lithographs, several of Moore's woodcuts, and two etchings by Ricketts after Legros.

On his writing table he has left the following books: Reynold's Discourses, a volume containing Voltaire's novels, Holroyd's recent book on Michael Angelo, Whistler's Gentle Art of Making Enemies, Letters of Matthew Arnold, Hallam's Middle Ages and a huge portfolio of reproductions of works of Albrecht Dürer. . . . The floor of this room is stained and varnished and upon it is a square of a kind of rush matting, very clean and cold. The double-ended sofa is covered with a tight shiny material striped in pale bluey grey and white. The iron coal box is of the old fashioned type . . . tall armchairs with spindle backs. There is a little air of austerity about the whole room, but with a group of people and a lady chanting to the twanging of one of Dolmetsch's psalteries, you forget the chilliness and enjoy the music of the verse, though not of the psaltery. Lady Gregory, Yeats, Binyon, the Miss Pyes, Smiths, Miss Wilson, Mrs Emery and the rest—will they gather here again when Marie Appia comes? It is time that girl Alice was here, I must go and turn the gas on at the meter.

Tom returned to his writing-table determined to finish the Dürer and prepare the selection of lyrics for Duckworth. He found himself fretting that Marie was not there and then by his side. Dürer was so much a part of the Appia cultural tradition that she could have helped him, much more than would be the case with Correggio in Italy. Still more he wanted to discuss the lyrics with her, perplexed as he was by the conflicting opinions on almost all of them except 'The Gazelles'. There were, of course, many distractions to relate. Shannon, having failed to produce the drawing, now demanded sittings for another portrait in oils, and coincidentally Will Rothenstein had pressingly renewed an earlier request to draw him. Ricketts needed help with the correction of proofs for his book, *The Prado and its Masterpieces*. It had seemed natural and right to resume writing the occasional verse for Sybil's little school, and he asked Marie to suggest suitable subjects. He attended two committee meetings of The Masquers; at the first an offer by Eleanora Duse to perform d'Annunzio's banned *La Città Morta* was discussed, and at the second the committee reluctantly decided to dissolve itself. As Gilbert Murray wrote to Yeats in Ireland, the committee had been 'very unlucky' in the way marriage and foreign travel had disabled its most active members at a critical period. Brother George's *Principia Ethica* appeared, and was firmly put aside for honeymoon reading. To the

yet greater excitement of the Moore family, two portraits submitted by Bertie to the Society of Portrait Painters were exhibited
at the New Gallery—*Sarah*, it was true, skied, but *Henrietta* hung
in a central position on the line. Hettie's future was a matter of
concern both to Tom and Marie. Her conviction that all ordinary
ladies should 'be philanthropical' had led her to consult her father
about a career in nursing: 'He says I am totally unfit physically,
and that the profession is already overburdened with ladies, who,
thinking they would like it, went into it without qualifications and
became simply a nuisance to themselves and others.' For the time
being she had decided to spend the winter with her parents, so
freeing Sarah to join Bertie in Rome for a spell.

'J'ai l'air de prendre pieusement les notes,' Marie wrote during
a meeting of the Synod, 'tandis qu'un de tes compatriotes fait des
lucubrations peu intéressantes en mauvais français.' She described
how the proceedings were interrupted for a moving little celebration of the fiftieth anniversary of the consecration in La Tour of
two pastors, her father and M. Gay; and how in the evening
Caroline had sung German *Lieder*, including 'Willst du dein Herz
mir schenken', which she had sung on the last evening of Tom's
visit to Paris in May, 'pendant que je regardais ta belle, douce et
grave figure et qu'il me semblait que tu ne me regardais jamais.'
This led her on to regretting the lack in English of the intimate
second person singular and wondering whether, as they were both
of Quaker stock, they might not 'thee and thou' one another. Tom
commented that the only person he knew who still used this form
of address was Mrs. Bertrand Russell, whose husband did not
reciprocate; he thought it would seem unnatural in everyday life
and would certainly create difficulties for their children. In his
letters he nevertheless tried to comply, never, however, achieving
the consistency habitual in his verse. An indisposition delayed
Marie's departure for the customary visits to the Swiss relatives
until 24 September. By the end of the month she had joined her
father in Paris, at the Maison des Diaconesses, for 119 bis was not
to be opened up until the rest of the family returned in three weeks'

time. Here she busied herself in bringing the accounts and register of members of her Y.W.C.A. branch up to date, helping her father in the compilation of a collection of her late brother's sermons, and spending time with the children in the orphanage.

Here, too, she heard from Tom of his mother's serious illness. Daniel had brought her up to 20 St. James's Square for a consultation with the woman doctor Mrs. Scharlieb. The final diagnosis was cancer of the bowel. An operation might prolong her life for a few years, otherwise she would probably die within months. Mrs. Scharlieb recommended a period in a nursing home to build up her strength for the operation; it could be arranged for Nellie to join the staff there during her stay and Daniel and Sarah would lodge near by. In spite of all Daniel's gentle persuasion, her dread of leaving her home for unfamiliar, clinical surroundings finally reduced Henrietta to so pitiable a state of distress that these plans were abandoned. Instead, Cheriton was to become the nursing home, in which Daniel and Nellie would carry out Mrs. Scharlieb's instructions aided by Hettie and Sarah. When this news reached the Valleys, Helen was prostrated with grief. Georges, too, had always retained a special regard for his sister-in-law, never forgetting her support on the trying American tour just before her wedding. At first Tom and Marie felt that their marriage should be postponed, at least until the result of the operation was known, but Henrietta protested against this being done on her account; nothing would, in fact, give her deeper satisfaction than that it should take place on 26 November, the anniversary of her own wedding. The Appias resolved to make every effort to meet her wish, though with an impending death now added to some continuing anxiety about Marie's health invitations could not yet be printed.

The announcement of the engagement had, however, had its own momentum and wedding presents had already begun to arrive. Marie received a huge number from the extended family and wide circle of friends in France, Switzerland, Italy, and Germany, and from co-workers in Paris, including all ranks of the

Y.W.C.A.: tea, dinner, and dessert services, table silver, framed engravings, photograph albums, embroidered table-cloths, cushions, and tea-cosies. Some of these, Marie was aware, did not quite conform to what Tom had previously laid down as to the furnishing of their home: 'We must veto all gimcracks of every description—nothing unnecessary and everything either extremely simple or else first rate of its kind. And you', he had continued, 'must take lessons from Ricketts to improve your notions; your taste is naturally good, but you have a lot of sophisticated notions . . . and these you must have killed. And as I love you far too much to do it myself you must let him do it.' To which she replied she would be glad to hear Ricketts's views, 'mais je n'ai pas de tout l'intention de me laisser imposer ses goûts et m'oblige à aimer ce que je n'aime pas'. Tom's presents, being fewer, were often described in detail: the Sheffield plate tea-caddy from the Michael Fields, sent with a quotation from Spenser's 'Epithalamion'; antique cut-glass water jugs from the Bertrand Russells; a rosewood table from Binyon and his fiancée; a panel of Greek embroidery from Mona Wilson; the promise of a glass-fronted bookcase from Bob Trevelyan; from the Pye family a 'tea basket' furnished with a kettle and spirit-lamp, a small meat-safe, a metal shelf for carving, and everything a travelling or picknicking couple could desire. When Nana saw the tea basket, she was 'in ecstasies, calling the tea caddies "little dears", just as though they were babies!' Nana herself gave a big white enamel hot-water jug, Alice a china toast-rack and the two maids at Cheriton 'a glorious sifter sugar basin in the shape of a silver coal scuttle washed with gold . . . it makes me blush to look at it, but it is really very good of them and shows how much they appreciated thee'. Ricketts and Shannon were both to give paintings, and Ricketts was already at work on the design of the promised pendant, inspired by a myth of inexhaustible fascination to Tom: 'He showed me a handful of beryls, aquamarines, pearls, amethysts, turquoises, sapphires, carbuncles, opals, emeralds, rubies, tourmalines and I know not what besides. He means it to be the most glorious of all his jewels.'

In the finished asymmetrical pendant (now in the Fitzwilliam Museum, Cambridge), the naked, golden figure of Psyche, very delicately modelled, descends into the jaws of Hades, against a green enamel background, studded and hung around with many of the stones mentioned here.

Louis and Caroline were to give Marie a piano, and Tom's brothers and sisters clubbed together to make a contribution towards the purchase of furniture. Harry sent his contribution separately, with a letter in which he hoped that 'Marie will not find it very unpleasant to meet me again; I dare say it won't happen very often as I think I am likely to be working up in the North for some time.' Tom wrote in answer that he was sure Marie would now have no objection to meeting him, but before sending his letter he enclosed it for Marie to see. 'I hope you will be able to forgive and think kindly of him at last. He has had a very hard time and much mental and bodily suffering since . . .' However callous his way of withdrawing from a foolishly contracted engagement might, in effect, have been, 'at bottom it was an act of courage; many men would have gone on merely from fear of wounding others or being ill-spoken of. Of course, sweetest, I don't want you to force your feelings in the least, I want you gradually to contemplate the possibility of new ones.' Marie agreed with the letter in principle, but nevertheless asked that the words 'I am sure that' should be changed to 'I hope that', and this was, of course, done.

Shortly before Caroline returned with her mother to Paris on 21 October, she had sent Marie another 'de ces inventions exquises'— a casket for Tom's letters. This box was covered with silk and lined with satin, on which carefully chosen verses from the Song of Solomon were painted in soft colours. Marie was deeply moved by this token of sisterly love and understanding. It was to her a symbol of the attachment between all the members of her family, hitherto so united in affection and purpose. Her own work for the Y.W.C.A., in which she found such satisfaction, was only part of the contribution both she and Caroline made to their father's and

Louis's ministry; they were both equally concerned with their mother in the harmonious running of the house. More painfully than ever before she realized the loss that parting would entail, both for her and for them. As she wrote to Tom, she was also now torn by conflicting loyalties. Although in many ways still identified with her family's way of life, she was no longer completely in accord with their religious views, nor could she fully accept his; she struggled to discover the common ground of faith without intellectual dishonesty. She desired Tom to join her in asking their 'spiritual Father' to give her 'le calme, la confiance et les clartés' that she needed.

Tom thought it right that she should voice her natural sorrow at the coming parting. To some extent he shared her sense of estrangement from those who had formerly been close: 'I cannot prevent my friends from feeling that I have fallen away from my intellectual standards, deserted them for your sake against my conscience.' He quoted Emerson on 'Worship': 'truth is our only armour in all passages of life and death. Wit is cheap, anger is cheap; but if you cannot argue or explain yourself to the other party, *cleave to the truth against me, against thee,* and you gain a station from which you cannot be dislodged. The other party will forget the words you spoke, but the *part you took* continues to plead for you.' If for the moment they both felt alone, when they were together might they not, as he had always argued, have 'more doors open' and attain 'wider hopes and loves'? As for the future practical problems particularly troubling her in regard to Caroline, 'The experiencing of such difficulties often reveals their solution and it is no use worrying about them too much in advance; especially, darling, be careful not to give way to morbid self-reproaches, the situation is common and is not the result of any fault in you.' Fearing that the return to life in full flux at 119 bis might cause a relapse in health, he added warnings against 'ill-judged kindnesses', sociability incommensurate with physical resources, and the unconsidered dissipation of spirit.

She did, indeed, become less well, but this was due to a form of enteritis for which she would have to follow a special diet for some weeks before it was completely cured. Because of this it was decided that the first month of the honeymoon should be spent quietly in a Swiss pension, before the exertions of the Italian tour. Again Tom became exercised about the inadvisability of an early pregnancy for Marie. To find out how this could be avoided he consulted this time, not his father, but several married friends. Two alternatives emerged from these inquiries: a pessary based on opium, known as the 'Wife's Friend', or separate beds and abstinence. In presenting these to Marie, Tom stressed that it was a moral duty not to conceive children unless one were in a fit state to bear and rear them properly; he knew he would find the second alternative extremely difficult, but if she felt the least repugnance to the first he would, of course, respect her wishes. 'Je suis ignorante sur toutes ces choses-la et je trouve bien dommage que le mariage consiste en autre chose qu'en "hugs and kisses".' Marie had, in fact, only heard of preventive measures in connection with the unfortunate women in Tante Louise's Refuge. This being so she admitted to feeling a certain initial repugnance, but, more importantly, she found it hard to believe that the introduction of a drug like opium into the body might not have harmful effects, such as the conception of a defective child. 'From the moral point of view I feel that if one wants to relieve oneself of the anxieties one should be able to deprive oneself of the pleasure.' Yet she understood that what was no sacrifice for a woman might be one almost impossible for a man. Therefore, provided Tom could obtain medical confirmation that the method was harmless, she would overcome her scruples and do as he desired. Tom then consulted Dr. Hulbert, now a house physician at St. Bartholomew's. In Hulbert's personal view the use of the pessary was harmless, effective, and fully justified; it was, however, not professional etiquette to recommend it in England, though very likely in France no such prejudice existed. At the same time another friend of Tom's assured him, with a conviction born of experience, that abstinence presented no difficulty where both parties considered it desirable. As this was clearly the course most acceptable to Marie, Tom decided to accept it without further ado, and so this question was settled.

By this time all hope of Henrietta's becoming strong enough for an operation had been abandoned. 'These are dark days,' Daniel wrote; he and the three daughters at Cheriton were providing what comfort they could as she grew slowly and painfully weaker. On hearing this, Marie impulsively suggested that after the wedding they should go straight to Torquay, so that Henrietta could be sure of seeing her eldest son together with his wife at least once before she died. This proposal had the reverse of the effect intended. The emotional agitation of such a visit would be more than Henrietta could now support, nor could she bear the thought of being seen in her wasted, disease-ridden state. In fact, she did not even feel equal to seeing Tom on his own before he left for France.

It was not only the shadow of death that now threw uncommon strain on all concerned in preparations for the wedding. At the end of October, 119 bis was a house of invalids. Helen lay in her room with a painfully swollen foot, injured on the journey from the Valleys. She was planner-in-chief, and her domestc standards and appreciation of social conventions demanded meticulous attention to detail. A week later, her aide-de-camp, Caroline, sprained her ankle. Then Louis was prostrated for three days with 'la grippe' and Marie for eight with a quinsy. At 20 St. James's Square, Tom had a heavy head cold and was being drastically treated for an attack of worms by Dr. Hulbert, without marked effect. Nevertheless, the determination to adhere to the date of 26 November if humanly possible did not waver. There was a great deal to be done, and the letters which crossed the Channel reveal a state of nervous tension.

The exigencies of the French marriage laws in the way of documentation, affidavits of parental consent, information for the Communauté de Biens and so forth, provoked Tom into describing them as one of the reasons why so many people in France 'dispense with the legalisation of their most intimate embraces'; in England 'it does not cost half what it does in France, and is simplicity itself'. Marie's wedding-dress had still to be made and most of her trousseau to be purchased. Knowing how reluctant Marie usually was to spend money on herself, Tom had secretly commissioned Caroline to supplement the trousseau as a present from him. Under the prevailing circumstances, the difficulties in performing this delicate task without her sister's knowledge were not minimized in Caroline's explanatory letters. Heroically hobbling, she eventually purchased 'un boa de plume d'autruche', '6 paires de jolis gants' and 'un manchon de petit-gris', but felt unable to take responsibility for the item generally considered *de rigueur*, 'une robe de soie noire'. There were several exchanges on the correct attire for the bridegroom. 'Mais jamais de la vie tu ne peut pas mettre des gants de *soie* blanche!' Though it was only a waste of money to try to make him look *comme il faut* like Julien Monod, Tom would of course 'buy kid gloves, or anything else that will make thee happy'. Appia opinion differed on the English equivalent to 'une redingote en drap'. At the end of a letter detailing the plight of her family while herself still weak from the quinsy, Marie suggested he should buy a ready-made coat in Paris: 'J'ai peur que tu ne me rapportes quelque'horreur d'Angleterre. Excuse cette petite sortie chauvine.' 'Petite chauvine', Tom replied, and proceeded to tell her that if she wanted to get well she should get married as soon as possible, 'en santé ou hors de patience, avec robe ou sans robe, trousseau fait ou trousseau à faire'. There would be no chance of her becoming robust if she remained in Paris and at home, and it would be more sensible for her family to make simpler arrangements for the wedding, instead of exhausting themselves. 'Si ta robe ne soit pas si splendide, je pouvais porter "a ready made coat". Que tu est une petite nigaude!' Did she not know that all the best clothes for men came from England and that ready-made clothes never fitted? 'O, comme tu m'embêtes avec ton chauvinisme, moi qui mets les Français au niveau des Hottentots en fait de coutumes et lois de mariage. Tu as un mari sévère, impatient, sombre et Anglais. Tu auras bien raison de dire "Non" devant M. le Maire. Mais si tu le dis, ton mari te mettre un couteau dans le cœur et après le même couteau dans le sien. Car il t'aime, avec ton chauvinisme et tes nigauderies, plus que lui-même, plus que la vie, plus que tout. . . .'

Marie could not be altogether displeased by this counter-attack, though she did take exception to the expression 'tu m'embêtes' applied to anyone's wife. When, however, Tom, who would have been quite content to be married 'after the manner of Friends and with only six Witnesses' like his Sturge grandparents before him, wrote direct to his aunt expressing his views about all the wedding fuss, apparently using the words 'stupid' and 'useless' in the process, Marie's temper cracked. She scolded him at length for presuming to give unasked-for advice to her parents, who were struggling for his mother's sake to celebrate their marriage on the date of her choice, and to celebrate it as was customary and fitting. He appeared neither to understand her father's position as a senior pastor of the Protestant church in Paris, nor her own natural desire, since she would be leaving her native land and the city of her birth, to include in this occasion the community of their friends and associates. Tom, though continuing to defend his standpoint to Marie, wrote a note of apology to his aunt, which under the circumstances was very graciously received.

By 8 November everyone was feeling better. Marie's doctor gave a favourable report. The date of the marriage was confirmed and the whole programme provisionally drawn up. It began three days before the church ceremony and included a reception for some 300 guests at the headquarters of the Christian Union immediately after it. The Appias wished to be assured that there was nothing in this programme that would seem insensitive to the Moores or lacking in respect for their sorrow. Tom could only say that he knew his mother would wish no alteration on her account and was sure his brothers and sisters would feel the same. On 14 November a report that Henrietta was sinking led to the cancellation of the reception.

Because of the uncertainty over the date, neither Binyon nor Bob Trevelyan was finally free to attend as all had hoped. So George, the best man, Hettie and Sarah, *demoiselles d'honneur*, who arrived in time for the civil marriage on the Tuesday, were the only representatives of the Moore connection. Cousine Hélène wrote an account of the proceedings for Tante Louise, regretfully absent in Cannes for the sake of her health. The dinner for some thirty 'intimes' at 119 bis that evening took place at a horseshoe table, spanning the salon, the landing, and Uncle Georges's study. There were 'de jolis discours, des vers, des paroles affectueuses'. Louis began his *Toast Fraternel* (one of the two speeches to have survived in manuscript) with humorous references to the *Entente Cordiale* and went on to trace how gradually Tom had become, both personally and culturally, the trusted link between their two countries. During his earlier spring visits, this English cousin had nevertheless been a puzzle to them; for in France, 'le pays de la méthode', the pursuit of any career was expected to follow a proscribed course 'de diplôme en diplôme'. 'Peut-être le remarquez-vous avec un sourire imperceptible, comptant bien nous montrer un jour que ce n'est pas pour rien que nos littérateurs ont dû emprunter à votre langue l'intraduisible expression de "self-made man".' Ernest Guy, speaking as an inquiring bachelor-philosopher, made a diverting exploration into the principles that governed the choice of marriage partners, and came to the conclusion that in Marie's case it was simply the logical outcome of her interest in Sully-Prudhomme and Leconte de Lisle.

And as for me, I say you are right, truly right, to marry a poet. *That* poet, who is a true poet for he transfigures everything he touches and animates it with a superior life. After leaving him one has the feeling of redescending to earth where everything seems colourless, except for the little blue flame that he has put in your heart and which continues to spread its sweet and beneficent light! Besides, you won't be leaving him. . . .

And in his closing words he gracefully introduced a tribute to

252

Hettie, the 'délicate présence féminine' that had animated the home where he had so often found refuge from the London fogs. 'L'image de ce foyer je la conserve précieusement parmi mes souvenirs les plus chers, et cette évocation du passé se trouve, me semble-t-il, en parfaite harmonie avec la perspective d'avenir.'

On Thursday 26 November, the church service was held in the Rédemption, 'avec un beau discours d'oncle Georges pour bénir le mariage'. Because, no doubt, of the cancellation of the reception, it took the congregation well over an hour to file out through the sacristy; the bride's veil was torn to shreds in the course of numberless embraces; the bridegroom's shoes grew tighter and tighter. In the evening the close friends and relatives accompanied 'le cher couple à la gare de l'Est et vu partir cette chère petite si profondément heureuse à côté d'un mari si bon et si sûr'. George, on his return to England, told mutual friends of the beauty of his brother's 'epic wedding', and Tom, writing to Bob Trevelyan a few days later from Pension Gerber, Paradiso, Lugano, conveyed how his father-in-law's spirit had so illumined the proceedings that he had not felt an outsider after all.

*

Henrietta died on 12 December. She had expressed a wish to be cremated, and Harry conducted the service at the crematorium in Golders Green; Tom and Marie read the service for the Burial of the Dead together at the appointed time on 16 December. Tom then wrote of his intention of attending the service at the deposition of ashes, which was to take place early in January at Honor Oak cemetery, near to where George and Jane Sturge were buried, but his father dissuaded him:

The sentiments of a burial can never attach to a deposition of ashes. Don't come I beg you. And do not imagine for an instant that I did not understand your absence before and see the justice of it. Your duty now seems to me to be to cherish your wife and not cause her trouble and anxiety by coming to England at the worst time of year on a quite unnecessary errand.

I wish you both a prosperous New Year, with new hopes as you have new duties. You are both in God's keeping, so I cannot but wish you both to live in Him.

The New Year saw them in Correggio country; through Milan to Parma and from there to Mantua and Bologna. Then, five weeks in all in Rome, a week in Florence and short stays in Orvieti, Mentone, Sienna, and again Parma. Ricketts wrote in envy, 'I suppose you have come in for a riot of flowers both in Rome and Florence and that your wife has become depraved on violets and cyclamen and taken incurably to fantastic irises and huge unnatural roses. We are with the crocus and the almond blossom and I pant for Italy. I feel wings inside my boots.' Other letters from England brought news of the pleasing reception of *The Gazelles and Other Poems*, of a fierce journalistic battle between Binyon and MacColl, of productions of Yeats's plays, and of the death of Arthur Strong. At the end of March the Sturge Moores were back in Paris. Here, after a few days, Tom left Marie and returned to England to check the redecoration of 20 St. James's Square, buy more furniture, find a replacement for Alice, now become Mrs. Jolly, and put the house and garden in order for Marie's arrival at the end of April. They then travelled down to Torquay for a week with Daniel and the sisters. Cheriton was up for sale, for a smaller home, strangely named Croom-a-boo, had been found near Exeter. Here Hettie and Sarah were to live with their father, and Annie was hoping again to find a teaching post in the neighbourhood.

When Tom and Marie returned to London the servant problem had still not been fully solved, so hospitality was restricted. But Yeats came for a poetry reading, at which Fisher and Mona Wilson were among the participants. Ernest Guy reappeared, 'now in Petroleum'. Ricketts and Marie enjoyed talking French together, and the Michael Fields were rapidly won over: 'Marie comes in—a topaz. Yes, she is a topaz. "Her eyes reign influence and cheat the skies". She has shone herself into marriage.' There was, however, then little time for Marie to savour these new relationships, for by the end of July she and Tom were at the

Airals Blancs. Though a summer holiday in the Valleys was to become part of the pattern of life for them and their children, it is hard to understand why this should have been inaugurated in a year so much of which had already been spent abroad, unless, perhaps, it was to assuage Helen Appia's grief at the death of a sister and the separation from a daughter. Early in August Tom heard from Hettie that their father was suffering from one of those mysterious bouts of pain, which he had now explained to her were due to gallstones. A week later he was seriously ill, the doctor had called in a surgeon, Nellie had come down from London.

Tom left for England on 17 August and arrived at Croom-a-boo to find all the family assembled, and his father dead. For fifteen years Daniel had kept to himself his progressively painful complaint for fear of distressing his wife; the accumulation of stone had finally led to death from blood poisoning. His children were left in a state of shock by this sudden bereavement. Hettie and Sarah had recovered from the strain of nursing their dying mother in planning a new life with their father, and now for them there was a blankness. There was, perhaps, no one they more needed to be with than Tom. He was, besides, co-trustee with Annie of his father's estate. Meanwhile, at the Airals Blancs Georges Appia was running a high temperature as a result of a poisoned hand. Marie urged Tom to bring his sisters out to the Valleys and he suggested that she should bring her father for convalescence at Croom-a-boo, but neither of these proposals was really in tune with the family situations.

So it was not until October that Tom and Marie were reunited at 20 St. James's Square and able to establish their 'foyer'. It was one such as Ernest Guy had rightly envisaged, where, whatever the trials they encountered, the pursuit of Truth, Goodness, and Beauty was sustained with warmth, disagreement, and a good deal of laughter. On their first wedding anniversary, Tom improvised a sonnet for Marie:

> One year of wedded life, my love, is ours:
> Not as we did intend its days were filled,

Nor have we realized what our souls willed
More than in other years; yet we buy flowers,
Invite our friends, prepare for joyous hours;
For Love's success lies wherein Love is skilled
And not to shape events, where breath is stilled.
The future cannot mock or cheat her powers
Who ne'er pretended to bring aught about.
Love's one ambition is to learn, and be
Inwardly prompt, to all experience free,
Yet not disturb that vision, set without
The bounds of worldly fret and sterile doubt,
Which entertained instills felicity.

Epilogue

THE Sturge Moores' son, Daniel, was born in 1905 (Ricketts, in the unfamiliar role of godfather, presented this infant with an orange-tree), and their daughter Henriette (always known as Riette) in 1907. In 1912 the family moved to John Constable's former home, 40 Well Walk, Hampstead, a gracious setting for the poetry readings and 'bachelor evenings' that are still remembered. They returned to this London home in 1927 after eight years in the village of Steep near Petersfield, where the children attended Bedales School as day pupils. This school and the community surrounding it provided a new circle for poetry readings at their house, Hillcroft, and Tom gave lectures in aesthetics to interested senior scholars. At Hillcroft he composed a number of his longer poems, verse-dramas, and lyrics, and continued to contribute vigorously to literary journals.

In Hampstead Marie was accepted as a member of the Friends Meeting, which Tom also quite often attended, without prejudice to a continuing allegiance to the Vaudois Church in Soho. Among the good causes she energetically supported were the University Women's Settlement in Islington and the work for poor children of the Caldecott Community. Dedicated though she was to every aspect of her husband's life and work, visits to Paris and the summer holidays in the Valleys were always for her a coming home. Her father visited 'les enfants' in London for the last time on his way back from a missionary conference in Edinburgh in 1910; he died that autumn at the Airals Blancs and is buried near to his son Henry in the Vaudois cemetery beside the River Pellice. Helen Appia, devotedly cared for by Caroline, lived on into her ninety-eighth year; she is buried not far from Lydia Sturge in the cemetery of Père Lachaise. The home of Louis and his wife, Louise Mehl, became the place of family reunions in Paris. If Ernest Guy was seen less frequently (he finally entered the diplomatic service), the bond with the cultured banker, Julien Monod, was strengthened; to him Tom owed his introduction to Paul Valéry, as Yeats owed to Tom his introduction to Adolphe Appia. Cousine Hélène, who during and after the First World War devoted her time to the missing persons records of the International Red Cross, retained her central position in the hearts of the Sturge Moores.

The Moore brothers and sisters in the main successfully pursued their various callings. George's eminence as a philosopher is well known; he also proved an eminently popular uncle. Annie found continuing satisfaction as a teacher of English and Latin, and was of considerable help to Tom as a proof-corrector. Harry became the respected vicar of Aysgarth in Yorkshire, where he was regarded as a confirmed bachelor until in 1913 he made a most happy marriage to his young parishioner, Elizabeth Blades; he then spent five years as a missionary in Japan, lecturing at the Theological College in Tokyo, and a further year in British Columbia before returning to his pastoral career in rural England. From 1905 Nellie worked for the Church of England Zenana Missionary Society as hospital physician and surgeon, first in Bangalore and then in the Punjab, bringing back beautiful Indian toys for her nephews and niece when on furlough. She died, aged only forty-five, at the teaching hospital in Sukkur, of which she had for several years been in charge. Bertie spent most of his later life in Florence, largely deflected from his career as an artist by acting as tutor and loyal general help to an English family. Sarah married George's friend and disciple, Alfred Ainsworth, in 1908; the Ainsworths and their two sons, the elder of whom was a severely brain-damaged epileptic, were near neighbours of the Sturge Moores while they were living in Steep. And Hettie, the sister with 'the unquenchable laugh', always looked after other people; she housekept for George when he was living in Richmond before his marriage to Dorothy Ely, relieved Sarah by taking charge of her younger son for long periods, and when later employed as a companion outside the family still remained the affectionate and perceptive link between all its members in her own generation and the next.

While family responsibilities meant a lessening of the intensive intercourse with some friends of Tom's bachelor days, most regretted in the case of Binyon, many of the outer circle were brought closer by Marie's sympathetic and sociable nature. She became warm friends with the 'ultra-modern' Dora Sanger, Gwendoline Bishop, by then Mrs. Bax, and the elderly Canon Wilson, Mona's father, and it was partly at her instigation that Arnold Dolmetsch, so often short of money, became a visiting teacher at Bedales. Selwyn Image, Will Rothenstein, Arthur Rackham, and that kindred spirit Lucien Pissarro were never lost sight of. Only with Roger Fry was there a lasting break, caused by another volte-face regarding an article for the *Burlington Magazine*. For Wyndham Lewis, Tom grew into what one biographer has described as a father-figure; Lewis bore with uncharacteristic good humour the 'picturesque expletives' heaped upon Vorticism and regularly sent his writings to the man whose judgement he valued more than any other. The correspondence with Ida Kruse appears to have tailed off. She became, not an actress, but the Head of the Department of English Literature at Denver University; as Mrs. Macfarlane she instituted an annual Drama Festival in the Central City Opera House which she and her family had presented to the University.

Sybil Pye, who never married, became one of the outstanding book-binders of her time, an innovator both in the arrangement of shapes in her designs and in their execution in inlaid leathers, richly harmonious in colour. Tom participated as eagerly in the progress of her work as she continued to do in his. Ethel Pye, too, told Marie that her sculptures 'did not exist' until Tom had seen them, and she carried out some of his designs for the costumes and masks in productions of his verse-plays. Tom's three early disciples all outlived him. If circumstances distanced Harry Mileham, Hugh Fisher remained ever a devoted and serviceable admirer, and Bob Trevelyan a generous and considerate friend. It was in the Trevelyan home near Dorking that Tom and Marie found refuge as 'evacuees' at the outbreak of the Second World War, when his health was already failing.

To Tom's sorrow other close friends of his youth pre-deceased him. The Michael Fields had moved to Well Walk before the Sturge Moores and there were no neighbours they valued more than Tom and Marie in the little time left them. Edith died of cancer in 1913 and Katherine, who had concealed from her that she was suffering from the same disease, the following year. After Edith's death, Ricketts broke with Katherine, and Tom remained the only former friend faithful to her. Another old friend is commemorated by the dedication of the Socratic dialogue, 'The Closing Door', (*Life and Letters*, February 1929) to 'the late Henry Poole R. A.'. Most deeply felt of all was the loss of Ricketts, always for Tom the maestro, and Shannon. Their partnership was tragically broken by the fall that fractured Shannon's skull and destroyed his personality in 1929. Ricketts only survived this blow for two years; until Shannon's death in 1937 Tom continued to visit him and send him simply worded picture-postcards. Over a longer span of years the relationship with Yeats deepened, Tom becoming the confidant for personal entanglements as well as a sounding-board for literary and philosophic theories. He devised book-plates for the Yeats family, ornaments for the Cuala Press, and from 1916 onwards designed the covers of many of Yeats's works. Yeats would suggest symbols that might be incorporated and then give the designer his head; the design for *The Tower*, a transformation of a stark photograph of Ballylee, the author found 'most rich, grave and beautiful'. Four years after Yeats's death in 1939 came Binyon's; Tom wrote to his widow of this friend as 'perhaps the most complete and perfect man' he had known, his 'best adviser', who had helped him both 'in my work as a creator and in the difficulties of living'.

Many of these friends had been involved in the projects in progress at the time of the marriage. The Literary Theatre Society was founded soon afterwards, with Binyon, Yeats, Pye, and Tom on the committee. In the two years before it was swallowed up by the Stage Society among its productions were *Aphrodite against Artemis*, with Florence Farr and Gwendoline Bishop in the cast, and Oscar Wilde's *A Florentine Tragedy*, for which Tom wrote the missing first act, and *Salomé*. Ricketts designed the scenery and costumes for all the Society's plays, as he did for Tom's *Judith*, performed by the Stage Society in 1916. The book on Dürer appeared in 1905 and also the collection of verses for children entitled *The Little School*, dedicated to Sybil Pye and printed by the Eragny Press. *Correggio* came out in 1906. Tom's marriage did not, after all, cause the Michael Fields to change their literary executor, and Ricketts made the same choice. In this capacity Tom edited a collection of Michael Field's poems in 1923 and ten years later, together with his son, the selection from their journal, *Works and Days*. Only a small part, however, of Tom's labours in assembling Ricketts's journals and letters and recording his multifarious artistic work is represented in the book entitled *Self-Portrait*, produced in 1939 in collaboration with Cecil Lewis; the rest is a quarry for later researchers. Two other continuing loyalties are demonstrated in the *Art and Life* of 1910 which presents a view of Flaubert reinforced by later writings, and in the 1939 volume of *Essays and Studies of the English Association* is one of the last things Tom wrote, a mellow, very personal reassessment of Matthew Arnold.

Tom died in 1944 after a long and painful illness. Marie survived him for thirteen years; she devotedly ordered all her husband's papers and gathered in material for a memoir until, too early, her memory failed her. Inheriting her father's artistic bent and following an Appia example, their daughter Riette has worked as a stage-designer and shared her experience with a great number of students; she taught at the Old Vic School under Michel St. Denis, with George Devine, and Byam Shaw, and, after its deplored closure in 1952, in the Drama Department of the Bath Academy of Art at Corsham Court and also at Dartington Hall. Her brother Dan has notably maintained the link between England and France, first by his work for the French Service of the BBC in the 1940s, a lifeline for millions of his mother's compatriots suffering under the German occupation, and then by the programme on French affairs for English listeners that he ran for many years from Radio Diffusion Française.

Family Trees

THE MOORES   THE STURGES

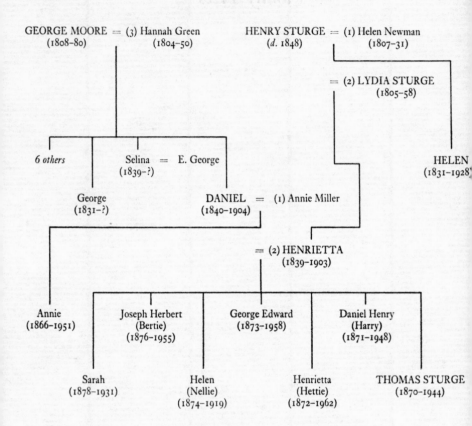

GEORGE MOORE = (3) Hannah Green   HENRY STURGE = (1) Helen Newman
(1808–80)   (1804–50)   (d. 1848)   (1807–31)

                                   = (2) LYDIA STURGE
                                       (1805–58)

6 others   Selina = E. George   HELEN
              (1839–?)   (1831–1928)

      George   DANIEL = (1) Annie Miller
      (1831–?)   (1840–1904)

                     = (2) HENRIETTA
                         (1839–1903)

Annie   Joseph Herbert   George Edward   Daniel Henry
(1866–1951) (Bertie)   (1873–1958)   (Harry)
             (1876–1955)   (1871–1948)

   Sarah   Helen   Henrietta   THOMAS STURGE
   (1878–1931)   (Nellie)   (Hettie)   (1870–1944)
                      (1874–1919)   (1872–1962)

THE APPIAS

(see over)

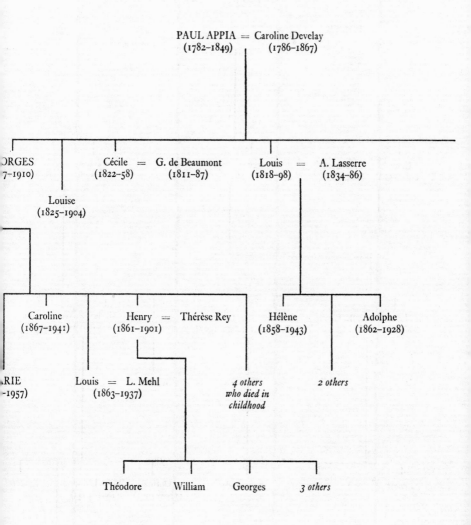

PAUL APPIA ═ Caroline Develay
(1782–1849)   (1786–1867)

...ORGES   Cécile ═ G. de Beaumont   Louis ═ A. Lasserre
(...7–1910)   (1822–58)   (1811–87)   (1818–98)   (1834–86)

                    Louise
                  (1825–1904)

Caroline   Henry ═ Thérèsc Rey   Hélène   Adolphe
(1867–1941)   (1861–1901)   (1858–1943)   (1862–1928)

..RIE   Louis ═ L. Mehl   *4 others*   *2 others*
(..–1957)   (1863–1937)   *who died in*
                                  childhood

          Théodore   William   Georges   *3 others*

THE APPIAS

(continued)

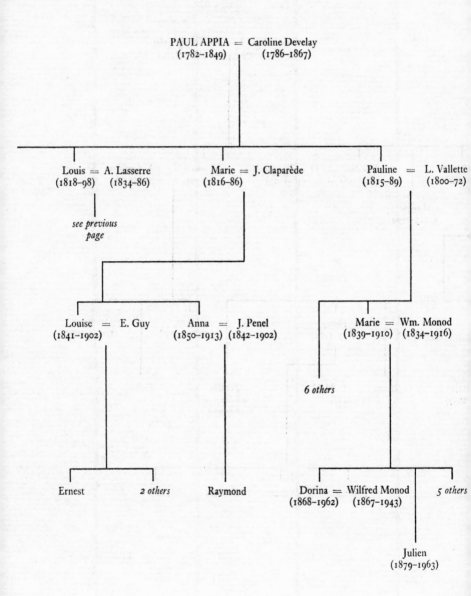

PAUL APPIA = Caroline Develay
(1782–1849)   (1786–1867)

Louis = A. Lasserre
(1818–98)   (1834–86)

see previous page

Marie = J. Claparède
(1816–86)

Pauline = L. Vallette
(1815–89)   (1800–72)

Louise = E. Guy
(1841–1902)

Anna = J. Penel
(1850–1913)   (1842–1902)

Marie = Wm. Monod
(1839–1910)   (1834–1916)

6 others

Ernest   *2 others*

Raymond

Dorina = Wilfred Monod
(1868–1962)   (1867–1943)

5 others

Julien
(1879–1963)

Index